HENRY VIII
and the
INVASION
of FRANCE

HENRY VIII
and the
INVASION
of FRANCE

Charles Cruickshank

ALAN SUTTON · Stroud

ST. MARTIN'S PRESS · New York

Copyright © in this edition Mrs M. Cruickshank 1990

First published in the United States of America 1991
All rights reserved. For information write:
Scholarly & Reference Books Division,
St. Martin's Press, 175 Fifth Avenue,
New York, NY10010

ISBN-312-04125-X

First published in the United Kingdom in 1990 by
Alan Sutton Publishing Limited
Phoenix Mill
Far Thrupp
Stroud
Gloucestershire GL5 2BU

British Library Cataloguing in Publication Data

Cruikshank, Charles
[240.4] Henry VIII and the invasion of France.
1. France, 1461–1515. Invasion, 1513 by England
I. [240.4] II. Title
944.027

ISBN 0-86299-768-2

Typeset in 11/12 Ehrhardt.
Typesetting and origination by
Alan Sutton Publishing Limited.
Printed in Great Britain by
Dotesios Printers Limited.

CONTENTS

LIST OF ILLUSTRATIONS

Photographs and illustrations were supplied by, or are reproduced by kind permission of the following: Windsor Castle, Royal Library, HM the Queen (6); The National Portrait Gallery, London (1, 12, 45); the Mansell Collection (5, 17, 46); Courtauld Institute of Art (11); The Bodleian Library, Oxford (3, 4, 9, 10, 23, 33, 34, 35, 36, 39, 40, 43, 48, 49); Society of Antiquaries of London (15, 16, 20, endpapers); Syndics of Cambridge University Library (2); Board of Trustees of the Royal Armouries (13, 14, 18, 19, 21, 22, 24, 25, 26, 27, 31, 32, 38, 41, 42, 44). Pictures 7, 8, 28, 29, 30 and 47 are reproduced by gracious permission of HM the Queen.

PREFACE

The plan followed has been to enfold in a narrative account of the 1513 campaign in France, which culminated in the capture and occupation of Tournai, the administrative, organizational, operational, and supply topics which seem worthy of separate treatment, without, it is hoped, seriously interrupting the flow of the narrative.

I should like to record my gratitude for help in various forms from Professor S.T. Bindoff, of Queen Mary College, London; Dr C.S.L. Davies, of Wadham College, Oxford; Dr Jeremy Goring, of Goldsmiths' College, London; Mr William Reid, of the Tower of London Armouries; and Dr Gabriel Wymans, Conservateur des Archives de l'État at Tournai.

C.G.C.

NOTE

The superior numbers in the text refer to the Sources which can be found at the end of the book.

The bracketed numbers in the text refer to the Notes which can be found at the end of chapters.

1 Objective

It was inevitable that Henry VIII should lead an 'army royal' into Europe within a few years of his accession, partly because he was by nature a bully, and partly to prove to himself, to his people, and above all to his peers the heads of state beyond the English Channel, that mastery of the art of war ranked high among his many accomplishments. Otherwise, he was but half a man.

The demonstration might be costly in terms of the wealth, effort, and lives of his subjects, but that was a secondary consideration. It would cost the king himself nothing. He would share none of the discomforts of the rank and file, and virtually none of their dangers. He would not suffer when 'grey-bearded winter began to show his face' and caused the 'decrepit shivering soldiers to complain and groan to each other'.[1] When he moved from one place to another he would not drag himself and his equipment on foot over muddy tracks, but would make the journey on horseback in the heart of a 'plump' of his most trusted guards, who would count it an honour to die in his defence. It was, however, unlikely that any would enjoy this privilege, since troops of light cavalry would scour the countryside to send back information about the movements of the enemy so that the king might be kept at a safe distance, 'for great honour consisteth in the safe-keeping' of the king and his Council.[2] Moreover, when there *was* the possibility of contact with the enemy, his royal person, unlike that of the yeoman archer or billman, would be protected by an ornamental steel casing weighing between sixty and seventy pounds. His table would be no less heavily laden than at Greenwich, nor his servants less numerous. Wherever the campaign took him he would sleep comfortably in his own bed, not necessarily alone, in a portable wooden house, the component parts of which needed twelve carts to carry them; or if he preferred it, in a palatial marquee hardly less magnificent than one of his bedchambers at home, and certainly not under a hedge or in a hut improvised from branches.

He would encounter few real hazards. Some tactical blunder by the higher command might suddenly engulf him and his bodyguard in a major battle from which there was no escape save through hand-to-hand fighting. He might be unlucky enough to find himself without armour in the path of a bullet fired at random from the walls of a besieged town, as did Sir Edmund Carew.(1) This indeed was a possibility envisaged by the Bishop of Durham when he drafted some notes about the plan of the 1513 campaign. He suggested that the king should not himself take part in any siege but remain with his retinue at a safe distance. In the bishop's view there were good reasons for this precaution: 'in the conserving of his noble person dependeth the weal and surety of his realm and all the nobles and others of his army, whereas of the contrary (which God

Henry VIII c. 1520

defend!) the loss and destruction of all may follow.'[3] The odds against this sort of mishap were very long, however. Indeed, bearing in mind the fate of Sir Francis Brian, who lost an eye in the jousts,[4] or of Henry II of France, who lost his life, it might be argued that the monarch was in greater danger in a tournament than on the battlefield, especially if he forgot to close his visor, as Henry VIII himself once did, leaving his face 'clean naked' and an inviting target for his adversary's spear.[5]

Nevertheless, the young king's burning desire to play a leading part in the affairs of Europe, fanned by the lingering influences of the code of chivalry, demanded conflict with more edge to it than jousting in the tiltyard. Existing rivalries happily provided him with an argument for moving from sham to real warfare. In November 1511 England joined the Holy League, an alliance with the papacy, Venice and Spain (and later the Empire) aimed at keeping France from dominating Europe; and in doing so she became involved in a war in which she had far less to gain than any of the other contestants.

Henry's father-in-law, Ferdinand of Aragon, had his eye on Navarre, a French possession straddling the Pyrenees; and if Henry wanted to offer himself as a cat's paw for furthering the aims of Aragon, Ferdinand certainly had no objection. Maximilian, the Holy Roman Emperor elect, who controlled the whole of what is now Germany, Austria, the Low Countries (through his grandson Charles), and a large part of north-eastern France, and was also

The coronation of Henry VIII and Catherine of Aragon

nominally responsible for some adjacent territories, saw in Louis XII's ambitions a threat to the security of his own dominions. He too was delighted to accept England as an ally, although he did not believe that her help would have much effect on the balance of power in Europe. In Italy Pope Julius II was the victim of French aggression, and also welcomed any support that Henry could provide.

There was, of course, no real need for England to become thus entangled. Henry had inherited peace with France under a treaty made by his father in 1502, which was renewed (as it had to be on the death of the sovereign if it were not to lapse automatically) on his accession in 1509. It would have sufficed for the moment if he had concentrated on developing his father's careful and unspectacular domestic policies, leaving the warring monarchs of Europe to sap each other's strength. It was too much, however, to expect the virile Henry, just into his twenties, to stand idly by, content to control the modest destinies of England from the Council chamber, when the spirits of St George and the illustrious fifth Henry held out the promise of honour and glory on the battle-fields of Europe; and if he had to pick a quarrel, France clearly selected herself as the most appropriate enemy. Her traditional links with the boorish Scots, who were always a potential menace to England's northern marches, her perpetual threat to the English town of Calais and to English shipping in the Channel, and her hostility to the papacy, which England still supported, all singled her out.

Henry made his first tentative interventions in the military affairs of Europe in 1511, when, in spite of the opposition of some members of his Council, he sent a force of about 1,500 archers under Thomas, Lord Darcy, to join Ferdinand in a campaign against the Moors of Barbary; and a force of the same size under Sir Edward Poynings, Warden of the Cinque Ports and former Lord Deputy of Ireland, to support Margaret of Savoy, Maximilian's daughter, against the Duke of Guelders. The latter expedition did quite well, in spite of having to operate in difficult territory, for the leader was a man of great experience and ability; but the former turned out to be a wild-goose chase.

As soon as it reached Cadiz in the south of Spain, Darcy was told by Ferdinand that he had decided to call off his campaign against the Moors and to keep his forces at home to defend the country against the French. The English commander was furious at this change of plan, but there was nothing he could do about it, except curtly to refuse Ferdinand's invitation to come to Seville to receive his thanks at a banquet, and head for home. It was just as well that his troops were not put to the test, as they found the heat of the Spanish summer too much for them. Hall records that they 'fell to drinking of hot wines and were scarce masters of themselves. Some ran to the stews, some brake hedges, and spoiled orchards and vineyards and oranges before they were ripe and did many other outrageous deeds.'[6]

In spite of this débâcle Henry sent a force in the following year under Thomas Grey, Marquis of Dorset, to join Ferdinand's troops in an invasion of Guienne. Grey had come near to execution as a traitor in the previous reign, but his jousting skill had restored him to favour in the eyes of Henry VIII. This expedition also accomplished nothing, partly because of the incompetence of the leader, partly because lack of pay and victuals induced the troops to mutiny, but mainly because Ferdinand again changed his mind. He now wanted to attack Navarre before turning on Guienne, which the English general refused to do. Henry decided that the English troops should winter overseas, but before his instructions reached Dorset he had taken the law into his own hands and embarked his men for England.

Once again foreign wines and food contributed to the undoing of the invaders. 'The Englishmen did eat of the garlick with all meats, and drank hot wines in the hot weather, and did eat all the hot fruits that they could get, which caused their blood so to boil in their bellies that there fell sick three thousand of the flux, and thereof died eighteen hundred men.'[7] The unknown author of the *Italian Relation*, a penetrating essay on the English way of life written some years before these expeditions, comments on this failing of Englishmen. After mentioning their great reputation as soldiers, which he considers must be well justified because of the fear they traditionally inspire in the French, he adds that he has it on the best authority that when war is raging most furiously the English soldiers will seek for good eating and all their other creature comforts without thinking of the great harm that may befall them.[8] The idea that the French feared the

Emperor Maximilian I (Montagu illustration 190.)

English seems to have been generally accepted. The Venetian ambassador in referring to the Earl of Shrewsbury said that he came from a noble and ancient family named Talbot and 'to this day in France they still their babes by threatening them when they cry with the coming of the Talbots.'[9]

If England was to make her mark as a military power something on a much grander scale than these minor expeditions was called for; and if Henry was to make *his* mark he must put himself at the head of his troops. Both propositions raised a difficulty.

A major attack on the most powerful monarch in Europe could not be contemplated without support from the country at large and from the king's advisers in particular. Several members of the Council considered that there was no case for intensifying the war with France, but their arguments cut little ice with the king, who was said to be so eager about the enterprise 'that no one can put it out of his head, unless it be God almighty.'[10] The queen wrote to Cardinal Bainbridge, the English ambassador at Rome, that Henry was so bent on the war against the French that he would never rest until their king was utterly destroyed;[11] and Lorenzo Pasqualigo, the Venetian consul in London, reported to his colleagues in Venice that Henry was wholly committed to the war and that he had made up his mind to lead his army in person. He understood that the Council were against the war, but not the queen.[12]

One way of winning the support of his advisers was to put France more clearly in the wrong; and Henry therefore sent an ambassador to Louis to warn him that unless he made peace with the Pope, on quite impossible terms, he would have to take the consequences. When the French king's inevitable dusty answer reached England Henry considered that his path was clear. He was now the Pope's chosen instrument against the excommunicate Louis, enjoying the backing of the Almighty (without which no wise sixteenth-century monarch went to war); and the anti-war party in the Council was able to use Louis's reply to justify a public change of heart, whatever their private opinion continued to be.

There was still, however, one important dissentient voice which questioned whether Henry should seek to become the champion of Christendom. John Colet, Dean of St Paul's, ventured to preach an anti-war sermon before the king on Good Friday 1513, the gist of which is recorded by Erasmus. The dean said, amongst other things, that those who went to war because of hatred or ambition, and slaughtered one another by turns, fought under the banner of the Devil. How could a man have the brotherly love needed to get him to heaven and yet bury his sword in his brother's heart? There was much more in the same vein 'so that the King was in some apprehension lest the soldiers whom he was on the point of leading abroad should feel that their courage was gone, through this discourse'. Shortly afterwards Henry summoned Colet to Greenwich, where they talked amicably about their different points of view in the garden of the Franciscan monastery and parted on good terms (to the disappointment of Colet's enemies), either because the king had successfully exploited the classical argument that the impending attack on France was a purely defensive measure, or because Colet had come to accept that discretion was the better part of valour.[13]

The second difficulty – opposition to Henry's proposal that he should lead the

Louis XII (Douce. D.244.)

army in person – was also disposed of only after a good deal of discussion. Although the risk that he would lose his life in a continental adventure was undoubtedly very slight, the fact remained that there *was* a risk. In the words of Polydore Vergil, the Italian priest who was living in England at this time, 'many considered it too perilous that the King in the first flush of his youthful maturity in arms should expose himself to the danger of so great a war.'[14] The king's advisers may have had Henry's own interests at heart when they tried to dissuade him from going to France; but they also saw very clearly that his untimely death might lead to a squabble about his successor which could plunge the country back into the anarchy of the previous century. At this time Henry had no son to be an undisputed successor and there were those who feared that in the event of his early death there might be an attempt to rescue the Yorkist Edmund de la Pole, Earl of Suffolk, from the Tower (into which Henry VII had enticed him with a promise of his life) and set him up as king. This powerful argument Henry VIII demolished with a single stroke of the headsman's axe shortly before the invasion of France started.[15]

Although the Privy Council pressed for the appointment of a general who would do the king's bidding, there was much to be said on the other side, and

Henry said it, no doubt with eloquence. In Polydore Vergil's account we hear him persuasively arguing the point from a position of great strength, as he had presumably made up his mind that nothing would stop him from being his own general. He must have the opportunity of creating 'such a fine opinion about his valour among all men that they would clearly understand that his ambition was not merely to equal but indeed to exceed the glorious deeds of his ancestors'. He reminded those present of the many occasions on which his predecessors had led English armies to great victories, and also of the times when battles had been lost in the absence of the king. Men were eager to face death when led by their sovereign: with any other commander, however able, they would be milder in their nature and would fight badly.[16] This was a considerable understatement in the light of the behaviour of the troops with Darcy and Dorset. Henry may have been tactful enough on this occasion not to refer to their failures (although earlier he had held an inquest into Dorset's expedition in the presence of the Spanish ambassador, in which he kept the leaders on their knees until they could endure it no longer and begged permission to stand up, at least until they had been proved guilty);[17] but they were certainly fresh both in his own mind and in the minds of his listeners. Finally, there was the incontrovertible fact that the king's life was in the hands of the Almighty, and the same Providence ruled everywhere.[18]

There were other important reasons why the king should act as his own commander-in-chief which were not touched upon during the Council's debate. Communications were impossibly slow, especially when they involved crossing the English Channel. As a rule a dispatch rider would cover no more than twenty miles a day,[19] and the journey from army headquarters in France to London and back might take two or three weeks. The messenger had to find his way, part of the time through hostile country, to a friendly Channel port. There he had to

Henry VIII, two years after his accession, rides in state to attend a tourney, 1511. From the original roll, Royal College of Arms

take ship for England. If he were lucky enough to coincide with a suitable vessel he might have to cool his heels for days on end waiting for a favourable wind. Most decisions could be taken on the spot by the king's lieutenant but sooner or later he must refer back to London for instructions. In August 1523 the Duke of Suffolk 'ordered all his captains to pitch their tents in the fields to the south of Calais, and there they lay for a month waiting letters from the King and his Council to tell them which way they should take to ravage France, in which matter the Cardinal of York took his time, for everything passed through his hands'.[20] The political and military situation might change drastically in a month, but it was not only a question of time. There was always the danger of misinterpreting even the most explicit instructions.

Again, if the sovereign were not the commander-in-chief it was possible that the army would act against his wishes, or that the council of war would disagree among themselves. The latter happened in 1522 when the Earl of Surrey, who had captured and sacked Hesdin, found his path barred by the Somme. He decided that in spite of the lateness of the season and the weakness of his men they should push on across the river deeper into France. Some of the captains agreed, but others thought his plan foolhardy (in which they had the support of most of the troops, who had suffered terrible privations and were on the verge of mutiny)[21] and their opinion prevailed. The army returned to England forthwith.[22] When the sovereign was in command he might receive conflicting advice but there would be no argument about the final decision. In his absence, however, a split in the council of war could upset the whole conduct of a campaign.

There were thus sound technical reasons why Henry should lead his troops himself, and they easily outweighed the single ill-founded argument against – that he would be exposing himself to danger. His insistence that he must go to France, however, stemmed not from military good sense, but purely and simply from his immense desire for personal glory. He might be a popular leader but he certainly was not a great general; and had the campaign been a military necessity he would have served England's interests best by staying at home. Thousands of his subjects might have to pay heavily to satisfy his craving for immortality; but if they succeeded in having his name inscribed in the halls of martial fame, no price was too high.

*   *   *

Part of the price had to be paid in hard cash; and now that the question of the commander-in-chief had been settled another important decision had to be taken. Just how was the hard cash to be found? For his war with France in 1492 Henry VII had a parliamentary grant of two 'fifteenths and tenths' – the tax on goods and chattels originally assessed at the rate of one-fifteenth of their value in the counties and one-tenth in the towns, but which since 1334 had been used to produce a flat £40,000. Parliament also agreed that if his campaign lasted more than eight months a third fifteenth and tenth should be levied; but in the event this supplementary provision was not required.[23]

Henry VII found parliament very cooperative in the matter of taxes for military

Henry VIII in parliament, 1515 by Sir Thomas Wriothesley

purposes, especially 'if it shoud be a case of glory, or necessity, such as a war with France or Scotland would be'.[24] It was one thing, however, for parliament to vote money and quite another for the tax collectors to get their hands on it. Those living in the more remote areas of the country did not yet consider themselves to be concerned with the welfare of the State as a whole. Taxation to pay for military aid to Brittany in 1489 was highly unpopular in the undisciplined northern marches. It caused a rebellion which was at first unsuccessfully tackled by the Earl of Northumberland (who was killed by the rebels) and had to be put down by the king himself. Six years later at the other end of the country the men of Cornwall refused to pay taxes for Henry's war with Scotland, which led to another sizeable revolt. The king had to divert his army from Scotland to deal with the rebels – again successfully.[25]

In fact, Henry VII's military expenditure, which was on a modest scale, turned out to be a good investment. At the end of his war with France the French king agreed to pay him £150,000 at the rate of £5,000 a year; his war with Scotland cost considerably less than the sums voted for it; and after the suppression of the two main rebellions of his reign he exacted a fortune in fines.[26] But although the country's finances were left in a healthy state by his careful budgeting, his son had no hope of paying for a major attack on France out of the ordinary revenues of the Crown. Substantial parliamentary help was needed. It was readily agreed to grant one-fifteenth and one-tenth (£40,000), the whole of which was to be devoted to the war, except for £6,000 set aside for the seaports; but because this was only a small part of what would be needed, parliament authorized a second and heavier tax which could be gathered in 'as well in shorter time as in more easy and indifferent manner'.[27]

This was a tax collector's dream, at least on paper: a combination of capital levy and income tax on commoners, with special provision for servants; and a rank tax on the upper classes. A knight paid thirty shillings; a baron or baronet, forty; an earl, four pounds; and a duke, ten marks (£6 13s. 4d.).

Commoners owning goods and chattels worth more than two pounds and less then ten had to contribute a shilling. Progressively larger amounts were exacted from the better-endowed, with a maximum of 53s. 4d. from those with possessions worth £800 or more. Unearned income was also taxed on a sliding scale, the top rate of twenty shillings being imposed on incomes of forty pounds a year and above. There was no exemption even for small unearned incomes, a shilling being levied on those below two pounds a year, which must have hit many widows. Labourers, journeymen, and servants – men and women – over fifteen years of age with wages of forty shillings a year or more were charged a shilling; and those less than two pounds a year, which must have hit many, sixpence, the lowest rate of all. Thus the great majority of servants and labourers had to forgo at least one week's wages to support a campaign in which few of them can have had much interest.

Naturalized aliens, and children of alien parents, were treated as native-born citizens, but all other aliens – for example, the many foreign merchants operating in London – were charged double the rates applied to native-born Englishmen. Thus the measure took in its stride every single person in the country with any money at his or her disposal.

The tax proposals now had to be presented to the people in such a way that they would enjoy the maximum support. Military expenditure in the sixteenth century was no more popular with those who footed the bill than in later times, and as the proposed war was manifestly unnecessary it was particularly important for the government to induce the citizens to bless their plans. To the extent that the invasion had the approval of the man in the street (without his necessarily understanding the true motive) the tax collectors – men nominated by Members of Parliament to cover their own constituency, but who were appointed by the king and were responsible direct to the Exchequer – would find their job the easier. In the event the north of England was again recalcitrant, but Henry profited by his father's experience. As soon as the signs of opposition became evident the burden placed on the north was reduced and serious trouble was averted.[28]

The usual method of putting proposals of this nature across to the public was to embody them in a royal proclamation; and this was duly done on 4 November 1512.[29] The proclamation leads off with an elaborate justification of the proposed enterprise, following closely the preamble to the statute authorizing the special taxation measures. Louis the French king, adversary to their most dread sovereign and liege lord King Henry VIII and to his realm of England, daily moveth and stirreth by all the means in his power to undermine the authority of the Pope, who has sought the assistance of the King of England and many other Christian princes against the French. Henry has answered the call, not only because of his blessed and godly disposition for the true faith, but also because of France's hostile acts against England; and he is now in all haste making ready 'divers and sundry great armies and navies'. If Louis cannot be made to see the folly of his ways, Henry in his most royal person will take the field against him. For this, a great deal of money will be needed.

The proclamation was printed and widely distributed, so that it might be read out and displayed in public places by the civic authorities. The taxpayers, in this case virtually the whole population, now knew that the great military expedition which had been rumoured for some time was shortly to be undertaken, and that it would be commanded by the king himself. Most important of all, they knew how deep each and every one of them would have to dip into his pocket.

Provision had already been made for the orderly payment of wages. As there was no standing army it meant that the organization and control of each expeditionary force had to be worked out afresh; or at least that the government had to ensure that the precedents still applied and were known both to those in authority and to the rank and file. The precedent for the issue of pay lay in a statute of Henry VII which had been passed for the purpose of his invasion of France in 1492,[30] and which was repeated almost word for word in 1512.[31] Captains were to ensure that their men were paid within six days of their receiving the company's wages from the treasurer-at-war, and also that the whole of the number of soldiers agreed with the king were present with the colours, on pain of imprisonment and forfeiture of their goods and chattels.

NOTE

(1) Elis Gruffudd provides another example, which may seem too good to be true. During the siege of Montreuil in Henry VIII's second personal invasion of France 'a number of the chief men in the town were sitting at dinner at the same table, when one or two messengers were sent from the mound [where the cannon were] to the town to tell them to make merry; which swept off the heads of all the people who happened to be sitting on that side of the table, except one' (Gruffudd (ii), p. 33).

2 Beach-head

At seven o'clock in the evening of Thursday, 30 June 1513, Dr John Taylor, rector of Coldingham in Lincolnshire, the king's chaplain, and clerk to the English parliament, mounted the seaward wall of Calais to watch the arrival of the last ships of the great fleet – the like of which Neptune had never seen before – carrying Henry and the final wave of the mighty invasion force he was leading to France.[1]

The previous day had been unpleasant, with incessant rain and gales. Shipping in the vicinity had been driven to take refuge in Calais harbour. The tents of the troops outside the town were severely damaged. So many poles were smashed and guy-ropes broken that Richard Gibson, yeoman tailor in charge of tents, was hard put to it to find replacements. Today, however, was perfect. A favourable wind brought the last of the English ships quickly and safely across the Channel.[2]

The fleet made its landfall west of Calais, which had the incidental advantage of terrifying the French garrison in Boulogne. They concluded that a direct assault was about to be made on them; but after a great deal of trumpet-blowing and firing of cannon, probably intended as much to entertain the king, who loved a good show, as to fray the nerves of the garrison, the ships turned eastwards

The Embarkation of Henry VIII. *The fleet setting sail from Dover; the five principal vessels can be seen in the foreground, with Dover Castle on the left. From a painting at Hampton Court, artist unknown*

towards the English port of Calais. As they neared the harbour they continued to fire salvo after salvo and were joyfully answered by the cannon on the walls of the town. The thunder of the guns could be plainly heard at Dover twenty-two miles away, and Taylor, right in the middle of it, wrote in his diary that the din was so frightful that the world might have been coming to an end.[3]

The king immediately went ashore, resplendent in a rich outfit specially chosen for the occasion. He wore a decorated suit of almain rivets – flexible armour in which the wearer could walk without too much difficulty, unlike the full-dress suit of the man-at-arms, which was a one-man prison needing a powerful horse to carry it. His hat was banded with crimson satin in which was pinned a brooch depicting St George, and over his armour he wore a tunic of cloth of gold embroidered with the red cross of England. He was ceremonially received at the top of the steps leading up to the jetty by the governor, Sir Gilbert Talbot, who offered him the keys of the town.[4]

The foot-combat armour, a tonlet for Henry VIII c. 1520. Helmet by Giovanni Missaglia, the remainder is Flemish

The governor, who had held the post for three years, must have been deeply relieved at the safe arrival of his royal master and the last of the invasion troops. He had been under a heavy strain in recent months, having been responsible for the preparations to receive the army in Calais, in addition to the day-to-day running of the garrison and other miscellaneous matters. These included keeping his ear to the ground to learn the intentions of the French government, for which purpose he had an allowance of 'spyall money' for rewarding those who brought useful information into Calais.[5]

A few weeks earlier he had broken down under the pressure and had gone to bed for a fortnight. His own explanation of his illness was that he had served the king so diligently that he had forgotten to serve God, for which he had been duly punished;[6] but perhaps not the least of his troubles had been providing for the wants of Thomas Wolsey, whose demanding presence was just beginning to make itself felt in English affairs. Talbot found it easy enough to lay in the tun of wine which Wolsey ordered for his own use in Calais, but none of the special black 'gown cloth' which he asked for was available locally. Every wish of the rising star must be meticulously attended to, however. Messengers were sent to St Omer and Bruges in search of the cloth, and eventually the governor was able to report, no doubt with a sigh of relief, that the material had been dispatched to Wolsey in England.[7]

As soon as he was safely on dry land the king was conducted by a crowd of civic and religious leaders across Paradise, the garden lying between the harbour and the town where nine-pins, dice, and the other gambling games of the day were customarily played, which derived its name not from the heavenly delights it contained, but merely from the Paradise family who lived near by. Then they passed through the main entrance to the town, the Lantern Gate, to form a great procession in which only the king and his sword-bearer were mounted. It was led by Garter King of Arms and other heralds in their brilliant uniforms to St. Nicholas' Church on the far side of the town; and after mass and a *Te Deum* Henry retired for the night to the 'right goodly and sumptuous' Staple Inn, which was to be his headquarters during his stay in Calais.[8]

It was not long before his sleep was interrupted. About eleven o'clock there was a commotion in the camp outside the walls which led to the sounding of the alarm in the town. The king hastened to the battlements to see for himself what the trouble was. An enemy agent who had contrived to get a job with the victuallers had led a force of about 300 Frenchmen from the neighbouring coastal towns of Wissant ('Whitesand' to the English residents in Calais) and Boulogne to the outskirts of the town. They had waited in the darkness until low tide, when it was possible to wade past Fort Risban which guarded the harbour entrance, and planned to set fire to the victualling tents pitched between the town and the encamped army. Fortunately the watch was well kept, which was to be expected on the first night the king was with his troops, and the attackers were spotted before they could do any damage. A company of English archers waded into the harbour and drove them off without too much trouble. After hearing an account of the affair from Richard Gibson, whose tents had been the objective of the attack, Henry went back to bed, well satisfied with the vigilance of the watch.[9]

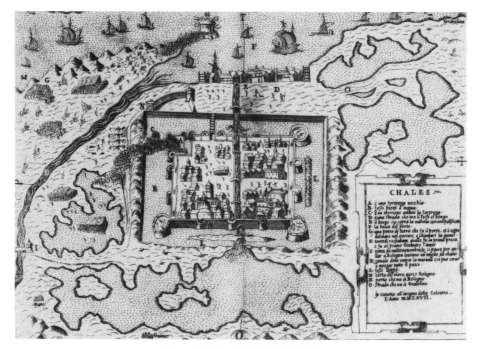

Plan of Calais 1567 (4°.B.49.Art.)

There had been a steady build-up of the English forces during the last three weeks. It was clearly impossible to get an army of any great size across the Channel in one move. Even if there had been enough shipping available the sudden arrival of between 30,000 and 40,000 men in Calais would have caused intolerable congestion. The army had therefore been transported in the three traditional divisions of fore-ward, middle-ward, and rear-ward, which were primarily intended to be battle formations, but could also be used to reduce problems of movement. When Henry again invaded France in 1544 the Privy Council advised him to use the same procedure.[10]

In 1513 a memorandum by the Bishop of Durham envisaged that the fore-ward, under the 45-year-old George Talbot, Earl of Shrewsbury, Steward of the Household and a member of the Privy Council, would start crossing on 15 May, wind and weather permitting; and estimated that it would take a fortnight to get the whole ward over to Calais.[11] In the event this timetable was not kept. It was not until 13 May that the command of the transports was given to John Hopton, a gentleman usher of the Chamber;[12] and it was another four days before Lord Mountjoy, William Hatclyffe, and Miles Gerrard were commissioned to provide the necessary vessels in the Cinque Ports, a complex and onerous task which they first tackled on 20 May.[13] At last on 6 June the fleet was assembled and began its job of ferrying the fore-ward across the Channel, which was safely completed in a mere four days. This left the transports free to carry the rear-ward, under Charles Somerset, Lord Herbert, starting on 10 June, and finally the middle-ward. The strict discipline, which was a feature of the whole expedition, applied even before the troops left England. Captains and men who failed to obey the orders of the commissioners to board the transports, and householders who harboured them, were liable to the death penalty.[14]

On 13 June the troops of the fore-ward, who by now had had a week in Calais to get properly organized, were summoned to the standard by the trumpeters, and marched out to make room for their comrades following on behind. Day by day the men of the middle-ward poured into Calais; and when the king himself arrived there on 30 June the ward which belonged to him by virtue of his leadership of the whole army was already assembled in the outskirts of the town awaiting his order to march.

* * *

Calais had been an English possession ever since its capture by Edward III 166 years earlier. In 1513 the town was the focal point of an irregular pale bounded by eighteen miles of Channel coast running from Gravelines in the east to Cap Blanc Nez in the west, penetrating at its deepest point nine miles inland, almost to the town of Ardres. The total area of the pale was about 120 square miles, and it had a population of about 12,000, no longer all the 'pure Englishmen' Edward III had insisted on, but a mixture of English, Picard, and Fleming.[15] The town was well fortified and protected on the seaward side by Fort Risban (probably 'Rushbank' originally), built on a promontory just outside the harbour. There were three other strong points within the pale: the castles of Hames and Guines, six and eight miles respectively to the south, and Fort Nieulay (then known as Newnhambridge) a mile or two outside Calais on the road to Boulogne.

The town and the pale were very much a part of England. 'Calais and the marches had never been considered as a mere fraction or relic of that kingdom of France which the kings of England claimed by right of inheritance under the Treaty of Troyes. The inhabitants were English subjects and their statute law was made at Westminster.'[15] The real value of the town lay in the protection it afforded England against attack by France, and in the easy access it gave English exporters to their markets on the Continent. These advantages were clearly recognized throughout the long period of English rule, and acts of parliament and royal proclamations show that the legislators in Westminster were anxious to provide for the security and efficient management of the outpost. Henry VII visited it himself in 1499 to be satisfied that it was properly run and that all the necessary precautions against sudden attack by the French were being taken.[16] One authority, writing not long afterwards, said that there were always about 800 chosen men in the town, 'and I do not believe that the castle of St Peter at Rhodes is more strictly guarded against the Turks than Calais is against the French'.[17] Because of the isolation of the place, however, it was difficult to be certain that the good intentions of parliament were always carried out.

During the middle years of Henry VIII's reign a decline in the prosperity of the town, caused principally by a falling-off in the wool trade, seriously affected the efficiency with which it was run; and an attempt was made to put things right in one of the most massive statutes in the history of parliament to that date. The preamble records that Calais is vital for the speedy and sure passage of all the king's subjects 'having intercourse of merchanting'; and also that the town, which 'hath been of long time, and yet is, one of the most principal treasures belonging to this his realm of England', is necessary both for the defence of the country and the control of the narrow seas.[18] In 1513, however, the high standards of administrative efficiency on which Henry VII had insisted were still being observed.

Possession of Calais made it easier to maintain an intelligence system that could keep abreast of any French developments directed against English interests. The Channel was a useful bulwark; but it was also a barrier that helped to protect French military secrets, and Calais was an admirable window for observing what the French were up to. Some idea of the potential scope of the intelligence network may be gathered from a manuscript in the Harleian collection which lists people in the neighbourhood of Calais who were still 'well-affected to the English nation' even after the town had been recaptured by France. For example: 'at Hames castle the brewer is a Calisian, sure; down in the marsh toward Hames, I think there be six Calisian soldiers, sure; at Oye along the downs are three Calisians, fishermen, sure also, but their names are forgotten; at Ark [Arques] there is an odd fellow, called monsieur de Prye, sure.'[19] If the English government could rely on so many potential informers after Calais and the pale had become French territory again, they must have had an even better source of information about troop movements, the state of fortifications, and so on, when these people formally owed loyalty to the English Crown, and were encouraged by disbursements from the governor's espionage fund.

The town, alas, was also a tempting base for hostile operations against France; and four times in his reign Henry VIII succumbed to the temptation – in 1513 and 1544 when he led his army in person, and in 1522 and 1523 when he sent Thomas Howard, Earl of Surrey, and Charles Brandon, Duke of Suffolk, as his commanders-in-chief. It was very like an English town, having had a mayor and council on the English pattern for a long time, and a flourishing commercial life founded on the activities of the merchants of the wool Staple, supplemented by the agriculture of the pale and herring fishing. The Staple was made responsible by act of the English Parliament for financing the garrison of the town and other strong points within the pale. This was only just. Without the garrison the merchants could not have survived a single day against the armies of France (although they were supposed to provide armed men free of charge to guard the town when the governor went on a foray – which he did from time to time to keep his troops fighting fit, and to remind the French that Calais had teeth);[20] and the £10,000 a year which they were required to pay for the soldiers was a sound investment.[21]

The military establishment worked in close collaboration with the civic authorities in managing the affairs of the town, but there was no doubt that the governor – 'the deputy of Calais' – had primary responsibility for the security of the pale as the direct representative of the Crown. His position at this time seems to have been very similar to that of the colonial governor of a later era, but the relationship between the Crown, the governor, and the city must have become less 'colonial' after Calais was given representation in the English

Parliament in 1536. In 1513 the unfortunate Sir Gilbert Talbot had about 700 troops under him.(1) Most of these, the 'great retinue', were stationed in the town and castle, but there were 17 in Fort Risban, 13 in Fort Nieulay, 40 in the castle of Hames, and 99 in the castle of Guines, the largest of the satellite garrisons, which was also nearest to the French border. The commanders of all the strong points were members of the governor's council, as were the high marshal, under-marshal, treasurer, comptroller and porter (the last holding a more important office than the name suggests).

The governor was responsible for seeing that justice was administered 'rightly and indifferently' in the king's courts (the judges of which were, however, like the garrison, paid out of the revenues of the town); but the merchants were left free to deal with commercial cases in the court of the Staple. Activities with a bearing on security – including the provision of food – which were in the first instance the responsibility of the civic authorities, were subject to the governor's approval. His powers were far from absolute, however, and a good many decisions had to be referred to London for final approval. For example, the king's permission had to be obtained before the governor could allow an alien to take up residence in the pale.

The high marshal had much the same functions as the marshal in the army when the troops were in camp. In addition to acting as second-in-command generally, and taking over the governor's duties when the latter was absent from his post (for which he needed special permission from the king), the marshal was particularly responsible for the administration of justice, and for ensuring through the under-marshal that the town was kept clean. He had also to see that good and true records were made 'of all manner of things that ought to be recorded'. The under-marshal's duties included posting the stand watch on the walls each evening, and making certain that it contained no interlopers; and, like the provost marshal in the army, he looked after the prison.

Between them the treasurer and the comptroller managed the financial administration of the garrison. The latter was required to muster the soldiers at least twice a year (more often if it seemed necessary to the governor and his council), and to satisfy himself that every man on the establishment was in post and adequately equipped with the appropriate armour and weapons. He then passed the certified muster book to the treasurer, who issued the amount of pay due, drawing on the funds he received from the Staple at six-monthly intervals. The treasurer was also in charge of the civilians engaged on maintenance of the fortifications, whose numbers varied from time to time. In 1513 there were sixteen masons and twenty-one carpenters, but later in the reign when the fortifications were being overhauled there were many more.

The last of the principal officers was the porter, who had charge of the keys of the town gates, and whose position made him an important source of inform-ation. News brought by people entering the town from the sea or from France was reported to him, and he passed on to the governor anything that seemed to have special significance, so that it might be incorporated in a report to London. He also had responsibilities in the sphere of customs. He was to prevent the imposition of unauthorized customs duties 'which might turn to the prejudice or hindrance of any person'.

The lieutenants of the satellite garrisons all had personal instructions on identical lines: to keep their castle and fortress 'true English' to the use of the king; to administer justice; to see that the peace was kept, and that there were no unlawful 'congregations, conventions, and conventicles'; and not to leave their posts without special permission from the king.

There were well-defined promotion procedures to ensure that the best men among the 'other ranks' got their due reward, and that corruption was kept to the minimum. At the apex of the other ranks' hierarchy came the five 'spears' assigned to the governor's retinue, and below them came the ordinary spears. Next were the archers on horseback, the scourers (scouts), the tipstaves, the 'vinteners' (the corporals of the later sixteenth-century army), the constables (who were civilian officers), the senior privates, who were paid 8d. a day, the ordinary privates, who had 6d., and, at the bottom of the list, the watchmen.

If there were a vacancy among the senior spears it was filled by the governor after he had examined the claims of all the spears in the garrison, but his final choice had to be ratified by his council. The vacancy thus created among the

The battle of Calais, where the English army was commanded by Sir Walter de Manny (Montagu illustration 195. No. 109.)

ordinary spears was filled by 'the most personable, sad, active and discreet' archer on horseback, and so it went on down the line. A tipstave vacancy was filled by the 'best-languaged' vintener; or, failing a suitable candidate among the vinteners, by the 'best-languaged' constable. On the lowest rung of the ladder stood the watchmen, whose first promotion was to the position of private soldier with a wage of 6d. a day.

All 'other ranks' promotions had to have the blessing of the governor, marshal, and comptroller, or any two of them; and when a promotion was made the clerk of the council gave the successful candidate a certificate signed by the comptroller and the treasurer, which was his authority to draw the pay of the higher post. For this service the promoted man had to pay the clerk a fee of twopence. Anyone who was not promoted in accordance with the procedure laid down forfeited his position, repaid all the wages he had received, and was liable to further punishment at the king's pleasure.

Promotions within the establishment of the treasurer were arranged separately, but on the same general lines. They also had to be approved by any two of the three – governor, marshal, and comptroller.

Calais was built in the form of a rectangle about three times as long as it was broad, the longer side running parallel with, and very close to, the sea and the harbour. As Henry sailed in he first saw the massive northern wall through a forest of masts. It was more of a series of linked towers than a wall, leading from the Beauchamp Tower on his left hand at the eastern end to the huge structure of the castle which occupied the north-west corner of the town, and was broken by the Lantern Gate with its beacons, and the Water Gate. Above the wall rose the tall closely packed roofs of the houses, and above them again soared the pointed spire of St Mary's Church, the towers of the town hall and the hall of the Staple, and finally, on his right hand, the square tower of the church of St Nicholas.

There were also substantial towers at the extremities of the southern wall and smaller towers at intervals round the whole perimeter. For the purpose of defence the wall was divided into six sectors, one of which was assigned to each of the principal officers. The governor was responsible for the Beauchamp Tower at the north-east corner of the town, where the highest ground was, and for the east wall as far south as the Milk Gate, which looked towards Flanders, and through which came the town's daily supply of milk. The marshal had the stretch from the Milk Gate to the south-east corner of the town, and also part of the south wall, and the comptroller the rest of the south wall to the Boulogne Gate. The short west side of the rectangle was in the hands of the treasurer; and then came the castle, which looked after itself. This left the north or seaward wall, which was shared between the under-marshal, who had the sector from the castle to the Rose Tower, including the Water Gate; and the porter, who had the rest of the north wall, including the Lantern Gate, through which Henry made his ceremonial entry.

A copy of the regulations for maintaining watch and ward in the town, which were drafted with great precision, is recorded in the Cottonian manuscripts.[22] They lay down which gates shall be open on which days, and for what hours, and the result is a highly complex timetable. They specify procedures for opening and closing the gates in which nothing is forgotten. For example, when the keys are being carried from one place to another they must be covered 'with a cushion or some other thing so that no man shall see the secrets of them'. They describe exactly how the various watches are to comport themselves, and the list comprises the stand watch stationed on the walls; the scout watch, which went the rounds of the town; the special 'burgess watch' on the castle hill, which was the responsibility of the town council; the banner watch used during the herring-fishing season, when many foreign vessels visited the port, which had to take into safe custody the armour and weapons of the visiting fishermen for the duration of their stay; and the search watch, which was responsible for policing the other watches.

Day-time guard duties included the ward at the gates, the daily ward in the market-place, and a special ward during Easter week, and were no less complicated.

Some idea of the thought that went into drafting the regulations may be gathered from a summary of the instructions to the search watch. At three o'clock every afternoon two tipstaves appointed for the week received the watchword for the night from the clerk of the council in the council chamber; and when the Flemish bell of the great hall rang in the evening one of them went to the east guard-house, and the other to the west. A constable with a company of nine men was waiting in each guard-house to receive the watchword, and the tipstave's admonition to 'keep good rule for that night'. The tipstaves then adjourned to the market-place, where the under-marshal was waiting for them. If the night was dark all three knocked on the flagstones until the sound of their staves brought them together. The tipstaves reported that the search watch was under way, and the under-marshal relayed this news to the governor.

At nine o'clock sharp two men set off from each of the guard-houses, only one in each pair having the watchword, and proceeded to inspect the stand watch on every part of the walls. When they came to the Water Gate, where the scout-watch guard-house was located, they had to call out 'Round! Round!' to which the scout watch answered 'Ye! Ye!' or 'Well! Well!' The two constables were expected to complete their tour in two hours (they were warned not to waste time playing dice or some other gambling game), and as soon as they got back to their guard-house two others left to take their place. This meant that for a period of ten hours during the night four constables were constantly moving through the town, keeping the other watchers on their toes. Any man who failed to do his stint on the search watch was imprisoned for eight days on the first offence, twenty days on the second, and dismissed from the service on the third.

If the search watch caught a member of the stand watch asleep three times in the same night, and succeeded in 'taking him by the nose', the fact was reported to a member of the council and the offender was duly subjected to a bizarre punishment which must have been very popular with the people of the town. On the next market day he was suspended from the wall in a basket ten or twelve feet above the waters of the harbour, and given a loaf of bread, a pot of drink, and a knife to cut the rope holding the basket when he had plucked up or imbibed the necessary courage. Meanwhile the dyke-keeper was standing by in a boat to rescue him when he eventually came down. Then, on the assumption that he did not go straight to the bottom of the harbour, he was returned to prison until the next market day, when he was released and banished from the town for a year and a day. A similar punishment (which seems to be singularly mild for the offence of falling asleep on guard duty three times in the same night) was prescribed in the garrison of Berwick, where there was also a convenient harbour.[23]

This then was the English town in which Henry was poised to push southwards to discipline the overweening French: an important strongly fortified trading-post with a well-organized garrison; a secure base to which the army could look for part of its supplies, so long as it did not roam too far afield; and a comforting escape route should a sudden withdrawal become necessary.

NOTE

(1) It appears to be suggested in *The Agrarian History of England and Wales* (vol. iv, p. 519) that the garrisons of Calais and Berwick in 1524 were both 20,000 men, but this could not possibly be right. In neither case did the normal garrison exceed 1,000. In Berwick in 1576, for example, there were 980 men (Cott. MS. Caligula B 1, f. 372).

3 Movement

Henry kept the middle-ward idle in Calais until 21 July, a grave error of judgement if his handling of the campaign is taken seriously. It meant that three weeks of high summer, the best part of the campaigning season, were wasted. It also meant that for a considerable period the English forces were divided, leaving the component parts the more vulnerable to any attack the French might mount. These criticisms of Henry's performance, however, apply only if the expedition is judged by normal professional standards, and if the outrageous luck of the rank amateur is discounted. As it happened, the French failed to take advantage of the chances Henry offered them to conquer his divided army; for which one of their military experts, who took part in the campaign, blames his fellow countrymen.[1] But rightly or wrongly the French higher command decided that their forces were too weak to risk a full-scale engagement, and the three

Margaret, Duchess of Savoy (present location unknown)

English wards were allowed to reunite without being subjected to a pitched battle. It also turned out that Henry's troops were able to gain their principal objective – to cover him with glory – before the campaigning season ended, although they had little time to spare and could well have done with the weeks he frittered away in July.

Not that the whole of his stay in Calais was unnecessary. There was work to be done, although it could have been done more quickly with greater profit. Much of the time the king was engaged in the business of state, discussing plans with members of his Council, reading and signing papers (many of which are preserved in a volume of the Stowe manuscripts in the British Museum),[2] meeting ambassadors, and generally organizing the middle-ward.

Henry got down to this work the day after he arrived, in spite of his disturbed night, when he received the ambassadors of the emperor and Margaret of Savoy in his dining-chamber in the Staple Inn. After they had delivered their messages they accompanied him to the church of St Nicholas and heard mass in the chapel of the Resurrection, where the body of Edmund Carew, a victim of the king's military ambitions, had been buried five days earlier.[3] In the same week he ratified the agreement about the campaign with the emperor before the high altar of St Mary's, and as usual made the most of the occasion. The ambassadors of Maximilian and Margaret were given a place of honour on either side of him as they rode to the church. Behind came the yeomen of the guard 'in their best jackets', the officers of the College of Arms in full uniform, and the corps of King's Spears marching on foot. The ceremony ended with a fanfare of trumpets.[4]

On market day, which fell on Wednesday in Calais, the statutes and ordinances of war specially prepared for the expedition were formally pro-claimed to members of the middle-ward, 'to the intent that no manner of person should pretend ignorance in them' – a precaution usually taken at the beginning of a campaign. On the following Friday the letters patent appointing Lord Lisle high marshal – second-in-command of the whole army – which had been issued to him at Westminster at the end of May, were read out by the Garter King of Arms in the market-place.[5] On the same day more ambassadors came, including the representatives of Ghent and Bruges, with offers to provide supplies for the invading army, on condition that the soldiers refrained from unfriendly acts towards their territories, to which Henry readily agreed.[6] Afterwards they were entertained by Henry to a show of his prowess with the long-bow. 'He cleft the mark in the midle and surpassed them all, as he surpasses them all in stature and personal graces', or at least so the loyal John Taylor claims in his diary. A few days later the Spanish ambassador put in an appearance and called on the king.[7]

In the first week in July there was an incident which Taylor thought boded ill for the success of the expedition. The town of Wissant, a short distance along the coast from Calais in the direction of Boulogne, having seen the tremendous power of the English army pouring across the Channel day after day, surren-dered without a shot being fired. Shortly afterwards, however, probably in the storm of 29 June, one of the English transports was driven ashore near the town and the inhabitants could not resist plundering the wreck. They took the crew prisoner and sent them off to Boulogne. Some of the ships of the English fleet, anxious for revenge, landed a force in Wissant Bay on Monday, 4 July, pillaged the town, and destroyed it by fire. Taylor reckons that because of their treachery the French deserved all they got, but nevertheless admits that many Englishmen were ashamed at the navy's ruthless action. He concludes that the Almighty must have shared their disapproval at the destruction of the town, for a terrible storm blew up on the following day and five English vessels were destroyed before the very eyes of the people in Calais, and their unfortunate crews perished 'after long struggling with the waves'.[8]

Henry regularly attended Mass in Calais, as he did throughout the expedition. The occasions are duly recorded, and so also are the sums he put into the collection. His usual offering, which came not from his own pocket but from 'our money appointed for the charge of our wars' in the hands of the treasurer-at-war, was the 6s. 8d. that had for many years been the traditional contribution of the sovereign. Even when he made his triumphal entry into the captured city of Tournai the standard offering was not increased, in spite of the importance of the occasion, although it is true that it was paid out three times during his progress.[9]

*   *   *

The fore-ward, under the Earl of Shrewsbury, whose family name – Talbot, the hunting-dog – was said to strike terror into the hearts of the French, left Calais on 13 June, having spent only a week there. Three days later the rear-ward, commanded by Lord Herbert, followed in its footsteps. This was part of the original plan. It had been intended that the fore-ward should spend as little time as possible in the town to avoid creating a shortage of food, but also that it should not push too far ahead of the rear-ward, as it was not considered to be strong enough to accomplish anything on its own.[10]

The two wards joined forces at Marquise, about fifteen miles west of Calais, and everyone assumed that Boulogne was their target. Suddenly, however, for reasons that are not clear in the surviving documents, they turned south and headed for Thérouanne. Had Henry been seriously concerned with the reconquest of northern France, Boulogne was the most obvious first objective. It looks as if he had in the first instance intended to attack it, but was persuaded to change his plan to one which would have greater benefit for Maximilian, who could do what he liked with the young Henry. The alternative that the English army was simply trying to mislead the French about their ultimate goal seems unlikely. The sixteenth-century army was hardly mobile enough to be used in a feint of this nature.

The march through Artois was uneventful. The scattered French garrisons sent out small forces to demonstrate against them, but the enemy did not venture far from their hastily reinforced strong-points and they made no attempt at a major attack. The fore-ward and rear-ward reached Thérouanne on 22 June and pitched camp near the town. The leaders, eager to get on with the job, immediately summoned a council of war. While this was in progress there was some desultory fire from the walls, and as luck would have it a bullet cut through the side of the tent and killed Edmund Carew as he sat at the council table. The members of the council of war were overcome with dismay, but Herbert reminded them that this was the chance of war. On active service the noble heart does not fear death; and even if he, their leader, were thus struck down, they must be prepared to take it in their stride.[11]

* * *

Henry at last gave the order to march on Thursday, 21 July, by which date the combined fore-ward and rear-ward had been sitting ineffectually before the heavily fortified town of Thérouanne for nearly a month. The king's ward was the biggest of the three, partly as a security measure, and partly because it included the vast household staff, few of whom contributed to the efficient conduct of the campaign. The fore-ward had about 12,000, not all of whom were fighting men, and the rear-ward about 7,500, but the total strength of the middle-ward may have been as high as 16,000. Over 2,000 of these, however, were there to serve the king in one capacity or another; and they would have been left at home had the expedition been commanded by a general appointed by Henry.

The king's 'wardrobe of robes' had a staff of 49; the wardrobe of the king's beds, 15; the king's chapel, 115; and the chamber generally, which included the knights and squires of the king's body, gentlemen ushers, sewers, grooms and pages, and a solitary luter, totalled 579. The king's household – those responsible for the provision of his food, the preparation of meals, and so on –

Charles Somerset, 1st Earl of Worcester by
George Harding

accounted for another 276 men. His eight trumpeters fulfilled an important military function, but the same can hardly be said for his minstrels and players, of whom there were ten.

The formation adopted for marching varied according to the particular circumstances of an army, but certain rules were generally accepted. 'The order to be had when a king goeth in battle'[12] ('battle' in this case being the term used to describe the marching formation, and not conflict with the enemy) assumes that the high marshal will march ahead of the main body of the troops, supported by his under-marshals and a company of 'valiant soldiers'. The main purpose of this advance guard is to spot important enemy concentrations and give the main force surrounding the king time to take up defensive positions should a major attack appear to be imminent.

Immediately behind this group come the officers whose functions require that they should reach the halting-place for the night in advance of the main body of the army – the harbinger (quartermaster of a later period), the sergeant of the tents, the victuallers, and the master of the ordnance. The rest of the troops are to ride or march 'where they shall be commanded' by the high marshal. The nobility accompany the king in the greatest strength possible, marching in order of precedence, their banners carried before them. Then come the king's trumpeters, from whose trumpets hang the royal arms, and the knights bachelor. The kings of arms, heralds and pursuivants (whose function was something between that of ambassador and dispatch-rider) march near the king 'ready to be sent here and there when need shall be'.[13]

These broad rules, laid down by tradition and common sense, were supplemented in the case of the 1513 expedition with more detailed procedural instructions that illustrate the great care with which the enterprise was planned. Indeed, so meticulous are they that they might have been drafted by a professional efficiency expert, and it must have been extremely difficult to observe them to the letter. For example, the cavalry were expected to saddle and mount their horses as one man. It was laid down 'that every horseman at the first blast of the trumpet do saddle his horse, at the second to bridle, at the third to leap on the horse's back to wait on the King or his lord or captain'. Men were required to keep close to the standard of their own company and not to mingle with other companies, unless, of course, like the harbinger and his assistants, they had business with the army as a whole. This rule had to be strictly observed at all times, especially when danger threatened, and when the troops had 'stalled' (that is, come to a temporary halt) and there was a strong incentive to alleviate the boredom of the occasion by passing the time of day with acquaintances in other companies. 'Also for no tidings nor for no manner of scry' (i.e. alarm) 'that may come in the host no man move himself in disarray out of the battle if they ride or go, but by leave of his chieftain.' If a man *did* leave a 'stall' without permission he was imprisoned, and lost any booty he was entitled to, one-third to his captain, and two-thirds to the commander of the troops he had left; and if anyone raised a banner to lead others from the army without authority, he was deemed a traitor and was drawn, hanged, and quartered.[14]

The order to be followed by Henry's battle – the middle-ward – was devised with particular care before it left Calais, no doubt simply because it *was* Henry's

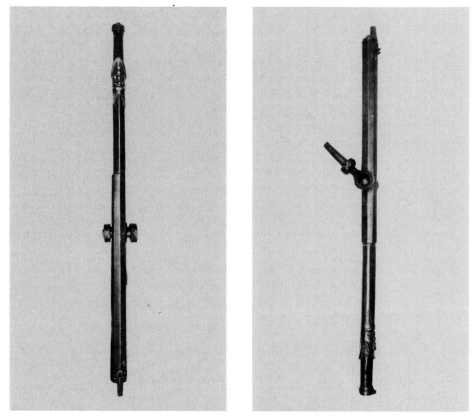

Bronze swivel gun; probably Flemish or German, c. 1520. Guns of this type were frequently carried on Tudor warships

battle. Several versions of the plan survive,[15] and although they vary on points of detail they agree on the broad pattern. They make it clear that the middle-ward, itself one of the three divisions of the whole army, was for the purpose of marching further sub-divided into three: a left wing, a right wing, and a centre, in the last of which the king was located. This arrangement was unusual enough to call for comment from the chronicler Hall, and it may perhaps be regarded as an early move in the direction of the regiment, which became properly established later in the century, and which made large armies much more flexible than when they were merely divided into three enormous 'battles'. A third of the middle-ward would in fact have been about 5,000 men, which was almost exactly the size of the early continental regiment; but the centre (6,700 or thereabouts), was larger than the two wings, so that the king would have the maximum amount of protection.

Some of the records suggest that the three component parts of the middle-ward marched one after the other, others that they marched abreast, and it may be that the formation adopted depended on the nature of the terrain for the time being. Some distance ahead of the main body of the ward rode the scourers (light cavalry scouts), the knight marshal, second-in-command to the high marshal, the provost marshal, the harbinger, and his assistants. The advance elements were protected by 'spears' from the garrison of Calais, 40 men-at-arms, 300 demi-lances (medium cavalry), and 200 mounted archers. These men were listed as a 'bill signed with the king's own hand', which shows that Henry had taken a close personal interest in devising the order of march. Then followed the heavy guns under the command of Sir Richard Carew, with his personal retinue and 1,000 men.

The two wings each had 3,000 men in two groups of 1,500. The centre was also in two sections: an 'avant-garde' under Lord Lisle, the high marshal, with 3,200 men; and surrounding the king 3,500, who included 800 members of the household qualified by birth to defend him at close quarters. An artillery screen protected the whole front and rear of the ward, and the baggage wagons 'meddled with ordnance' covered the flanks, so that a defensive position could be taken up at very short notice. Finally, there came another detachment of light cavalry to ensure that any danger of attack from the rear was spotted in good time.

The whole formation was designed to provide the maximum security consistent with mobility, security especially for the king, the heart and soul of the ward. If the enemy were to get anywhere near him they had to fight their way through the light cavalry escort, past the protecting wall of wagons and cannon and the billmen and archers of the wings, before they reached the 3,500 men immediately surrounding him, who included his standard-bearer and personal bodyguard.

A detachment of German troops, supplied through the good offices of Maximilian, but paid for by Henry, occupied a key position in the left wing, thanks to their reputation as tough fighters, which was recognized throughout Europe. 'They render excellent services on a day of battle,' says one contemporary authority, 'or when the camp is to be pitched near the enemy, or when the army is in retreat, as they are well-disciplined and obey their officers.' This was only one side of the picture, however. The same writer goes on to say:

> But such is their beastliness and arrogance that unless they are commanded by a captain of their own nation whom they know to be generous and courageous, and who holds a commission from the Emperor, they are rather a firebrand and a source of trouble than any real advantage.[16]

The English higher command fully recognized that the Germans were difficult allies. It was firmly laid down in the regulations that:

> ... no Englishman intermeddle or lodge himself within the ground assigned to the Almains for their lodging, or to give them any reproach or unfitting language or words by the which noise or debate might ensue, upon pain of imprisonment and further to be punished as the case shall require ... And over that, the King's highness commandeth that all Englishmen and other of his army friendly and courteously do treat the said Almains after like manner as though they were his proper subjects.[17]

It is possible to deduce a rough idea of the 'shape' of the king's ward as it made its ponderous way down through the rolling plains of Artois. Even if we assume that the three sub-divisions of the ward marched one behind the other we arrive at a formation with a singularly broad front. We know that each of the wings had 200 men in a rank, so that if they marched in the 'order' of the second half of the century, which allowed 3 ft between the files, each wing would have a front of 200 yards. 'Order' also stipulated a distance of 6 ft between the follower and leader, so that if we take the total strength of the king's ward to be 16,000 men (the probable maximum) it would have no more than 80 ranks. It would thus have a front of 200 yds (200 men) and a depth of only 160 yds (80 men).

If, however, the component parts marched abreast, if the wings really acted as wings (and at least some of the records suggest that they sometimes did), the front would have been extended to nearly a third of a mile (600 men), while the depth was reduced to a mere 50 yds (say 26 men). These 'shapes' are perhaps surprising, but they become less so if we bear in mind that the army was uninhibited by the need to follow roads, although it is true that forests, hills and rivers must from time to time have dictated changes in the chosen formation. Again, the narrower the front, the more the troops, and especially the gun-carriages and the wagons, would churn up the ground; and there was therefore positive advantage in spreading the ranks as wide as possible. Finally, the more the army was extended from front to rear, the more vulnerable it was to a flank attack at the critical moment when it was about to halt and set up camp.

The shape of the ward would of course be different if it were marching in 'open order' (12 ft between the files, and the same distance between follower and leader); or in close order (the files shoulder to shoulder, and only 3 ft between follower and leader).

The vehicles used were mainly two- and four-wheeled wagons. The latter were 10 or 12 ft long and consisted of a floor with rails round the perimeter. Sometimes if the load was very long – tent-poles, for example – the back and front rails were removed so that the load could project at either end. Perishable stores were normally covered by a tarpaulin made from several horse-hides sewn together. The number of horses pulling the wagons varied from two to seven, depending on the weight of the load, but many more were needed to drag the heavy guns. The lighter cannon were carried on wagons, but the heavier had their own gun-carriages, and some of them took as many as twenty-four Flanders mares – which were much more powerful than English horses. The wagons were supposed to be used only for guns, stores and tents, but privates often tried to ride on them, which was against regulations. It was laid down for the 1513 expedition that captains were to limit the number of men 'attending upon their carriages' to the minimum needed to set up their tents. If they assigned more than the minimum to this work they were liable to lose a month's pay, and the super-numerary men were to be imprisoned.[18]

* * *

Hardly had the trumpet call summoning Henry's ward to the standard died away when it became apparent that it is difficult to plan for every contingency. As the troops were falling in, there was a stampede among the cavalry. Sir Henry Marney, captain of the king's guard, had his leg broken and a number of other gentlemen were injured. The incident was serious enough to upset the whole departure plan – 'it was long ere ever the army might be set in order according to the bill devised by the council'; and when darkness fell the troops had covered no more than three miles.[19]

Camp was pitched between the townships of Fréthun and Old Coquelles in an area protected by impassable marshland; but the army faced no real danger from the enemy, as it was still within the pale of Calais. The king had chosen a bad day to start his adventure, for after a clear morning (which had been devoted to restoring some semblance of order among the troops) it rained heavily all afternoon and night. The tents, which had already suffered from the weather, particularly in the storm of 4 July, were further damaged and began to leak. Perhaps this was the reason why the king did not go to bed, but instead rode round the saturated camp in the small hours of the morning encouraging the unfortunate watch who had to stand in the downpour, saying to them, perhaps with unjustified optimism, 'Well, comrades, now that we have suffered in the beginning, fortune promises us better things, God willing.'[20]

The middle-ward remained where it was next day, still within sight of Calais. This may have been to give the tents time to dry out, or it may have been because it was Mary Magdalene's Day. It can hardly have been because the men were worn out after their three-mile march. Mass was heard in the camp, and attended by Henry.[21] The French, who had been waiting patiently for the king's ward to emerge, sent a small force from Boulogne to reconnoitre but they were met by Sir Rees ap Thomas and the light cavalry and beat a hasty retreat.[22]

On Saturday, 23 July, the troops restarted their march, but once again they could cover no more than three miles, although on this occasion there was no untoward incident to delay them. They spent the night at Hames, still inside the pale, and remained there all day, Sunday, while Henry went off to nearby Guines to see the state of his fortress and garrison there.[23]

Although the distances covered in the first two days were a good deal less than normal, it was in fact impossible for an expedition to march more than a few miles in a day. Small mounted groups could in theory cover between twenty and thirty miles a day. In 1542, for example, a company of 100 cavalry were expected to cover nearly thirty miles a day to get them from York to Newcastle upon Tyne – which compares very favourably with the official posting journey of seven miles in summer and five in winter;[24] but it was quite impossible for a whole army to move at this rate. Daylight was one limiting factor, for troops could not be moved with any degree of safety at night. There was also a limit to the distance a man could march. The king and his senior officers, and also the captains and petty-captains, were mounted and could cover much greater distances than the heavily laden infantryman; but the effective progress of the army as a whole was limited to that of the slowest element, the artillery. To allow the artillery train to fall behind the main body of the army, or to send it off an hour or two earlier in an attempt to lengthen the day's march, would have left the guns vulnerable to attack by the enemy, and it would also have denied their protection against any attack launched on the rest of the army. So the speed of the march was the speed of the slowest of the cannon.

The army had no detailed maps of the territory they passed through, and it was therefore necessary to recruit expert guides. These were as a rule natives of the country invaded, as it was unlikely that the invading force would have anyone who knew the country well enough to advise on the best routes. This posed a grave security risk, for it was never easy to decide with certainty where the loyalty of the chosen guides lay. They were assigned to a guide master, responsible to the high marshal, who was adjured to treat them well so that they would not be tempted to steal away, taking with them information of untold value to the enemy. They were to be promised great rewards if they did a good job, and threatened with the most condign punishment if they let the army down through either treachery or incompetence.[25]

Camp was struck on Monday, 25 July, and the ward marched about six miles to the neighbourhood of Ardres. They were now approaching enemy territory, although the town of Ardres was supposed to be 'patised'. That is to say the inhabitants had agreed to pay some form of tribute to the invaders in return for which they would be unmolested. In spite of this the Germans accompanied by some English troops began to pillage and burn the town, and desecrate the churches. Henry immediately issued an order that anyone found guilty of stealing from the people of Ardres would suffer the death penalty; and he ordered the troops to leave the town within the hour. They paid little attention to his order, however, thereby illustrating the point made above,[26] and the city was cleared of the rioting troops only when Henry in person led a detachment of his guards against them. Three Germans were hanged on the king's instructions.[27]

Now that the middle-ward was outside the pale it was frequently subjected to nuisance attacks by the French. The first substantial encounter occurred when a considerable force based on Boulogne and Montreuil engaged the English troops near Tournehem. According to one authority their objective was to kill or capture the king, but the ward stood its ground and used its artillery to great effect. Fleuranges considers that if the French had been able to reply to the English cannon they would have won this 'grand and triumphant' skirmish; but they had no guns – they could scarcely have dragged them from Boulogne with the small forces at their disposal – and they were eventually beaten off.[28]

When the ward moved on again it marched in 'close order' (i.e. shoulder to shoulder), so that it would be less vulnerable to surprise attack by detachments of French cavalry; but some of the heavy guns were allowed to fall behind – perhaps because the constant attention which the troops were now receiving from the French encouraged the majority to move rather faster – and St John the Evangelist, one of Henry's beloved twelve apostles, lagged further and further behind the main body of the ward and was finally allowed by the team in charge to slip off the track into a stream. The apostles had been bought in Flanders specially for the expedition, and to lose one of them before it had been fired in anger was a major disaster. St John weighed more than three tons, and as the water was quite deep it was clearly going to be a long job to bring him back into the fold again. However, George Buckemer, the master carpenter of Calais who

The Emperor Maximilian hunting on horseback with a crossbow. Engraving by Hans Burgkmair from Der Weiss Kunig, *1516*

was accompanying the ward, insisted that he could make the necessary lifting tackle and get the gun on dry land again. The ward accordingly pressed on, after a hundred workmen had been assigned to help the carpenter; but a powerful French force which had watched the incident from a safe distance emerged from its hiding-place as soon as the coast was clear and fell upon the unsuspecting labourers with spears, crossbows and hand-guns. The unfortunate men had no chance of defending themselves and were all killed or taken prisoner. Hall, perhaps a little unfairly, blames the master carpenter, 'who would work all of his own head without counsel',[29] but had to pay for his wilfullness with his life.

Meanwhile the rest of the ward had reached Tournehem, 'where there is a fair castle standing in a woody country'. Their way was barred by the river Hem north of the town, and when his officers hesitated to cross, Henry had to set a good example by wading in first. They were still in the neighbourhood of Tournehem on Wednesday, 27 August, when news came that the English spy who had been sending information about the French forces had been caught and killed; and that the enemy who had been skilfully using the woods for cover were now approaching through a mist so dense that the English troops could hardly see each other. Henry at once ordered the trumpeters to 'blow to the standard', and 'with the ardour of a youthful knight'[30] led the middle-ward to a defensive position on a near by slope, where he personally supervised the planting of the artillery. According to the English authorities the French infantry halted two miles away, concealed by a low hill, while the cavalry tried to tempt the middle-ward into a trap; but Henry ordered his men to stand their ground. During this period a French knight approached and issued a challenge to single combat, showing that the age of chivalry was not yet dead, but the challenge was not accepted.

The whole of the enemy force then revealed itself and was met with artillery fire, to which it had no reply. The English cavalry launched a spirited attack and a general mêlée developed, of which John Taylor observes: 'It was a pleasant sight, if a man's skin had not been in hazard.' At noon, when the engagement had been in progress for six hours, Sir Rees ap Thomas, who had been away on a reconnaissance, turned up with his light cavalry (to the alarm of the middle-ward, who thought they were French reinforcements); but his appearance was decisive, and the enemy withdrew.[31]

According to Taylor, one English soldier and twenty French were killed, but the weather was also responsible for casualties. Early in the day the fog gave way to blazing sunshine, and the Englishmen, 'unaccustomed to great heat',[32] were kept in battle array from six o'clock in the morning until three in the afternoon, with no shade and no drinking water, and 'were burned about the mouth with heat of the stomach'. Some actually died 'for lack of moisture'. The day was afterwards known as dry Wednesday.

The French have a different version of the encounter, which illustrates the point made below that it is difficult to build up an accurate picture of any fight. According to the *Histoire du bon Chevalier* Henry reached Thérouanne only after he had had a 'bad fright' at Tournehem, where he was nearly attacked by 1,200 mounted men-at-arms. Unfortunately the French had no infantry, whereas

Henry had nothing *but* infantry – 12,000 of them, including 4,000 *Landsknechte*. As soon as the two armies got within cannon shot of each other the king 'eut paour d'estre trahy: si descendit a pied, et se mist au meillieu des lansquenets'. There was no question of treachery, however, and the chronicler can only mean that Henry was afraid that he was going to be done for, and that he therefore dismounted and found an inconspicuous and safe position in the middle of the German troops, whom he regarded as better fighters than his fellow country-men. The author of the *Histoire* considers that it was the English rather than the French who laid a trap, and says that most of the French wanted to walk right into it. Even Bayard several times urged de Piennes, the French commander, to charge, claiming that there was no risk. If the English line broke, they would be routed: if it held firm, the French could easily escape, as they were mounted and the English had no cavalry. De Piennes firmly refused to charge, however. He said that he had been ordered by the king to take no chances, but 'to keep the field', that is to say to maintain intact a force that could be used to keep the countryside free from marauding bands of Englishmen; and he would not agree to an attack. He won the argument, and the English ward was allowed to march away unmolested 'under the very noses of the French'.[33] John Taylor supports Fleuranges and Bayard in the view that had the French taken their chance they might have won a considerable victory, and perhaps prevented Henry from joining the other two wards at Thérouanne; but all the evidence shows that de Piennes was under the strictest instructions not to become involved with the main English force.[34]

As they left Tournehem Henry (unaware that the French were forbidden to attack in strength) ordered the main body of his cavalry to ride behind the ward as a precautionary measure, but no attack materialized, and they were able to pitch camp about two miles from St Omer without further interruption. While they were in the neighbourhood of St Omer many of the English captains visited the churches in the town, which were considered to be very beautiful; and according to Robert Macquereau they also took the opportunity to stock up, not with food, which was plentiful in the camp, but with shoes, stockings and other articles of clothing.[35]

Henry had been most upset by the loss of St John the Evangelist, and his anger increased when the news came in that the French had captured a second gun – a bombard known as the 'red gun' – which seems to have been left in the care of the labourers deputed to retrieve the sunken apostle. The Earl of Essex and Sir Rees ap Thomas were sent back to see if they could recover the two cannon. They found that the bombard had been removed to safety by the French but the apostle still lay in the stream. Lord Berners, the master of the ordnance, who was also in charge of the pioneers, succeeded in bringing it up and a team of Flanders mares was harnessed to it; but before they could move off a large French force came on the scene. Essex was tempted to attack it, but Sir Rees ap Thomas restrained him, pointing out that they were heavily outnumbered. In any case their orders were to recover St John, and they must leave it at that. Essex reluctantly agreed, but as they began the return journey to camp, 'softly and not in flying manner', the French cavalry launched an attack on their rear. The English companies retaliated with great spirit and the French were soon in retreat, leaving Essex and Sir Rees free to convey St John back to the king in triumph.

The middle-ward then spent three days at Arques, and on Monday, 1 August, marched to Thérouanne, where they set up camp a mile from the city – with difficulty, for the great heat of the last day or two gave way to a violent rainstorm which lasted a day and a half, and produced a sea of mud in which the men could hardly move.[36]

4　Camp

In friendly territory the army might be quartered in the towns and villages through which it passed, on the authority of 'billets' issued by the knight harbinger – the quartermaster. This gave the yeoman soldier a roof over his head for the night, without impairing his mobility, as he was able to join the company standard the instant the trumpet call sounded in the morning.

There was no question, however, of billeting the troops in France, and tents were the only alternative to sleeping rough; but tents were reserved for the officers. To provide them for the rank and file would have seriously reduced the mobility of the army, partly by increasing the total weight the baggage wagons had to carry, and partly by lengthening the time taken to strike and pitch camp; and it would, of course, have substantially increased the cost of equipping the expedition. Nevertheless, about this time captains were taking it upon themselves to provide better shelter for their men in spite of the objections of the higher command. On the expedition which besieged and captured Boulogne in 1544 there was a general order forbidding them to provide tents or marquees for private soldiers, on the grounds that it would hinder the movement of the army. The common soldiers were expected 'to make their own lodging as the men of other nations did'.[1] This meant either sleeping in the open or improvising a simple hut out of branches brought from the nearest wood and perhaps covered with straw or a linen or canvas sheet. To get himself ready for the march a man would have to do no more than fold and stow the sheet among his few possessions, and finally set fire to his lodging so that it would be of no use to the enemy.

It was in fact possible to live fairly comfortably in huts, provided that the weather was not too bad. Elis Gruffudd, perhaps a tougher-than-average Welsh soldier, heaps scorn on men who were not prepared to take the trouble to make a hut. Writing of the troops in France in 1523 he says:

> . . . And yet they had no reason to complain except of their own sluggishness and slovenliness. For there was no lack of food or drink or wood for fire or making huts, and plenty of straw to roof them and to lie on if they had only fetched it; but there was many a man weak in body who preferred from sheer laziness to lie under the hedge rather than take the trouble to make a snug warm hut . . .

Gruffudd also records that tents could be very comfortable, and at the same time

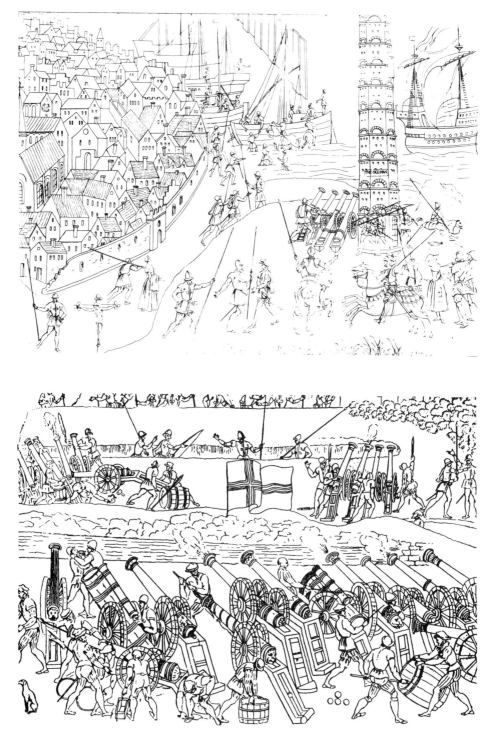

The siege of Boulogne 1544. Details from an engraving of the wall painting at Cowdray House (now destroyed)

shows that the hardships which the private soldier has to face change little with the centuries. He speaks of himself lying in a tent during freezing weather 'as snug as a small pig', when the man next to him:

> ... got up to make water in the door of the tent or the hale and shouted, 'Ah, sirs, if I had known at the beginning of the night that there would be as much frost and snow as this I would not have taken so much trouble to search my shirt for lice, but I should have hung it out in the wind and let them die of cold as we shall do if we stay here any longer.'[2]

The officers, however, including the captains, lived in tents, the handling of which was a big job on any expedition. It was a much bigger job on a 'royal' expedition, when provision had to be made for the many members of the household without whom Henry's daily routine could not have proceeded, and also for many services which could be dispensed with when the commander-in-chief was the king's lieutenant. The accounts of Richard Gibson, yeoman tailor in charge of tents on the 1513 expedition, give some idea of the magnitude of the task and provide further evidence of the care with which every aspect of the expedition was planned.[3]

The tents were not very different in design and construction from some of those in use at the present day. The majority were made of canvas, although the royal tents were of richer materials, including damask and say. The most magnificent of all, which was reserved for Henry's ceremonial occasions, was completely fashioned from cloth-of-gold.

There were four main types: 'Tents' resembled bell tents as we know them, with a single central pole and a circular floor about 20 ft in diameter, and were sometimes known as 'round houses'.[4] 'Pavilions' were roughly the same size as tents, with a square base, vertical walls supported by poles at the corners, and a pyramid-shaped roof leading up to a single pole. 'Hales' were very large, with almost exactly the same shape as the present-day marquee; that is to say, they had walls which were usually 6 ft high, supported by a series of poles of the same height, a rectangular floor, sometimes with semicircular ends, and several tall poles running down the middle. Finally, there were 'tressans' or galleries, connecting the other tents, which were often spacious and constituted shelters in their own right. All these forms were held erect by guy-ropes leading from the top of the tent-poles to metal pegs hammered into the ground – 'pins of iron', to give them their contemporary name. Some of the guy-ropes, divided into three branches, were sewn into the canvas of the tent. This 'crowfoot tackling' is clearly seen in the drawing referred to below.[5]

Most of the senior officers' marquees were of double canvas and they sometimes had an inner tent to give even greater protection from the elements. For example a marquee 30 ft by 15 might contain a smaller tent 24 ft by 12. The actual living-space was thus surrounded by an insulating passage 18 in wide at the sides and 3 ft wide at the ends. The dimensions of all the four types of tent varied, but there were standard sizes, of which 24 by 12, 30 by 15, and 50 by 20 ft were the most common for marquees, and 18 or 20 ft diameter for tents and sides for pavilions.

Tents were allocated to the higher command on the same principle that governs the size of the carpet upon which the administrator of today wages the battle of government. The individual officer's entitlement as a rule accurately matched his rank. Inevitably Henry had by far the most magnificent quarters, in which the *pièce de résistance* was not a tent but a prefabricated timber house, complete with fireplace and chimneys, the component parts of which occupied twelve carts. The approximate size and shape of the house may be deduced from an inventory of the parts made in December 1537 when the then master of the king's tents (Sir Thomas Cawarden) was examining hales and tents which had been in store since they came back from the siege of Tournai twenty-four years earlier. The tents were in poor condition but the wooden house had lasted well.

It had two rooms, one 27 ft by 14, with walls 8 ft high to the eaves, and the other smaller, with 7-ft walls; a pitched roof about 14 ft from floor to apex; and windows of 'lantern horn', which admitted some light but at the same time gave privacy. (Glazed windows were common at this time, but horn had the advantage for this special purpose that it was more durable than glass.) The component parts were standardized to facilitate assembly and dismantling. The thirty roof panels were all 8 ft by 3. There were two sizes of wall panel – 8 ft by 3 ft 4 in (twenty panels) for the larger room; and 7 ft by 3 ft 10 in (twelve panels) for the smaller. Other parts included joists, rafters, beams, posts, and made-up sections of flooring. To enhance the appearance of the house, and make it look more solid, the outside was painted 'in manner of brickwork'.[6]

It is not clear if the king used the house when the army was on the march and remained no more than a night or two in one place. Common sense deems this an unwarrantable waste of effort, but few of Henry's actions on the 1513 campaign were governed by common sense, and it may well be that the pavilioners' first task when the army halted was to assemble the 'King's house of timber'.

Henry also had two wagon-loads of tents (apart from his great tent of cloth of gold, which occupied a whole wagon) with a total area of more than 4,000 sq ft. They included a porch, three pavilions, two marquees ('the first chamber' and 'the great chamber'), and several connecting galleries, one of which led from the great chamber to the timber house. Finally, in one of the galleries there was a small canvas room 25 ft sq which, according to the antiquary Francis Grose, was used either for stowing baggage, or as a bedroom, although it is difficult to understand how Grose thought that a man of Henry's height could sleep comfortably in a 5-ft bed. The purpose of the room was in fact to house the king's close-stool,(1) which the *Oxford English Dictionary* delicately describes as 'a chamber utensil enclosed in a stool or box', a facility provided for only five members of the king's retinue – Wolsey, the captain of the yeoman of the guard, the treasurer-at-war, the lord chamberlain and the master of the horse.

A German account of Maximilian's visit to the camp at Thérouanne on 14 August provides a vivid picture of Henry's tents. They looked like a castle or little town, and guards with drawn swords were stationed at intervals around them. 'Entering a gateway, one passed into the tents, first a tent, then a passage between, then another tent covered here and there with gold, until one came to the King's tent, which was of a handsome size.' Inside, all over from the ground to the roof, it was covered with rich cloth of gold of pure drawn gold thread. There was a beautiful gilded sideboard, on which stood large vessels and flagons, including drinking-cups of solid gold 'which are looked after by certain persons thereto appointed' – the officers of the ewery. From the king's main tent, 'the great chamber', a passage covered inside and out with cloth of gold led into 'a council house which puts together and takes to pieces again' – an accurate description of the king's portable wooden building. 'It is painted red outside and within is hung with golden tapestry. Therein stood the king's bed hung round with very precious cloth-of-gold, the gilt woodwork being carved and very well finished.'[7]

Although the accommodation provided for Henry's senior officers diminished according to their rank, there were exceptions to the rule. Wolsey was officially no more than the king's almoner, but his group of tents, the biggest of which was known as the Inflamed House, occupied more than 1,700 sq ft, about half as much again as the records show for Lord Lisle, second-in-command of the whole army; but Wolsey had played an important part in the preparatory work for the expedition, and it is perhaps to be expected that he would find himself in more generous quarters than his place in the chain of command warranted.

Sometimes a group of officers shared a tent. These groups included the king's physicians, surgeons, and their assistants – thirty-one of them in all[8] – his trumpeters, the harbingers, and the kings of arms, heralds, and pursuivants. Others who shared were the king's secretaries and the gentlemen ushers. The provost marshal had a tent which was also occupied by any prisoners committed to his charge, which he cannot have found entirely satisfactory. Two marquees were provided for the ambassadors from friendly states who accompanied Henry on the expedition. Their tents were among the few that were provided with partitions, perhaps so that there might be some semblance of security when their occupants were discussing matters of state with their secretaries and drafting dispatches to their governments.

One of the more unusual marquees was the Jewel House, which was necessary only on a royal expedition when the king wanted to be able to hand out tokens of affection and esteem as the spirit moved him. The Jewel House was one of the 'marquees within a marquee', and the fortune that Henry carried with him in precious stones and ornaments on the 1513 expedition, and so generously disbursed, was probably protected by guards sleeping in the narrow corridors between the inner and outer tents.

Most of the household services – the bakehouse, pantry, scullery, buttery, woodyard, laundry, ewery and so on, were accommodated in standard marquees 24 ft by 12; and although these tents were primarily intended to house the equipment needed for the various services, it is likely that the servants were accustomed to sleep in them in spite of the general rule that only the officers should enjoy the comfort of a tent.

The larder had a much bigger marquee, as did the clerk of the kitchen, who was responsible for looking after the 'store for the King's mouth' – the provisions reserved for the king's own use. Henry's 'wardrobe of beds' and his 'wardrobe of robes' each needed a marquee of 700 sq ft, which is hardly surprising in view of the splendour with which the king dressed on all occasions, and the elaborate nature of the bed-coverings under which he slept.[9] The large number of men concerned with the erection and maintenance of the tents – the pavilioners – had a tent to themselves, a 1,000 ft marquee in plain white canvas.

To make it easier to identify the tents, both when they were packed up in the baggage train and when they were erected in the camp, they were given names that as a rule had some connection with the purpose of the tent or the function of the officer who occupied it. The chaplains' tent was known as The Chalice, the surgeons' as The Beds, and the carpenters' marquee as The Hammer. The master of the armoury had The Gauntlett and the captain of the yeoman of the guard The Red Sword.

The biggest marquees, which had 1,000 sq ft of floor space, were called Shields – Red, Blue, Green, Gold, Black and White – much as a class of destroyers might be named at the present day. Others read like the names of inns – The Wheat Sheaf, The Greyhound, The Flagon (which was in fact the Jewel House), the Red Rose and The White (the larder), and The Leopard's Head (the wardrobe of robes). The tents had signs illustrating their names, so that soldiers carrying messages from one part of the camp to another might readily find their destination. The king's lodgings, of course, were easily found. They were much larger and more magnificent than the others, and the king's beasts, the Lion, the Dragon, the Greyhound, the Antelope and the Dun Cow squatted on the tallest of their poles holding vanes bearing the royal coat of arms.[10] They must have been a permanent source of wonder and admiration to the rank and file, who probably counted themselves lucky if they got through a night without being soaked to the skin.

Even so it was not all plain sailing for the élite who qualified for a tent. The sixteenth-century tent was just as vulnerable as its modern counterpart. In spite of the fact that virtually all those on the 1513 expedition were specially made for it – Richard Gibson's accounts record how many ells of material went into them, and how much they cost – a good deal of modification had to be made in the course of the expedition, which suggests that the original designs left something to be desired. Nearly 5,000 'buttons of timber' had to be bought in France for buttoning the walls and doors of the king's tents. Some occupants seem to have suffered from the cold, for in several cases walls were doubled and extra partitions added. Whenever there was a stormy night – and the summer of 1513 had a lot of bad weather mixed with good – guy ropes were broken and canvas ripped. Gibson was constantly making emergency purchases to repair the damage. On at least one occasion a tent was partially destroyed by fire. Even the 'strange ambassadors' posed a problem. They ran true to form and were dissatisfied with the accommodation originally provided for them. They prevailed on those in charge of the tents to double the walls of their marquee, and, more important, to add the stool place which had been denied them.

The vulnerability of the tents was vividly portrayed in one of a series of contemporary paintings which decorated the great hall at Cowdray before it was destroyed by fire at the end of the eighteenth century. A detailed description of this painting, which shows Henry's camp at Marquise on his second expedition to France in 1544, was recorded by Sir John Ayloffe in 1773, not long before it was burned; and his account is supported by a pen-and-ink drawing now in the possession of the Society of Antiquaries. In Ayloffe's words:

> The front or foreground of this piece represents a champaign country, covered with baggage and ammunition wagons, artillery, and a great number of different sorts of tents, labouring under the utmost distress from a violent and incessant storm of wind and lightning, which is expressed in a masterly manner. Here we see several tents blown down and lying on the ground; whilst the soldiers and women, in all the pangs of fright and horror, are endeavouring to creep from under the shattered ruins, and seem apprehensive of being again buried under the neighbouring tottering tents. Others have their tent pins drawn, and are represented as falling; whilst the soldiers and artillery-men, harassed by the stress of weather and scarce able to stand against the force of the wind, weakly endeavour to keep them up. Of those that are left standing, some are torn in pieces by the wind, and others have their curtains blown open and waving in the air.[11]

Ayloffe has perhaps imported more alarm and despondency into the scene than the unknown artist intended. The collapse of a tent, as modern campers know, can be irritating, but it is hardly catastrophic. Moreover, if the sketch referred to above is faithful, Ayloffe seems to exaggerate the part played by women in the camp of 1544. It shows only one woman, who does not look much like a camp follower, dispassionately surveying the scene of destruction around her, her voluminous skirts singularly undisturbed by the gale.

*   *   *

The high marshal, who had ridden ahead with his attendants, had to choose the camp site. This was a tricky business. If he came across an ideal place too early in the day he must turn a blind eye to it, since to stop there would curtail the day's march. On the other hand he might find as nightfall approached that they were in countryside unsuitable for a camp, and the army would have to press on through the twilight, becoming hungrier and more bad-tempered, and perhaps finally they would have to settle for an unsatisfactory site. The marshal was in fact faced with something like a game of musical chairs. If he decided to stop too soon he would delay the army's arrival at their ultimate objective; and if his decision were made too late in the day the troops would have to erect the tents and build their shelters in the dark, and their vulnerability to enemy raiding-parties would be greatly increased.

Ideal sites were few and far between. 'Lodge the army where they may be lords of the three commodities which cannot be spared,' says Thomas Audley, 'that is, wood, water, and pasture.' This was easier said than done. In the first place, a large reasonably level place was needed. It must be free of trees, to leave a clear field of vision against the possibility of enemy attack; but, as Audley points out, it must be near a wood from which logs for the camp kitchens and branches for the construction of huts may be readily brought. It must also be near a stream that will give plenty of water for the horses and for washing (which has to be done downstream so that pure water for drinking and cooking may be available near the camp); but it must be on elevated ground, to provide a dry foundation for the tents, and to put the encamped troops in a satisfactory defensive position. Thirdly, there must be good grazing nearby, so that the horses and any live cattle driven with the expedition can feed.[12] Only rarely can the high marshal have found a site that conformed to this exacting specification, at the moment when the army was ready to halt for the night.

A standard plan of the camp was prepared before the army left England. There is a copy in the British Museum with explanatory notes, which show that the theory later set down by Thomas Audley – 'pitch your camp four square, dividing the same in four parts by great streets marching across the camp from one side to the other'[13] – was followed on the 1513 expedition. Usually there was a clear space at the intersection of the two main streets, which was used as a market-place, and also as the place of assembly when there was a general alarm. The main streets were to be not less than thirty paces wide. Guy-ropes and tent-pegs were to be kept well clear of them, so that if there were an alarm the troops would be able to hurry to the assembly-place (which would ideally be the highest point in the camp) without tripping over them.[14] On a royal expedition the market-place was moved nearer the perimeter and the central area was reserved for the king, so that he might be made as safe as possible from surprise attack; and so that he would also enjoy privacy, it was laid down that there must be a minumum of 200 ft between the ends of the guy-ropes of his tents and those of the tents next to them.[15] The floor area of the middle-ward tents totalled over 65,000 sq ft, and when provision had been made for the 'great streets', for the 200 ft of no man's land surrounding the king's own tents, and for the clear area between the other tents, to enable the soldiers to walk freely about the camp without tripping on guy-ropes, a very large area indeed was required.

There was a well-established procedure for setting up camp. As soon as the order to halt had been given the cavalry ranged themselves in a defensive position and remained mounted until the infantry, the king's innumerable attendants, the baggage train, and the artillery had arrived and taken up their appointed positions. Scouts were sent out in all directions and remained on the alert until arrangements could be made for posting the routine watch.

If the army halted for only a single night it was considered unnecessary to provide any protection in the form of earth-works: it was enough to surround the camp with the carriages and wagons interspersed with the artillery. If, however, it was decided to remain in the same place for a considerable period (when the site chosen would have to be very good indeed), it was desirable to entrench the camp, especially if the enemy were in the neighbourhood in any strength. One expert recommended the construction of a trench 12 ft deep by 15 ft wide. This needed a tremendous amount of excavation, far more than the pioneers, the pick-and-shovel brigade of the sixteenth-century army, could possibly accomplish in a reasonable time, and it was therefore understood that every available man must lend a hand.[16] The 1513 expedition, however, was never completely entrenched while on the march, although once or twice it did remain in the same place for a few days. The threat from the enemy was not great enough to make trenches essential.

Another precaution taken when the army camped in the same place for several days was the adoption of special sanitary measures. It was recognized that there was a connection between filth and disease, and disciplinary codes as a rule made a point of reminding the troops about the importance of maintaining a high standard of sanitation. This point was covered in the royal proclamation which embodied the disciplinary code for the 1513 expedition, as follows:

> Also the King straitly chargeth and commandeth that if it happen that his host tarry by the space of three days or above in one place or ground, be it at siege or otherwise, that then every man keep clean his lodging, not suffering any carrion, filth, or any other unwholesome or infective stinking air to be in or near the same his lodging, but forthwith to bury the same deep in the earth upon pain to be punished after the discretion of the marshal.[17]

It seems that in the practice this regulation was considered inadequate, for in a further proclamation at the siege of Thérouanne, commanding the army in general terms to abide by the ordinances lately 'openly read, published, and declared unto them from article to article and from point to point', the licence to do nothing about the disposal of garbage until after three days in the same place is withdrawn. Instead it is laid down that 'if any person will ease himself, to go out of the compass and precinct of the field, or else to bury it in the earth upon pain of imprisonment after the discretion of the marshal'.[18] In the 1544 expedition, when standards generally fell far below those of 1513, there seems to have been little effort to deal with the problem of sanitation. Elis Gruffudd speaks of the:

> . . . stink of the carrion of the mares and the horses that died among the host which were left to rot on the ground for want of anyone to bury them as the discipline of a host demands. This stench struck within and filled the vital senses and spirits with rotten air which made great havoc with the heart and the mind, and for all these reasons, as well as the displeasure of God, there fell a great pestilence among the soldiers.[19]

When camp was pitched, priority was inevitably given to setting up the king's tents. Henry would certainly not expect to be kept waiting in armour for any length of time after a strenuous day's ride – the memorandum referred to above makes this very clear. The marshal's first task was to select the ground for the king's lodging, making sure that it was dry, and then to order those responsible for erecting his tents to get on with the job without delay. Thereafter the other tents were to be erected according to the agreed plan.[20]

While the pavilioners were busy with the king's tents and those of the senior officers, and the rank and file were cutting boughs to make their shelters, the watch was being organized. As in the garrison towns, there were two main types of sentry: first, the stand watch stationed immediately inside the line of wagons surrounding the camp; and second, the scout watch, sometimes mounted, which was posted about a hundred yards from the perimeter of the camp, to give an early warning of the enemy's approach. The scout watch was in groups of five men, who were supposed to be near enough to see each other on a moonlit night. On a dark night they had to be within hailing distance, and were to 'sound' each other every 'half quarter of an hour'. The watchword for the night was entrusted to only one of the group of five.[21] A special guard was provided for the king's tents, and also for the tent where the council of war held their deliberations, 'so that no man may come within a certain distance of the same; and those that ward the place must be honest and secret'.[22] Sentries were also posted at the wagons carrying the army's pay and round the ordnance stores.[23]

The high marshal decided on the watchword in consultation with the king, and the word was written on small slips of paper ('little bills') and circulated to the council of war and to the captains. The word 'in the secret keeping of which consisteth the assurance of the whole army' was also communicated to the provost marshal for transmission to the officers of the watch. At nightfall the king's trumpeter sounded a call, which was answered by all the other trumpeters in the camp. At the first call those assigned to watch duties made themselves ready for the night's vigil and as the last call died away proceeded to their posts. When all were in position – scout watch and stand watch – a culverin was fired to give the signal for absolute silence, so that the sentries might easily hear the sounds of an approaching enemy. At dawn the king's trumpeter stood by the royal tents and sounded the call for the watch to dismiss; but when the army was besieging a town the trumpeter was stationed elsewhere, to avoid giving the enemy a clue as to the king's whereabouts – a rather meaningless precaution, as Henry's tents could hardly be mistaken.

The members of the watch also had to maintain complete silence, except when the scout watch called to the neighbouring group to assure themselves that all was well. If any persons approached the camp the first duty of the sentries was to challenge them and ask for the watchword of the night; and if this was not given they were to be regarded as enemies. The scout watch was to fall back to the perimeter of the camp, defending themselves as they went. The stand watch, who would be alerted by the noise of fighting in front of them, were to do what they could to support their retreating comrades, and they had to take the greatest care not to injure them in the dark. The scout watch were also warned to be wary of giving false alarms, which could very easily lead to serious panic. If the enemy did succeed in reaching the perimeter of the camp the captains of the middle-ward were at once to lead their men to the king's quarters, unless they found themselves face to face with the attackers, in which case they were to stand their ground and send for help.[24]

NOTE

(1)   The wardrobe accounts of the following year contain a warrant signed by Henry which gives a detailed specification of this piece of equipment. It commands Sir Andrew Windsor, Keeper of the Great Wardrobe, 'that ye prepare and ordain for our use these parcels following. First, a chamber stool of timber with clasps of iron with sufficient gilt nails, ribbons and fringes of silk, covered with tawny velvet of our Great Wardrobe. Item, two basins of tin for the same stool. Item, a sheet of linen cloth two ells long with two breadths at 8d. the ell. Item, a mail of leather to truss the same stool and stuff.' (PRO E 101/418/5, f. 47.)

5 Supply

VICTUALS

In the sixteenth century few foodstuffs could be preserved for any length of time. Biscuit had a relatively long storage life but it was by no means indefinite. Even in a garrison town like Berwick, where it was much easier to handle the rations than with an army on the march, the biscuit issue could cause difficulty. In 1545 stocks were deteriorating so rapidly that the Privy Council ordered the bakeries in the town to close down temporarily, to force the troops to eat up inferior biscuit before it became totally unfit for human consumption.[1] Bread kept for only a few days. Salt fish – staple fish, stock fish, ling, salmon and herring – had a fairly long life, but bacon and salt beef did not. Bacon could be kept for a short time if 'laid in bran for the preserving thereof', and beef would last indefinitely in the form of live cattle. The troops moved so slowly on the march that it was possible to drive cattle with them, but an enormous herd would have been needed to feed the whole army. It seems inevitable that any live animals which accompanied the 1513 expedition were reserved for the king and his senior officers. On the whole, however, the expedition fared well in the matter of food. At least there were few complaints about rations, which cannot be said for the next invasion of France ten years later, when Elis Gruffudd recorded that:

> . . . the bread, of which there were five kinds each more bitter and worse than the other, was very hard, and the common soldiers and workmen got the worst, except for those who could pay cash, and there were few of those, for they all got 6d. a day . . . . It was an abomination to weak bowels to have to eat hard dry bitter bread baked from the powder of grey corn, and old meat which had got spoiled in the air and was fly-blown before it was put in salt. Or old butter gone so mouldy and of so many colours that a man had to hold his nose before coming near to it, or old hard dry cheese.[2]

Beer, still a peculiarly English drink, was an important item in the yeoman soldier's daily ration, a fact supported by the *Italian Relation*, which tells us that:

> . . . the common people make two beverages from wheat, barley and oats, one of which is called beer and the other ale; and these liquors are much liked by them, nor are they disliked by foreigners after they have drunk them four or six times; they are most agreeable to the palate, when a person is by some chance rather heated.[3]

The English troops became very heated under the burning sun of Spain in Dorset's expedition of 1512, and mutiny followed swiftly after the beer ration dried up and only the local wines remained. Even when supplies of beer were plentiful the men could be fussy about quality. The victualling commissioners in Plymouth reported to the Privy Council in May 1513 that the lord admiral had ordered that no more beer was to be brewed in the West Country, because the soldiers preferred London beer (especially if it had been brewed in March, the best month). It kept better because it was brewed from barley rather than oaten malt. It was added, however, that if there was nothing better available than West Country beer the troops were perfectly content with it.[4] Beer in general could be kept for up to five or six months provided that it was brewed strong and stored in good casks.

The difficulty of preserving food is illustrated by the victualler's accounts on the 1513 expedition, which indicate that substantial quantities of all the principal foodstuffs bought by the king for the use of the troops had either to be written off as a total loss or sold for nominal sums. One of these accounts shows that 496 pipes (a pipe was the equivalent of four barrels) of salt beef, which had cost £1,150, were sold for £260; 23 pipes were buried at Calais because the beef was 'so corrupted that no man would buy it'; quantities of ling were sold to a number of buyers 'rotten and broken'; and bacon was 'clearly lost rotten' – that is to say, it was a total write-off. The whole loss on this particular account amounted to £3,500.[5]

The limiting factor, however, was not the storage life of the army's rations but the sheer bulk of the food supply. Even if it had been possible to preserve indefinitely the whole of the daily ration of the rank and file – as can be done at the present day – it would have been quite impossible to carry it with the army. The magnitude of the problem is demonstrated quite simply. A typical daily ration might include, say, a pound of biscuit, a pound of beef to go with it, and 8 pints of beer, making a total weight of about 10 pounds a day, or something like 2,000 lbs a head for a six-month's campaign. Thus at the outset 30,000 men would have needed a baggage train to carry 60,000,000 lbs – say between 10,000 and 15,000 wagons with double that number of carters, as there were usually two to the wagon, and several times that number of horses. Provision had therefore to be made for regular daily supplies, which had to be carried over steadily increasing distances as the army penetrated deeper into enemy territory. It was no longer possible for a large expeditionary force to live off the land as the smaller forces of medieval times had as a rule been able to do.

The defending army might consider itself too weak to take on the invaders in a pitched battle, but they could nevertheless inflict a great deal of damage at small risk to themselves simply by concentrating on the supply lines; and this is what the relatively weak French forces did in 1513. The English higher command were alive to the danger and made special provision for escorts for the victuallers based on Calais and on Flanders, 'for without sufficient conduct no creature durst bring any victual to the army'.[6] The fact that Henry was able to get some food supplies from Flanders much simplified the victualling problem, since the route he followed never took him far from friendly and well-stocked territory. On the other hand, an English expedition was always liable to be held to ransom by victuallers from the Low Countries, who were well aware of the strength of their bargaining position.[7]

Even before Henry crossed the Channel with the middle-ward the daily victualling train from Calais to the other two wards at Thérouanne was being attacked. On Monday, 27 June, a convoy variously estimated at twenty-four,[6] eighty,[8] and a hundred[9] wagons was safely escorted by a detachment of troops from the garrison of Calais as far as Guines, where the escort duty was taken over by 300 troops under Sir Edward Belknap accompanied by sixty men, of whom twenty-four were mounted, and from Guines, under the command of Sir Nicholas Vaux, captain of the castle there. There was no sign of the enemy as the victualling wagons slowly approached Ardres, and discipline became relaxed. The small body of cavalry, paying little attention to their charges, halted to slake their thirst, and the infantry also fell into disorder, so that the carters were left quite without protection.

A powerful French force was enjoying this spectacle from concealed positions in the forest of Guines; and choosing their moment carefully, they suddenly fell upon the victualling train. The carters, who were not equipped to defend themselves, fled as one man, pausing only to loose their horses, which they used to escape the more quickly. The few cavalry in the English force manfully attacked the French with their spears, and the archers sheltering behind the wagons, which they drew up in a circle, kept firing as long as they could; but they were hopelessly outnumbered. Sir Nicholas Vaux tried to rally the infantry and lead them to the rescue, but they had been so badly caught off guard that nothing could be done about it, and Vaux and Belknap were forced to flee for their lives with the shattered remnant of the escort troops back to the safety of Guines.

This defeat, which in Hall's view would never have happened had the cavalry not stopped for a drink, or if the infantry had kept order, cost the lives of many Englishmen – 8 from the garrison of Guines and 30 archers in Hall's account,[10] 100 (Polydore Vergil),[11] 200 (Dr John Taylor, who says that the victims' bodies were stripped and their faces mutilated),[12] 300 (the *Chronicle of Calais*),[13] and 500 (the Venetian ambassador to France).[14] Whatever the true figure, it was a heavy reverse, and in addition to many tall men the English lost all the wagons and the supplies they carried. The French also suffered some losses, but far fewer than the victualling train.

The news of the disaster was badly received at the camp before Thérouanne, for it was absolutely essential that a high proportion of the daily supplies should get through. Sir Rees ap Thomas was at once despatched with his light cavalry to seek out the French raiding forces, but the enemy had wisely retreated to their strongholds, taking their booty with them. The English cavalry had to return to base without the chance of avenging their comrades. After this episode the invaders provided a much stronger escort for the daily victualling train to Thérouanne – so strong that it was believed that the French would hardly dare attack it; and discipline was much better kept. Moreover, arrangements were made to increase the supply of victuals from the Low Countries because of the greater safety of the routes from there, and in spite of the higher cost.

Nevertheless, further attempts were made to cripple the besieging army by attacking the Calais–Thérouanne, supply line. On Monday, 1 August, the commander of the garrison at Boulogne, knowing 'that daily victuals were brought out of England to Calais to succour the camp' at Thérouanne, and no doubt encouraged by the success of the raid at Ardres four days earlier, decided to launch an attack on Calais itself. About three o'clock in the morning he led a powerful force to Fort Nieulay on the edge of the Calais pale, and had the good fortune to find that the men guarding the draw-bridge were fast asleep, perhaps on the assumption that any French attacks would be made further south. The enemy made short work of them and quickly lowered the bridge which gave access through the marshlands to the pale proper. They left half their force by the fort while the rest went into the fields to drive away the cattle. Those who ventured as far as the town of Calais were spotted from the walls, where the guards were rather more alert than they had been at Fort Nieulay, and the alarm was raised.

The rank and file in Calais guessed that Fort Nieulay must have fallen and were all for leaving the town to attack the enemy. Sir Gilbert Talbot, however, was not going to take any chances. He realized that an engagement with a French force that might heavily outnumber the troops at his command could be disastrous; and if Calais fell the king's main line of retreat would be cut off. He therefore ordered that the gates should remain closed until dawn. The raiders thus found it comparatively easy to round up many cattle.

Before they could get them out of the pale, however, victuallers in charge of provisions destined for Thérouanne, including some of the officials of the acatry (the household office concerned with the supply of meat and fish) who were sleeping outside the walls, were aroused by the disturbance. They awakened the king's bakers and coopers, also bound for Thérouanne, and some of the sailors from the nearby harbour, and together they set upon the marauders with a will. Having slain all they encountered – Hall tells us they took no prisoners – they made for Fort Nieulay and managed to get possession of it, although they could not drive away the substantial body of French troops who remained there 'in a stall' waiting for their companions to return.

About five o'clock, when dawn was breaking, Talbot considered it safe to send out the under-marshal of Calais with 200 archers, who found that the victuallers had done their work so well that there was virtually no opposition left. They hurried to Fort Nieulay to join forces with the civilians there and marched against the remainder of the French troops. The latter, unable to believe that a handful of civilians could have disposed of their colleagues, assumed that the approaching troops were their own raiding party, and it was only when they saw the banner of St George that they knew that 'they must needs fight or die'. They were routed in the skirmish that followed, two dozen being killed and more than 200 taken prisoner. The guns of Fort Nieulay, which were already on their way to Boulogne, were recovered, as was most of the booty, and the prisoners were put up for sale in Calais.[15] Undaunted by this reverse, which fully compensated for the defeat at Ardres, a French force shortly afterwards attacked Bonningues-lès-Calais within the pale and made off with all the cattle in the village.[16]

Of the two stages in the victualling process – first, the purchase and transport of bulk supplies, and second, their distribution to the individual soldier – the latter seems to have remained more or less the same throughout the Tudor period, but the former varied from reign to reign. Henry VII relied on the

Crown's right of purveyance (the element in the royal prerogative which allowed the king to take from his subjects provisions, horses and carts at his own price) to feed the army which he led against the rebels in the north of England in 1487. A royal proclamation ordered people dealing in foodstuffs, and the king's subjects in general, 'to provide and make ready plenty of bread and ale, and of other victuals as well for horse and man, at reasonable price in ready money', so that there would be no shortage as the army moved north. The proclamation stressed that a fair price would be paid for all victuals taken for the army.[17] Purveyance worked well in England, and it minimized the storage problem. There was no need for the purveyor to take up more than a few days' supplies at a time and he was under no obligation to buy any victuals that were not in first-rate condition. When Henry VII led his troops into France in 1492, however, he relied on private individuals who undertook to supply food under ordinary commercial arrangements without enjoying the support of purveyance.

These contrasts were very rigid. A typical indenture required three London merchants to buy and consign to Portsmouth by a given date two pipes of wheat flour, two pipes of beef, two butts of Malmsey, six pipes of beer, ten flitches of bacon, ten quarters of oats, four weys of cheese, two quarters of beans and four barrels of salt, all 'good sufficient and wholesome for man's body'; and if the merchants failed to carry out their part of the bargain they were made liable to forfeit to the king 'all that they may forfeit in body, lands, and goods' – a heavy penalty.

Although these transactions were carried through by private enterprise, they had the strongest blessing of the Crown, whose officers were ordered to give the contractors and their servants all possible help in locating and buying food. Port officers were instructed to allow the supplies to be shipped without let or hindrance, and free of customs duty. Further, it was stipulated that if the merchants could not make their rendezvous with the army because of 'dread and fear of enemies' (i.e. the French), they should send a message to the higher command by one of the barks assigned to coastal duties, which included liaison with the victualling merchants. Escort vessels would then be provided. If in spite of this the victuals were captured, the king bore half the loss.

The protection which the Crown afforded in English coastal waters continued when the victuallers reached France. The merchants undertook to offer the victuals for sale 'in open market' in the army at such time and place as the provost marshal decided, and in the meantime the king guaranteed their safety; but if they sold outside the army they were fined double the value of the goods disposed of, and imprisoned at the king's will. The carrot was left almost to the end of the contract:

> . . . and that at their coming to the host and during the time of their abode there they shall be so well entreated and have such reasonable prices set upon their victuals with such reasonable gain for ready money as the said William, John, and John shall well live and be right well content and pleased; and shall in like [wise] in good surety be conducted again from the host unto their ship.[18]

Although this particular contract does not spell out the fact that the merchants financed their purchases themselves, it is clear that this was so, and that the dividend to be reaped from the money they laid out depended on the reasonableness of the retail prices determined by the provost marshal – prices which ideally were pitched at a level that would give the merchants a satisfactory profit margin without forcing the rank and file to go short of food, which they had to pay for out of their wages of sixpence a day. In another similar contract the merchant clearly undertook to finance the purchase of the food.[19] He agreed to provide the supplies specified – three pipes of flour, fifteen pipes of beer, and a single pipe of beef – 'at his proper cost and charges', and it may be that these words were omitted from the larger contract described above as a result of a clerical error.

At the end of the Tudor period, when the intensification of the war in Ireland imposed very heavy strains on the army's victualling arrangements, the government experimented with a variety of contracts in which the financial and other responsibilities were shared between the Crown and the merchant in varying degrees. Some of these were very similar to Henry VII's contracts. Over a period of years, Elizabeth I's government took on more and more of the work of providing and shipping food to the army, but the system did not work well, and the Privy Council made a sudden decision to return responsibility for the purchase and distribution of rations to the contractors 'from the beginning to the ending'.[20] But for the 1513 expedition there was nothing like the contracts of Henry VII and Elizabeth I, which may seem strange in a century when most branches of military organization show signs of a steady development.

Why did Henry VIII rely so heavily on purveyance when the first and last of the Tudor monarchs preferred to enter into contracts with merchants? It is easy to understand Elizabeth's position, for by her time there was a growing dislike of purveyance, among the people and while her government steadfastly opposed encroachment by parliament on the prerogative of purveyance they did allow its impact to be reduced by compounding the Crown's rights.[21] In any case, purveyance was beginning to outlive its usefulness, Edward Baeshe, the navy victualler under four monarchs, suggested in 1562 that it would be better and cheaper to forget about purveyance as a means of feeding the royal household and the navy. Although at first sight it might seem to be very economical, by the time all the extra costs were added in it was no cheaper than direct contracts. He therefore recommended that the Crown should make bargains with butchers, bakers and brewers for the supply of food.[22]

The explanation may be that, when Henry won the battle to lead the 1513 expedition in person in spite of the opposition of his councillors, it was considered logical that the household staff should play a big part in victualling the enterprise. Feeding the Court was not quite as formidable a task as feeding an expeditionary force or even the higher command, but it was nevertheless a big job; and as something like 2,000 Court officials and servants accompanied the king to France it was natural that he should rely on his normal household services, including those of the purveyors. He was certainly not going to lower his own eating standards by putting his table in the hands of the ordinary army victuallers and camp cooks; and if the household officials were to be called upon to purvey victuals for the king and his huge entourage, it was a relatively simple matter to extend their commissions to provide at least to some extent for the

Henry VIII in council, a wood engraving from Hall's Chronicle, *1548*

army as a whole. Private victuallers, however, were also used both from England and from the Low Countries.

The first important administrative act in connection with the victualling arrangements for the 1513 expedition was the issue of a royal proclamation in December 1512 announcing that the king was commissioning 'divers his trusty servants to purvey and buy for his money, at reasonable price, wheat and other victuals'. These supplies were ostensibly required for the fleet, which was being fitted out to meet the threat of invasion from France, but the controls imposed by the proclamation were also fundamental to the provisioning of Henry's proposed expeditionary force. No person was to 'engross, forestall, or regrate' victuals (three words which meant to corner the market to make an excessive profit); and food was to be exported only by those holding commissions from the king. Offenders against the regulations forfeited any victuals they had illegally acquired, or the proceeds, if they had sold them, half to the Crown and half to the informer; and the guilty parties were also liable to imprisonment.[23]

As the winter dragged to an end the purveyors appointed to take up victuals 'at reasonable prices' went into action throughout the country. In February, for example, William Hades and William Tego were commissioned for two months to provide wheat and other necessaries.[24] William Hatclyffe and John Henkyn had a commission for wheat and salt fish.[25] The pace quickened in March when numerous commissions were issued; and in April the number of the king's agents travelling the countryside in search of food for the armed forces again increased. John Ricroft, the sergeant of the larder, was engaged to provide 20,000 quarters of malt, 3,000 quarters each of beans and oats, 300 oxen and 1,000 sheep over the next six months;[26] and the yeomen purveyors of the avenary were to provide 'hay, oats, horse-bread, litter, stabling, and carriage' for Henry's horses.[27]

The very heavy purchases inevitably had an effect on food prices, even in 1512, long before the army's demands had reached their climax. Lorenzo Pasqualigo reported to Venice that 25,000 oxen had been salted, with the result that the price of meat had been driven up from a penny to threepence a pound.[28] In January 1513 Nicolo di Favri had the same tale to tell. The price of bread was high because of the war. The price of meat had more than doubled because of the hugh quantities salted for the use of the army.[29]

There is no detailed account of how the arrangements for the bulk supply of victuals worked in 1513, but some idea at least of the theory in Henry VIII's time may be gathered from draft instructions to the 'chief victualler' of the garrisons at Boulogne and Le Havre at the end of the reign. Anthony Aucher was made responsible for 'all the whole mass of the victualling there' and had a commission to take up supplies in England, including butter, cheese and all kinds of grain. He had to agree reasonable buying prices and to record in duplicate the sellers' names and the quantities and prices of food bought. One copy of the record was certified by the local constable and a justice of the peace and sent to London for the information of the Council, and the other was retained locally as a warrant for payment, which had to be made in the presence of the constable and justice. A special procedure was provided for the wholesale purchase of 'oxen, steers, and suchlike', which normally were found only in markets and fairs. Aucher was to be given enough money to buy these for cash without going through the normal drill, under which the seller had to wait, perhaps a very long time, for his money. The victualler had also to arrange shipment, and to get licences for everything he exported. An exception was made, however, for the hides and fells of cattle and sheep slaughtered in England, which he was allowed to export freely to any country with which Henry was at peace, so long as the proceeds found their way to the Crown.

A precise drill was also provided for dealing with the victuals when they reached their destination. The customs officials were to record all arrivals and notify them to the council in the garrison at least once a week. Before bulk cargoes were broken down they were to be inspected, so that if they were unsatisfactory they could be returned to England, or a claim made against the victualler; and this inspection was also used to ensure that victuals 'which may worst be kept may be first spent'. The grain was received off the ships by two 'grainers', one representing the victualler and the other the council, who made weekly returns of receipts and issues, and was stowed in 'garnets' (granaries) with double locks, so that the stores could be opened only when both the grainers were present. Stocks of grain had to be turned regularly to keep them sweet, and to save the expense of hiring grain turners the victualler was assigned a squad of soldiers to do the work for him. Under these proposals the victualler was given charge of all the bakers, brewers, millers, carters and labourers needed to feed the troops, so that the only individual directly responsible to the council was the grainer they appointed as a watchdog. A 'meater' had a similar function in connection with the supplies of meat.

Provision was also made for the care of live cattle destined for the army's rations. Pasture was to be allocated to them near the town walls. All other cattle, for example the property of local butchers and commoners, were to be grazed further out, so that they would afford some protection to the Crown herds in the event of an enemy attack.[30]

Although the make-up of the private's rations was laid down by the central authority, it was quite impossible to ensure that each man daily received his precise entitlement. Indeed, the gap between theory and practice which existed in many branches of sixteenth-century military organization was probably very wide in the sphere of the commissariat. Even if purveyors were commissioned to buy the range of foodstuffs needed to support the official daily ration, it seems most unlikely that supplies would ever come forward in just the right proportions. In any case, some consignments would be lost *en route* (as in the débâcle at Ardres); some would go bad and have to be destroyed; and private victuallers, whose contribution was vital, would bring to the camp the food that would show them the greatest margin of profit, and not necessarily the types needed to balance the official ration. Even in Elizabeth I's time, when the use of large bulk contracts made it easier to match supplies with the theoretical components of the ration issue, there were often serious discrepencies; and it must have been much worse in Henry VIII's reign, when the idea of a balanced ration was relatively new.

Responsibility for food within the army rested with the high marshal, but the day-to-day decisions were taken by his subordinates, the provost marshal and the clerk of the market. The provost marshal had, of course, other duties – he had to see that the camp was kept clean, to arrest and imprison those who offended against the regulations, and so on – but the clerk of the market had a full-time job looking after the receipt, storage and issue of victuals. Handling the daily victualling trains from Calais presented no problem, but supplies brought by private victuallers, especially those from the Low Countries, might raise difficulties. It was so important that the army should be regularly provisioned that considerable security risks were taken in dealing with private victuallers, who might even be enemy aliens; and it was constantly stressed that these people must always be given the benefit of any doubts about their integrity and treated with the greatest courtesy.

As far back as King John it was formally laid down that no victuals should be distributed until those who had brought them to the camp had been paid; and the whole army from the barons down to the humblest retainers had to swear to obey this rule.[31] A treatise written towards the end of Henry VIII's reign recommended that 'all men must honestly entreat and suffer generally all kinds of victuallers, friends or foes'. They were to be given ready access to the market-place, and they were to be allowed equally freely to depart with the money they received for their goods. Enemy aliens could supply the army with useful information in addition to the food they brought. It might be possible, by using 'gentle language' and 'wittily enquiring questions necessary to be known', to gather some idea from them of the opposing army's intentions, a risky proceeding if the same victuallers were also providing food to the enemy.[32]

The importance of keeping on the best possible terms with private victuallers was recognized in the disciplinary code prepared for the 1513 expedition, which provided the death penalty for robbing a merchant 'coming unto the market with victual or other merchandise for the refreshment of the host'. The regulations also provided for the sharing of foodstuffs found by the army on the march. Those who came across them were allowed to take a reasonable amount for themselves, but the balance had to be handed over to the clerk of the market for the general use of the troops. Any soldier who disobeyed this order lost all his goods and chattels and was imprisoned.[33]

MUNITIONS

The expedition could not carry all the food it needed, but at least it could be virtually self-supporting in the matter of artillery, arms and equipment generally. It was physically possible to carry enough of these stores to see an army through a summer campaign, and most of them were durable, although there were some exceptions. Reserve stocks of bow-strings (which were made from silk or hemp) might rot if they were stored in damp conditions for any length of time, especially if they were imperfectly waxed. Gunpowder would also deteriorate if it was not packed in sound waterproof casks. Although bills, pikes and swords were often found to be ruined after years in store they could easily survive a six-month campaign; but the new 'weapons of fire', with their precision mechanisms, were vulnerable both to damp and to rough handling. If the chests in which they were carried were knocked about, which was inevitable given bad roads or no roads at all, they were bound to suffer damage. Even the most careful private must have found it difficult to maintain properly the hand-gun issued to him, and the expedition's accounts show payments for repairs to harquebuses from time to time.[34] It was better, however, for the army to carry with it all the munitions it was likely to need and to take the chance of damage or deterioration than to rely on supplementary consignments from its base.

The plans for the 1513 expedition did assume, however, that there would be a 'great staple of powder and shot' provided at Calais, or some other suitable point to be designated by the king and Council, which could be drawn on in emergency;[35] and the wisdom of this sort of precaution was borne out in 1544, when Henry found himself committed to an exceptionally long and heavy bombardment at the siege of Boulogne. Additional supplies of gunpowder had to be rushed from every available source, including the castles of the Cinque Ports and all shipping, English and foreign, lying in the Thames.[36] In theory there should have been little difficulty in making an expedition self-supporting in respect of tenting equipment, but in fact Richard Gibson had to make local purchases of canvas, rope, tent-poles and fittings in almost every town the troops passed through, perhaps because the damage to the tents from storms was much greater than had been anticipated; and in spite of the large number of spares carried by the expedition, quantities of a good many general stores had to be purchased *en route*.[37]

Each of the three wards had its own ordnance establishment, including gunners, pioneers, artificers, wagoners and carters. (Wagons were larger vehicles with anything from four to eight horses, and the wagoners were paid a standard fee of 10d. a day for every horse they provided with their wagon. Carters were engaged to drive horses and carts owned by the army. The ordinary carter had a daily wage of 6d., and the 'headmen carters' 8d.) There seems to be little relationship between the original estimates of the ordnance departments and their actual complement in France. One estimate of the gunners and supporting troops required for 15,000 infantry and 3,000 cavalry – admittedly larger than any of the three wards were in the event – is about 100 officers, 160 artificers, 480 gunners and trench makers, 200 miners, 500 pioneers, 1,500 carters and an unspecified number of ordinary soldiers to guard the ordnance.[38] But the accounts of the middle-ward, which are a reliable guide, as there was at this time virtually none of the chicanery which put large numbers of fictitious names on the muster rolls so that captains might pocket 'dead-pays', show a very different picture. In August and September, when the campaign was well under way, wages were being paid to 300 gunners, 1,600 pioneers, 600 carters and 120 wagoners – all very different from the estimate. There were only about 90 artificers – the technicians needed to service the guns and other weapons, and to maintain the carts and wagons, who included smiths, carpenters, joiners, wheelwrights, bowyers, fletchers, harness-makers and so on – compared with the estimate of 160. Finally, there was the master of the ordnance (Lord Berners in the case of the middle-ward), a lieutenant, a provost, a surgeon and their servants.[39]

There are several possible explanations of the discrepancies. The estimates were only estimates; the numbers available from the Low Countries, the main source of gunners and wagoners, could not be accurately assessed in advance, and may have turned out to be quite different from the Privy Council's expectations; there may have had to be some improvisation for other reasons as the campaign proceeded; and wastage through casualties must have had some effect.

Although the estimates should be treated with caution, it is possible to derive from them some ideas of the size and complexity of the munitions supply problem, even in 1513. They set out details of the allocation of equipment to the three wards, and suggest that the total provision was intended to be shared equally between them in spite of the difference in their sizes; and they also provide details of the number of vehicles needed to carry the stores.[40]

It was by no means easy to find the carts and wagons, the horses to pull them, and the men to drive them. The army's requirements – something in the region of 2,000 vehicles, with the appropriate complement of horses and drivers – were small in relation to the total in use in England; but the individual farmer could not readily afford to lose a single cart, especially at harvest time, and any campaign that began in the summer was bound to clash with the harvest. The whole of England, except the most northerly counties, which were expected to keep an eye on Scotland (or at least to be neutral!) rather than to take part in overseas campaigns, was scoured for carts and carters for the 1513 expedition, but it was impossible to get enough of them and the search had to be extended to the Low Countries.[41] Indeed the provision of vehicles continued to be a problem in all Henry's expeditions. This was part of the price he had to pay for not establishing a standing army, complete with transport and other services.

Although it was important not to denude England of carts and men needed for the harvest and for the transport of produce generally, it was a costly business to equip the army by buying or hiring carts overseas, which were the only alternative. This raised no serious difficulty in 1513 when money was still plentiful and no one in authority had the slightest intention of counting the cost, but later in Henry's reign it was recognized by some that the provision of carts outside England was bad for the balance of payments. A memorandum dealing with the preparatory work for the expedition against France in 1522 proposed that strenuous efforts should be made to find transport vehicles and their drivers in England rather than to hire them on the other side of the Channel.

The argument was supported by detailed costing. To hire 1,000 wagons and the necessary 'limoners' (draught horses) for six months from, say, the Low Countries would cost a total of £26,800. But the same number of wagons could be bought in England, where 'one with another' they cost £10, for £10,000; 1,000 limoners in England would cost £2,000. Even when the English carters' wages were taken into account the king would save £5,200, and at the end of the campaign would still own the surviving horses and carts. Furthermore, the army would benefit from the presence of 2,200 'tall men, Englishmen' who would be able to serve as pioneers, or even to fight side by side with their compatriots if occasion demanded, which carters hired from the Low Countries could hardly be expected to do. It was therefore proposed that commissioners should be appointed to provide wagons and limoners 'within the realm'.[42]

The importance of leaving the farmers free to get on with their work of feeding the nation was again in mind in 1544, when the individuals commissioned to find horses and carts for the invasion of France were instructed to take only those 'as might be conveniently spared without disfurniture of necessary tillage and husbandry of any man'.[43] Moreover, the same balance-of-payments point was made in a paper demonstrating 'how much more commodious it shall be to take carriages within this realm than to hire the same in Flanders'. The total cost of 1,200 wagons, including harness, half of which were to be drawn by teams of ten oxen, was put at £20,600. The same wagons hired in Flanders would cost £30,000, so that by making provision in England the Crown would save £9,400. On this occasion it was estimated that even when the carters' wages were brought into the account there still would be a saving of £400, and – the point which was made in 1522 – 'all the oxen, horses and carriages remain the King's majesty's'.[44]

Gunpowder had been in use for the better part of two centuries and by 1513 heavy guns were standard equipment in most armies. Henry VII had not been particularly interested in artillery, which was to be expected, as he was committed to peace rather than to war (although his reign was not entirely devoid of military effort) and to economy rather than extravagance. The art of

An English bronze culverin, dated 1542. It has an overall length of 11 ft 9 in and fired on 18-lb shot. It was recovered from the Mary Rose in 1840

gun-founding made some progress in England in his time, but the country adopted new ideas and new weapons more slowly than the rest of Europe. This national characteristic was recognized by Sir Richard Morison in 1539 in the Preface to his translation of *The Strategemes, Sleyghtes, and Policies of Warre* by Frontinus – one of England's first military books. He says 'the noble captains of England have oft declared that they little need any instructions, any books, to teach them to touse[(1)] their enemies',[45] and it was partly this attitude that meant that in 1513 the country had to look overseas for some types of heavy artillery. Guns were, of course, made in England and Henry VIII did what he could to encourage the industry. In January 1513 Nicolo di Favri, who was attached to the Venetian embassy in England, said in a report on the preparations for the expedition that 'by day and night and on all the festivals the cannon founders are at work';[46] but the continental makers had greater experience and Henry looked to them, especially the great master of the art, Hans Poppenruyter, for supplementary supplies.

There were many types of cannon, single- and multi-barrelled, breech-loading and muzzle-loading, cast and forged, for the men who made them and the cannoneers who fired them were still feeling their way, and individual experience and prejudice led to the production of many varieties – too many for all practical purposes. It is difficult to be dogmatic on this point because of uncertainty about nomenclature, but even if we consider only the sizes and calibres of the guns in use, and forget about the multiplicity of names attached to them, it seems clear that there was no real need for the long range of graduated sizes, starting with modest weapons that fired 2-in balls, and working up to monsters hurling a ball of 9 in diameter. There were at least eight distinct sizes of straightforward single-barrelled heavy gun, which in England were known as the falconet, falcon, minion, saker, demi-culverin, culverin, demi-cannon and cannon. The smallest of these, the falconet, weighed about 300 lb, and the largest, the cannon, between 4,500 and 6,000 lb.[47] Different names, however, were in use for the various sizes. The cannon, for example, was sometimes known as the bombard, the culverin as the curtows, and so on.

It is possible to isolate four main functions for the heavy guns in the army, and only four types of gun were needed. The main use of cannon at this time was for battering fortifications, for which two sorts of weapon were required. If the town besieged was itself well equipped with artillery it would be difficult for the besiegers to come close to their objective in safety, and they would therefore need cannon with a long range, which would be able to fire only a relatively small missile. This was the position at the siege of Thérouanne, where the defending guns, which were in excellent condition, were manned by skilled professional soldiers, who were able to keep the English army at a respectful distance. They were so far away from the walls, in fact, that their artillery made heavy weather of the work of demolishing them.

On the other hand, if the besieged force had no cannon to speak of, or if they were in the hands of inefficient cannoneers, the besiegers could come very close to the town walls with impunity, and what they then needed was a heavier short-range gun with the maximum destructive power. This was the position at the siege of Tournai, where the defending guns (which were in any case

Crowned Tudor rose engraving surrounded by the garter carried on a Saker gun cast in 1529 for Henry VIII by the Arcamus family of gun-founders in London

antiquated) were in the hands of amateurs, and gave little trouble to the besiegers. Siege warfare also called for a third type of gun – a weapon to be used not against the walls, but against the people and buildings inside them: one that could, for example, lob a fused bomb, which would have a serious effect on morale, in addition to causing physical damage. These pot-guns, or mortars, were used with great effect at Tournai, and helped to bring the townspeople to the point where they were thankful to throw their hand in.

The fourth class of gun tactically necessary was an anti-personnel weapon which could be used in the field, probably to fire diced or grape shot. A variant of this was the 'organ', a many-barrelled piece which could be highly effective, for example, when aimed at a breach in the wall of a besieged town through which the defenders launched a sudden attack. There were more organs in the 1513 expedition than any other type of heavy gun – forty of them in each of the three wards, each in its own cart – and it seems likely that when the invading force came face to face with a substantial body of the enemy in the field (as for example they did in the neighbourhood of Tournehem)[48] it was the organs,

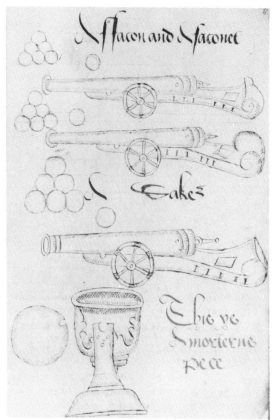

A diagram from a sixteenth-century manuscript, showing falcon, falconet, saker cannon and mortar

whose spread of fire could do a great deal more damage to infantry or cavalry than the single shot of the heavier cannon, that were called upon.

The heaviest guns in the expedition, which are described as bombards, were very much bigger than the next biggest. They fired an enormous iron ball weighing 260 lb and took a charge of 80 lb of gunpowder; but it was reckoned that they could not be fired more often than five times a day. It is not clear how this theoretical rate of fire was determined – whether it was related to the time taken to bring the gun back into position after the recoil (which in the case of the bombard must have been spectacular), or to cool the barrel enough to take the next charge, or to manhandle the huge cannon-ball into the muzzle; less probably, it may have been the belief that a higher rate would bring the gun dangerously near to bursting-point. The slow rate of fire made it absolutely essential that the heavier guns should be accurately aimed. A very little carelessness could easily waste a whole day's effort. There were six bombards, two in each of the three wards; and each was pulled by a team of twenty-four Flanders mares – English horses simply were not strong enough.

The most interesting guns of the 1513 expedition were the twelve apostles, to which Henry was obviously very much attached, and which present something of a mystery. None of them is known to survive – although they were made of bronze and therefore had a chance of survival if they escaped the melting-pot – and we are therefore forced to rely on documentary evidence about them. It has been generally considered that they were twelve pieces of the same size, the supporting evidence being an authority to pay for 'twelve apostles' weighing a total of 67,225 lb at £2 per 100 lb, or £1,344 10s. per gun, and for twelve apparently identical gun-carriages for them at £12 each.[49] Martin du Bellay, not the most reliable authority, when describing how St John the Evangelist fell into the water[50] says that the piece was a double grand culverin 'of which the army had twelve of the same calibre, which took cannon-balls'.[51] John Taylor, who usually gets his facts right, records that the king had twelve guns of unusual magnitude each cast in the image of an apostle.[52]

So far so good. But some of the lists of guns in the 1513 expedition show that only two apostles were attached to each ward, making a total of six, and that they were the heaviest siege guns after the bombards.[53] In another list, however, each of the wards is given 'two apostles of the greater sort' and two 'of the smaller sort'. The former are said to be for 'battery of towns and fortresses' and the latter 'for closing of the field', i.e. they were to be used at close quarters in battle. No details of the performance of the smaller guns are given, but in assessment of the quantity of gunpowder needed to maintain an all-out bombardment for eight days there is some information about what must have been the heavier apostles. They fired a 20 lb iron ball thirty times a day, and they took a charge of 20 lb of gunpowder. Further, it is recorded that the smaller apostles had twenty-one horses (apparently to pull their ancillary equipment and ammunition) while the greater had thirty horses.[54] To sum up: the truth probably is that there were twelve apostles, and not two sets of twelve; that six were siege guns, and six much lighter field pieces, and that each of the wards had two of each size. This is supported by the accounts of the middle-ward, which show four gunners in charge of four apostles – Peter, Bartholomew, Simon and James the Less. The four gunners were all paid the same, however (16d. a day), and they all had one assistant, which may suggest that their responsibilities were equal. (There were gunners' posts in the ward which carried wages of 8d. and 10d., and it might therefore be expected that those in charge of the smaller apostles would be entitled to a lower rate.) The only difference between the four apostles is that seven and eight carters were allocated respectively to Peter and Bartholomew, whereas Simon needed nine and James the Less ten.[55] We might therefore guess that James the Less (paradoxically) and Simon were the great apostles attached to Henry's ward, and that Peter and Bartholomew were the 'smaller sort'; but whatever the names attributed to the various guns, there seems to be little doubt that there were six large and six small.(2)

The wards had over sixty guns each, in addition to their forty multi-barrelled organs. The heavier weapons – bombards, apostles, curtows, and 'Nuremberg pieces' – were all drawn by Flanders mares; and the ligher – demi-culverins, serpentines, falcons, falconets – had teams of English horses ranging from two for the falconet to ten for the demi-culverin. A battery which used all the siege guns in all three wards firing at their maximum rate required about 32 tons of gunpowder a day. The expedition seems to have carried with it 510 tons, so that it was probably in a position to maintain an all-out battery for sixteen days without drawing on outside supplies.(3)

The provision of ancillary ordnance stores presented its own problems. Those in charge of the planning of the 1513 expedition, none of whom had any experience of supply on this scale, were faced with the acquisition of a multitude of small items, shortage of any one of which might precipitate a crisis, but which might be easily enough overlooked in the preparatory stages. These items included sickles and scythes for clearing the undergrowth at the gun sites; shovels, spades, and scoops for making trenches to protect the artillery and for building mounds from which the guns could fire down into a besieged town; balances and weights to measure out the charges of gunpowder required for the various sizes of heavy gun; 300 leather buckets to carry powder from the dump to the guns; ladles for charging them; miscellaneous materials without which the cannoneers could not do an efficient job – axle-grease for the gun-carriages, vinegar for cooling the guns in action, barrels of nails, soap, candles, lanterns, cresset lights and so on. There were also four wagon-loads of coal to be used in the forges of the smiths who were responsible for the maintenance and repair of the guns and equipment. One item, the purpose of which is not quite clear, is described as 'great spikings for the great gun wheels', of which there were six barrels in each ward. These spikes cannot have been used to improve the traction of the gun-carriages, as they were not automotive, but were pulled by teams of horses, which leaves the possible explanation that they were spikes fixed into the gun-carriage wheels to help to control the recoil; or they may have been a device to hold the gun in position after it had been aimed.

Under the Statute of Winchester of 1285 all able-bodied men were supposed to possess weapons on a scale related to their wealth. This law was generally reaffirmed by Henry VIII in one of the first acts of his reign, but it would have been quite unrealistic to assume that it was implicitly obeyed by every citizen, and that in the event of mobilization the levies would turn up on the due date with the equipment that the law required them to have; or that, if they did, it would be in serviceable condition. This is confirmed by Thomas Audley, who proposes that the Crown should maintain a stock of equipment for 4,000 men, which would hardly have been necessary had the arms provisions of the Statute of Winchester been universally observed. Audley points out that the Emperor Charles V has accepted responsibility for maintaining government stocks of arms, and recommends that England should follow suit. He admits that it may be argued that this provision will cost as much as the Crown jewels, but when the day of battle comes, weapons and equipment will be worth a great deal more than diamonds.[56]

In 1513 the government seem to have gone on the assumption that new weapons would have to be provided for the whole of the force; and they also made provision for substantial reserve stocks, which would, of course, have been increased to the extent that the recruits who obeyed the law were able to bring serviceable weapons with them. This lavish provision, which suggests that the Crown had little faith in the Statute of Winchester, markedly contrasts with its cheese-paring attitude later in the century, when the responsibility for equipping the troops was more and more transferred from the central authority to the

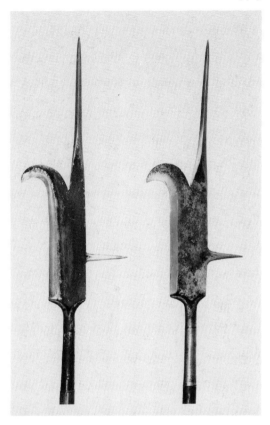

Bills: probably English, early sixteenth century. The length of the head is 33½ in

shires; it was possible only so long as the fortune left by Henry VII was there to be drawn upon.

The great majority of the infantry were still equipped with the bills and bows that had done yeoman service for centuries and which were made in England (although partly from imported materials). Pikes, now the leading weapon on the mainland of Europe, were found only in small numbers in the 1513 expedition, and were carried mostly by the mercenaries engaged by Henry – the Almains and Burgundians. In the months before the expedition crossed into France substantial purchases were made of all types of equipment for the infantrymen, including quantities of the new firearms. Thus John de Castro, a merchant of Spain, was commissioned to supply eighty hand-guns, each complete with its powder horn, for which he was paid 6s. a gun, and there were many similar transactions. These hand-guns were relatively light and simple, but there were also purchases of harquebuses, more powerful weapons, which cost about twice as much as the 'hand-gun'. Thousands of 'complete harnesses' were bought at this time also. These were suits of 'almain rivets' for infantrymen, comprising breast-plate and back-plate, pairs of splints to protect the arms, gorgets for the neck and shoulder, and helmets, which cost around 16s. the set.[57]

Each of the three wards had ninety vehicles reserved for the transport of spare

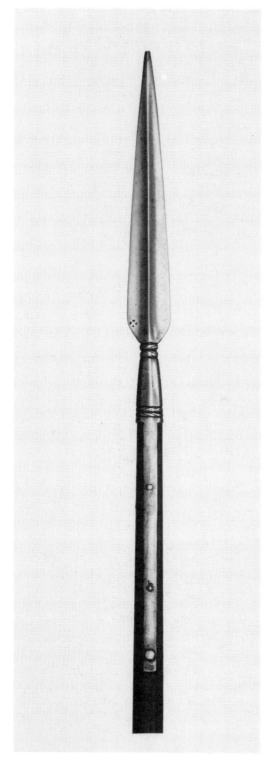

*An early sixteenth-century small spear or
javelin, possibly for Henry VIII's guard*

equipment and weapons. The estimates of the requirements of the wards vary, but one of the more modest allows 5,200 bows divided into parcels of 400 in 13 wagons; 86,000 bowstrings packed in 20 barrels which needed 2 wagons; and 10,000 sheaves of arrows that had a further 26 wagons. There were 2,000 demi-lances (medium-sized cavalry spears) and 1,400 'whole spears' – 200 to a wagon in each case; 4,000 pikes in 8 wagons; and 5,000 each of bills and 'archers' stakes' – the long stakes fitted with sockets and spikes, two of which were carried by each archer to be stuck into the ground to form a sort of abatis to give protection against a cavalry charge in terrain where there was no natural cover. There were also quantities of 'casting caltrops' – multi-spiked weapons which could be strewn around in open ground when a force was compelled to retreat and would damage alike the feet of infantrymen and the hooves of horses.[58] Thomas Audley would have approved of this, for he was still recommending the use of the caltrops in the middle of the century.[59] Even the most modest estimates proposed the provision of quantities greatly in excess of the numbers of men in the ward, so that if not a single yeoman brought with him the weapon he was required by law to possess the force could have been equipped several times over from new purchases.

Audley also describes the qualities required in the officers of the ordnance. The master must be 'expert and skilful in all points cannonry', able to instruct his subordinates in their art. He is responsible for seeing that the heavy guns are

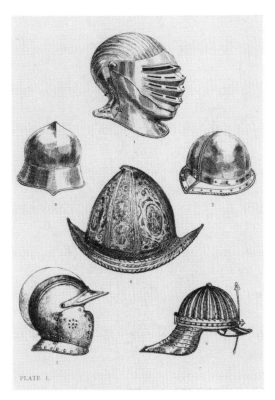

Helmets from the beginning of the reign of Henry VIII (23152.c.3 plate L)

'well and strongly stocked, and mounted upon strong axle-trees, and wheels well-shod and strongly bound with iron'. The lieutenant of the ordnance as second-in-command understudies the master in all respects. The master gunner's main job is training the cannoneers. He has to satisfy himself that 'every cannoneer appointed to any piece of ordnance is able to govern the same as to that cunning science appertaineth'. Finally, the individual cannoneer must be 'skilful in the weight of his powder and shot, and also in the height of the mouth . . . skilful in the receipt of his powder, and know the authority of the same'. When he takes over his gun at the beginning of the expedition he must 'diligently search and try that she be clean from honeycombs, right bored and that the barrel be clean, and the touch hole clear and to the same a close cover'. He is also to make certain that he has all the requisite charging ladles, sponges, priming irons, moulds for making hail shot and so on.[60]

Henry's anxiety that England should make up the leeway lost in the heavy-guns arms race was matched by his interest in the development of the hand fire-arm, in spite of the implications for the long-bow, a weapon which he himself used with great skill. For many decades the Crown had worried about the decline in the use of the bow and there had been a series of statutes designed to keep it going, not only because of its importance for national defence, but because it was seen as an antidote to the gambling craze, which was considered to be assuming dangerous proportions. If the able-bodied men of the country devoted their spare time to practising archery, not only would the physique of the nation as a whole benefit, but less time would be available for gambling games with all their attendant evils. But if the bow was to be kept going indefinitely in the interests of the health of the people it meant that the new weapons of fire must be shunned.

Alternatively, if it was accepted that the new weapons had come to stay, the government must face up to the disappearance of the long-bow. This was not easy, for it was England's traditional weapon, and no government likes to interfere with tradition, unless it is absolutely inevitable. More important, even if there was disagreement about the value of weapons of fire on the battlefield, they had proved to be highly effective in the hands of the robber, the poacher, and the murderer. Therefore if the government went all out to replace the long-bow with fire-arms, at a time when the country still relied on a citizen army, they might be opening the door to an era of lawlessness, which could prove much more serious than gambling. This problem became acute during Elizabeth I's reign, for by that time the development of fire-arms elsewhere in Europe left no doubt in the mind of the Privy Council about the proper course; but in Henry VIII's time the controversy was only just beginning, and the government line was to err in favour of the long-bow – which was hardly surprising when the relative efficiency of the long-bow and that of the early fire-arms were compared, to say nothing of their relative costs.

One of Henry's early statutes, 'An act concerning shooting in long-bows',[61] praised the traditional weapon, condemned the cross-bow (which was considered to be evil because it was so deadly), and repeated the traditional objections to illegal games, including tennis and bowls. It also reaffirmed the Statute of Winchester, requiring men to possess and practice with the bow. This

An English buckler of wood faced with concentric circles of brass rivets c. 1520

was the position at the time of the 1513 expedition, but later in the reign the government made a daring experiment by throwing open the use of hand-guns to a wide section of the population. It was laid down in a royal proclamation of 1544 that the king, considering that it was expedient to have:

> . . . some number of his subjects skilled and exercised in the feat of shooting in handguns and hagbusshes,(4) as well for the defence of the realm against enemies as annoying of the same in time of war . . . gives licence and liberty to all and singular his majesty's subjects born within his grace's dominions being of age of sixteen and upwards that they and every of them from henceforth may lawfully shoot in handguns and hagbusshes without incurring forfeiture loss or damage for the same.

It was, in fact, to be quite legal to use fire-arms, despite the earlier statutes. There were, however, some provisos. It was still forbidden to shoot game ('deer, partridges, pheasants, herons, shovellers, teals and hares') in the neighbourhood of any of the king's palaces, and in any other place without the licence of the owner of the ground; and it was also an offence to use fire-arms in any city, borough, town or village 'where habitation of people is', unless 'it be at butt, hill, or bank, certainly appointed therefor'.[62]

It quickly became evident that his move was much too liberal for the times, for two years later there was a further proclamation cancelling the arrangement, ostensibly on the ground that 'it hath pleased God to remove from us the plague of war and to send unto us a right honourable and profitable peace'. The generous licence was revoked and the citizens were once again forbidden to use hand-guns, except as permitted by an act of 1541 or through a licence under the Great Seal.[63] It is conceivable that the Crown's liberal attitude to the use of fire-arms was changed for the reason stated in the proclamation – that the danger of war had receded and that there was therefore no need to encourage the people to familiarize themselves with the new weapons; but it seems likely that the change of heart was as much a social as a military decision. If too many people had guns it would encourage lawlessness in a variety of forms; and in the long run it would put dissident groups into a position to challenge the authority of the Crown.

NOTES

(1) The suggestion that Bartholomew was a field gun is weakened, however, by Robert Macquereau's evidence that at the siege of Tournai Henry personally directed the firing of Bartholomew at the towers of the cathedral (below, p. 145).
(2) These figures must be treated with caution, as the various estimates of the number and size of the guns in the three wards differ a good deal from each other.
(3) Harquebuses.
(4) Treat roughly (*OED*).

6 Siege

The formal siege of Thérouanne began with the summons of the town by
Bluemantle pursuivant on Saturday, 25 June, three days after the fore-ward and
rear-ward had arrived there. This was the standard opening gambit, which could
in theory lead to the surrender of a garrison without a shot being fired, but in
practice was no more than a courteous intimation to those within that they were
about to be subjected to a siege. Even in the reign of Elizabeth I, when most
chivalric niceties were a thing of the past, strong traces of chivalry lingered on in
the realm of siege warfare. A treatise written in her time, more than sixty years
after the 1513 expedition, still assumes that the proper courtesies will be
observed by both sides. The herald from the besieging army sounds his trumpet
thrice, whereupon the garrison commander greets him with much honour,
refuses to surrender, and suggests that he depart in peace, after receiving 'an
honourable reward'; and before the siege can begin in earnest the herald is
expected to have a second parley with the town.[1]

Bluemantle, having demanded permission to enter the gate, was taken to
Antoine de Créquy, the officer commanding the garrison, whom he addressed in
the names of Henry, King of France and England, and of the Earl of
Shrewsbury, lieutenant general of the English army before Thérouanne. He
explained in formal language that he was instructed to summon the garrison to
surrender within twenty-four hours, and that he was authorized to promise that
if they did so Henry would spare their lives and property; but, he went on, 'in
case that ye refuse so to do, and if he take it by strong hand and army he shall do
all to be put to fire and blood, and upon that take ye advisement. And I desire
you to make me an answer of your will and intention touching this same.'[2]

This was the correct approach, and up to a point de Créquy also observed
protocol. He duly consulted his council of war, and then informed Bluemantle
that Thérouanne would never surrender to the enemies of France. He then
added that the pursuivant had better clear out quickly, unless he wanted to enjoy
the hospitality of the town for an indefinite period – a thinly-veiled threat which
a stickler for the etiquette of chivalry would have ruled out of order. Bluemantle
promptly returned to the English camp to pass on the garrison's reaction to the
summons, and the siege was under way.[3]

As soon as the English herald left the town de Créquy sent a messenger to
Louis to bring him up to date with the latest developments; and in due course
received his best wishes, a generous amount of money, and a promise of massive
help. This caused a wave of enthusiasm among the garrison. 'Better to die on the
walls', cried de Créquy, 'than to surrender.' His shout of 'Vive le roi!' was taken
up by the bystanders and trumpets and drums were sounded. The uproar could

be clearly heard in the English camp, and the commanders, thinking that a major sortie was imminent, ordered the troops to the standard. It was only when some French prisoners explained what was happening that they were allowed to stand down.[4]

There were four main courses of action open to the besiegers. The most usual was to bombard sections of the wall until they were reduced to rubble, and then to send in the assault forces through the breaches, while other detachments used ladders to scale the walls that had been left intact. (The expedition carried with it fifteen cart-loads of scaling-ladders.) It was of course essential that the breaches should be big enough to allow the attacking force to be deployed on a wide front. If they were required to pour through a narrow gap they would meet a devastating concentrated fire. Further, the masonry had to be broken down reasonably fine so that men could scramble over it and still carry their weapons without difficulty. If these two conditions were not fulfilled disaster was inevitable. At the siege of Leith in 1560, for example, the assault was ordered long before the breaches were ready, and despite great heroism among the rank and file the English attack was repulsed with heavy losses.

Secondly, the walls could be breached by the detonation of a mine underneath them, which was highly effective when it came off. If the attackers were lucky and the activities of their miners were not detected, it was possible to create an instantaneous breach and rush in the assault troops before the garrison could assemble its forces where the wall was broken. If a breach was being made by cannon fire it was obvious where the assault must come and the defenders could concentrate their troops at exactly the right spot before the attack materialised. Not so with a successful mine, which would leave the troops in the immediate vicinity of the breach in a state of confusion; and in the interval when their fellows from other parts of the garrison were being marshalled the assault troops had a good chance of consolidating a position within the walls. Mining, however, was a risky business.

Thirdly, a garrison could be starved into submission, provided that a complete blockade was maintained, and that the besiegers were strong enough to ward off any attack in their rear. Finally, it was possible in theory to break the morale of those within a beleagured city by concentrating the bombardment on the houses rather than on the wall; but this could succeed only where the town was small and where there was a large civilian population.

Very little happened between the issue of the summons and the arrival of the middle-ward under Henry on 1 August, which confirms the point made when the expedition was planned that it would succeed only if all three wards worked as a team.[5] While Henry was frittering away his time in Calais the rest of his troops lacked the strength to strike a decisive blow; and they came in for a good deal of criticism during this period. According to one report the garrison refused to believe that the Englishmen posed any real threat. They told Louis that they had plenty of food and could easily hold out until All Saints' Day (1 November). Indeed, they considered that they were better provisioned than the besiegers, whose supply lines they thought very vulnerable. The writer of this report added that the English troops might just as well have been in Ireland for all the impression they were making in France.[6] On 11 July, Roberto Acciaiolo, the

Florentine ambassador to France, wrote to the Signory that the English were making little progress with the siege, partly because of the incessant rain which hindered operations, and partly because they were suffering heavily from the guns defending the town.[7]

A rather more optimistic view of the situation was taken by one of the English soldiers, Humphrey Rudyng, in a letter to his friend William Micklow in Worcestershire. He assured Micklow that every word he wrote was the truth and that he could vouch for most of his account from his own observation. On Sunday, 10 July, the bombardment was 'so fierce and thick against the town wall and the gates' that the garrison was convinced that the assault was imminent. The alarm bells in the town were rung, but in fact the assault never materialized. The civilians of Thérouanne did, however, meet a great disaster on the same night, for 'the fairest young women within the town, many dozen in number, were slain by the falling of a house'. Rudyng may have exaggerated this episode, but he insisted that the walls were 'sore beaten with guns' and that many houses were destroyed. Perhaps his account was more biased than those of the diplomatic observers, but at least he was an eyewitness of the events he described, and often found himself in the middle of them. He was no less certain about the outcome of the siege than were the garrison – 'I trust that by St James's Day (25 July) the lord captain and the army shall drink wine in Thérouanne of the best.'[8]

A fortnight later the Florentine ambassador was still deriding the English troops' performance. They had now been under the walls of the town for over a month and had nothing to show for their labours. They had not attempted a single assault, nor had they been engaged in any noteworthy feat of arms, and their reputation was suffering badly as a result. He considered that if they had captured Thérouanne quickly they would have put the French in a very awkward position, but in fact their blockade was so imperfect that it was a simple matter to send reinforcements into the town. On 21 July, 200 men-at-arms forced their way in, losing only ten of their number, and took with them 100 pioneers to help to repair the damaged fortifications.[9] Acciaiolo did admit, however, that there had been panic when the English troops first appeared before Thérouanne, and in this he is supported by the chronicler Robert Macquereau, who says that the civilians in the town and the garrison troops were all terrified when the siege began.[10]

There is no doubt that Thérouanne was a formidable objective, although one writer, also anxious to disparage the efforts of the invading army, claimed that it was the weakest garrison town in France.[11] This was nonsense, for it was recognized to be the key to Picardy, and was traditionally one of the few pillars on which the King of France could sleep in peace.[12] Situated in the rolling valley of the river Lys about six miles upstream from Aire, it was 'strongly fortified with walls, ramparts, bulwarks, with divers fortresses in the ditches which were so broad and so plumb steep it was wonder to behold'.[13] The fortress was well provided with artillery and expert cannoneers, who took a regular toll of the besiegers; and it had a powerful and well-disciplined garrison. A Welsh eyewitness of the siege testifies to the strength of the town's defences. The trenches surrounding it were so deep that men were afraid to walk too near the

Maximilian in the workshop of Conrad Seusenhafer. An engraving by Hans Burgkmair from Der Weiss Kunig, *1516*

edge in case they fell in; and their banks were covered with impenetrable quickset hedges. There were more trenches inside the walls to provide a last-ditch defence, should the enemy succeed in passing the main wall, and there were also ramparts made from timber and earth. Some of the trenches had deep pits to make 'fumigations, to the intent that the men upon the assaulting of the same should have been poisoned and stopped'.[14] Even if the danger to the attacking force of this early attempt to use noxious fumes in warfare is discounted, there is no doubt that it would have taken a superhuman effort to break through the town's defences.

At first the English fore-ward, under the command of the Earl of Shrewsbury, occupied a position to the north-west of the fortress, and the rear-ward under Lord Herbert was stationed to the east. Both wards were in full view of the enemy guns, and trenches had to be dug to allow the artillery to get anywhere near striking distance of the walls. Rudyng tells us that the trenches 'near hands compassing three parts of the town', supplemented by a natural hollow in the case of the fore-ward, enabled the English guns and miners 'to get within a birdbolt(1) shot to the walls';[15] but even so, the range was such that little impression could be made on the fortifications.

Moreover, the frequent sorties made by 'the stradiots', light cavalry with short stirrups, beaver hats, small spears, and swords like the scimitars of Turkey, with whom 'many a staff was broken and many a proper feat of arms done', made it difficult for the besiegers to keep up a steady rate of fire. There was also a contingent of German mercenaries who sallied forth from time to time with hand-guns and pikes and inflicted casualties before they were driven back to the safety of the town by the English archers.[16] In these encounters, some of which were intended by the garrison to tempt the besiegers within harquebus shot of the walls, men were slain on both parts, but 'the more part Frenchman'.[15] On one occasion the Frenchmen actually contrived to capture an English standard – a shameful thing for the English company concerned; and they took a steady toll of the besiegers from the Green Rampart, a high mound outside the north-east corner of the wall that carried a powerful battery.[17]

It soon became evident that it was going to be a long job to create a breach that could be assaulted with any chance of success; and, indeed, it seemed possible that the garrison, which had plenty of pioneers, might succeed night after night in making good the damage done by the English guns during the day, and thus produce a stalemate which would end only when the French king had amassed a strong enough force to raise the siege. The only way to deal with walls that could not readily be breached was to mine them. A single mine could take as much gunpowder as the whole battery of cannon used in weeks of bombardment, and if it were properly placed its effect could be even more devastating. Sir Alexander Baynham, captain of the pioneers of the rear-ward, was therefore ordered to dig a mine that would demolish a sector of the wall wide enough to admit a powerful assault force.

The work proceeded satisfactorily, for the rich soil of the Lys valley presented no problem to the pioneers; but, unfortunately, the French were well informed as to what was going on, either through their spies outside the town or from their own shrewd observation of the activities of the English pioneer corps. They knew that their wall was being mined, and they knew just where the enemy were working. It was therefore easy enough to drive out their own shaft far enough from the English tunnel to keep the sound of their pickaxes and shovels from the English pioneers, far enough from the wall to avoid any risk of damaging it by exploding a counter-mine, but near enough to the enemy tunnel to destroy it when the time was ripe. As soon as the French mine reached the strategic point, the end chamber was packed with gunpowder, a train was run back into the town, and there was now nothing to do but to wait for the moment when the maximum number of Englishmen were working in their mine. The moment was well chosen, for the besiegers' tunnel was completely destroyed and the men in it either entombed or seriously burned. Of the bodies brought out, two had been burned to death. 'Three others of them lie burned, more likely to die than to live.'[18]

This setback must have lowered the besiegers' morale, for it was now clear that little could be done until the middle-ward joined forces with them; but Henry was still sitting comfortably in Calais. The counter-mine was sprung on Monday, 18 July, three days before he was due to start his ponderous march south. The only encouraging feature at this time was the success of the light cavalry under Sir Rees ap Thomas. Their job was to scour the wooded plains in the neighbourhood of Thérouanne to keep the French contingents there on the alert, and if possible to discourage them from grouping to mount an all-out attack on the besieging army. This 'keeping of the field' was vital to the safety of any besieging force, and it was nobly carried out by the spirited Welshman and his 'northern horse', even if on occasion small detachments of French troops did contrive to threaten the English army. Hall sums up their contribution thus: They 'many times encountered with the Frenchmen and slew and took divers prisoners so that the Frenchmen drew not towards the siege but turned another way'.[19] On Saturday, 16 July, for example, a body of French troops (which Humphrey Rudyng puts at 6,000, surely a gross exaggeration, in spite of his protestations of accurate reporting) which approached from the north-west was fended off by a wing of the light cavalry that 'slew three, drowned two, and took four live prisoners', not a very impressive bag if there were in fact 6,000 in the French force.[20] Only when Henry arrived with the middle-ward was it possible to encircle the fortress completely and embark on a serious attempt to starve the garrison out. The Florentine ambassador reported to his government on 10 August, however, that Henry's arrival had made little difference. The guns of the middle-ward had made it possible to intensify the bombardment, but even so it was making little impression. The besiegers had several times threatened an assault, but it was never actually made, and the garrison were becoming more and more confident that the town would not be taken by storm. Louis, who was in Amiens at this time, was grateful for the breathing-space thus afforded him, and pressed on with the task of putting his available forces in order, so that they might challenge the English army in the field. He was hoping that he would be joined by the Duke of Guelders, when their combined army would number as many as 25,000 men – quite enough to risk an engagement with the invaders.[21]

Writing from Beauvais on 8 August, Juliano de Medici suggested that the English might well be on the point of abandoning the siege. He had heard that they planned to make an assault in the next day or two, and that if it failed they would withdraw and try their luck at Montreuil or St Quentin, which would be easier nuts to crack. He thought that even now the French had gathered together a strong enough force to take them on in a straight fight, but to make quite certain of success Louis was waiting for the Duke of Guelders to join him, which he was expected to do in a few days. On the same date yet another Italian added that the English had accomplished none of the things they had set out to do, and that they were thoroughly demoralized.[22]

Two days later the Florentine ambassador continued his pessimistic account of the besiegers' lack of progress. He now considered that even if they captured

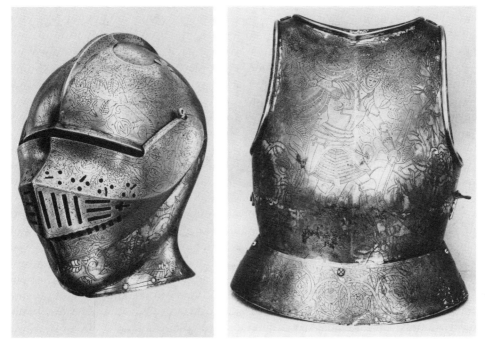

The silvered and engraved helmet and breastplate (engraved with the figure of St George) from Henry VIII's armour Made in England c. 1514–15

Thérouanne it was so late in the campaigning season that it would be impossible to capitalize on their success; but he saw little chance of the town's falling. The blockade was still incomplete, in spite of the arrival of the middle-ward, and a French force under Captain Fontrailles had had little difficulty in fighting its way in. The captain had a leisurely discussion with the garrison commander, who was still confident that they could hold out. When it was suggested that the visitors might remain to help with the defence of the town de Créquy said that he wanted no more than 80 men-at-arms on foot to be left behind. The remainder of the contingent fought their way out as easily as they had entered, after Fontrailles had made a thorough inspection of the state of the fortifications, so that he might report on them to Louis.[23]

It seems likely that the garrison were in a less happy position than Acciaiolo would have had his government believe. Perhaps it was because the garrison commander was worried about food supplies that he asked for infantrymen (and only a small number at that), in spite of the damage he had inflicted on the besiegers with cavalry sorties. Horses had to be fed, and maybe fodder was beginning to run short. Further, the date to which the garrison could survive with comfort was brought foward from 1 November to the beginning of September, another indication that things were becoming difficult.

Henry's arrival had made little difference to the conduct of the siege, but a fresh impetus was given on Wednesday, 10 August, by Maximilian's appearance on the scene. When the news came that he had reached Aire tremendous preparations were made for his reception. The tent of cloth of gold, which was erected only on great occasions, was brought out and taken to the chosen meeting-place – the village of Rincq, midway between Thérouanne and Aire. The nobility donned their most beautiful clothes, fashioned from richly-ornamented cloth of gold and cloth of silver. Hall singles out the Duke of Buckingham, who was in purple, for special mention. His horse's bard was 'full of spangles and little bells of gold marvellous costly and pleasant to behold'. Henry's own coat was adorned with pearls and precious stones and over it he wore a suit of light armour. His helmet and the component parts of his heavy armour were carried behind him by nine of the henchmen, who wore white and crimson cloth-of-gold covered with golden ornaments,[24] and as he rode the golden bells on his harness, which weighed as much as two ounces each, dropped off one by one and were left as souvenirs for the emperor's bodyguard. According to one estimate, Maximilian was escorted by 1,500 men and Henry by 2,500.[25] Alas, all the effort that had gone into this pageantry was wasted, for as king and emperor met the heavens opened, and what was to have been a splendid occasion was limited to the briefest of conferences between the two bedraggled monarchs in a rain-sodden tent. They did no more than 'confirm their good league for the annihilation of the King of France' before they went their separate ways in search of dry clothing.

A further meeting was arranged three days later. This time the weather was kinder; not that it mattered, as the conference took place in Henry's portable wooden house, which stood up to the elements much better than the tents. Maximilian had a much smaller bodyguard '300 all clad in one colour who ran with him on foot'. Before sitting down at the conference table he had to inspect the whole of the besieging force – 'really big strong men' according to a German observer – whom Henry had lined up three or four deep. The tent of cloth of gold, surmounted by a golden lion holding the arms of England in its paws, had had a chance to dry out, and was much admired. The emperor's tailor reckoned that it must have cost 33 florins an ell to make. Maximilian dined in the tent, the meal being prepared as usual by his own cook. Afterwards he adjourned to the wooden house, where he discussed the plan of campaign with Henry until eleven o'clock, at which hour he returned to Aire for the night.[26] They got on so well on this occasion 'that one might have thought them father and son', but they did have a difference of opinion. Henry was convinced that Thérouanne must be assaulted, and said that there would be adequate breaches in another three days. He himself would lead the assault. Maximilian, however, saw only too clearly how difficult it would be to take such a powerful fortress by storm.[27]

At this moment, when things were going far from well with the expedition, it became apparent that the trouble from Scotland that had been anticipated before the expedition left for France was likely to materialize. Lyon King of Arms came from the Scottish king to inform Henry that, unless he withdrew from France, James would enter England from the north. Henry listened in silence, and when the herald had finished said that he could not readily believe that his brother of Scotland would thus break his solemn oath; but if he were misguided enough to invade England, there was no doubt that he would regret it. He could not very well say less, but he must have had serious misgivings about the security of England at a time when the flower of her manhood was with him in France.

While the siege was in progress Henry had little time to spare for private correspondence, even with his queen back in England. He had written to her while he was in Calais, but it was simply about a minor business matter raised by the Bishop of Winchester, and the letter was addressed to her in her capacity of Regent and not of wife.[28] The ill-starred Catherine, however, was a regular and solicitous correspondent, writing as a rule to Wolsey because she hesitated to trouble the king himself. Her letters show her to be a humble, loyal, and affectionate wife, ever anxious about the comfort and safety of her husband, like any other wife whose man has gone to the wars. She wrote to Wolsey from Richmond on 26 July, saying that now that the middle-ward had left Calais it would no doubt be difficult for the king to find time to write to her, and that she would therefore send a succession of messengers to bring frequent news of him. She trusted that before long he would come home to her with as great a victory as any prince ever had.[29] She constantly worried about his welfare and at the beginning of August asked Margaret of Savoy to send a physician to attend him.[30] A fortnight later she wrote to Wolsey expressing her thankfulness that Henry had safely accomplished the dangerous march to Thérouanne, in spite of the attentions of the French, and saying 'I trust to God it shall be so continued that ever the King shall have the best on his enemies with as great honour as ever king had.' She added that she had been very troubled to think that Henry was so near to the siege – she must have agreed with the Council's earlier proposal that he should be compelled to watch all military operations from a safe distance – but she now thanked God for Wolsey's assurance 'of the good heed that the king taketh of himself to avoid all manner of dangers' and begged him to do everything in his power to keep the king safe.[31] But she need not have troubled. Henry himself had every intention to avoid 'all manner of dangers', particularly in the solitary battle of the expedition which was only a few days away.

NOTE

(1)   A kind of blunt-headed arrow used for shooting birds (*OED*).

7   Discipline

It was relatively easy to maintain good discipline before Thérouanne, in spite of frequent and successful French sorties. A besieging army has as a rule a strong moral superiority over a besieged enemy, unless it is liable to be threatened by a powerful relieving force; and the English soldiers knew that they were capable of matching any army that the French could put in the field at that juncture. Moreover, the weather was tolerable. It rained a great deal, but this was no particular hardship to Englishmen. There was no question of trouble among the yeoman soldiers because of constant blazing heat (as there had been the year before in Spain) or because of severe frost and snow (as there was to be in the next invasion of France ten years later).

Discipline on the 1513 expedition was in fact exceptionally good throughout. On the few occasions when the troops did fall from grace it was due to slackness rather than to a calculated attempt to disobey regulations. (The indiscipline which led to the rout of the food convoy from Calais to Thérouanne is a good example.[1]) In this respect the army of 1513 was markedly different from the unhappy force commanded by the Marquis of Dorset in the previous year,[2] and indeed from English sixteenth-century armies in general.

The reasons are not difficult to find. That Henry was to be commander-in-chief meant that the best type of man willingly offered himself for service – in so far as there was a choice in the matter. The young king was a popular figure and the idea of following him into battle and sharing in the spoils of war appealed to many adventurous spirits. More important, those responsible for selecting the recruits worked to a very high standard, knowing that the king would see at first hand the result of their efforts. There were none of the rogues and vagabonds who plagued many of the overseas expeditions of the latter part of the century and who were swept into the army simply to rid the country of their unwelcome presence. Nor was there any of the war-weariness which affected England's forces towards the end of Elizabeth I's reign, when the barrel was scraped year after year and many of those who had not been able to dodge conscription in the first place employed every conceivable trick to escape from the army.

Nevertheless, regulations were needed. The usual practice was to issue a code, enumerating offences and the penalties attaching to them, on the eve of the departure of an expeditionary force, although it was impossible before the introduction of printing to give these codes a very wide circulation in the army. Manuscript copies were issued to the principal officers, who were responsible for having the regulations read out to the troops under their command, so that, in the words of the preamble to Henry V's code, 'all those concerned may not pretend ignorance of the said constitutions'.[3]

There are several examples of disciplinary codes before the sixteenth century. The first comprehensive body of regulations still extant was issued by Richard II in 1385, but a hundred years earlier Richard I had promulgated a handful of rules 'for the government of those going by sea to the Holy Land', dealing simply with the offences of murder, wounding, assault, theft and cursing. The convicted murderer was bound to his victim's body and thrown into the sea; the thief was banished from the army, after his head had been shorn, smeared with boiling pitch and feathered; and the man who struck a comrade without wounding him was ducked thrice.[4]

Richard II's code, which like the others was drafted after 'good consultation and deliberation' with the nobility and knights with special experience of warfare, has twenty-six articles covering most aspects of military life; and it provides the basis of the later codes, including those of Henry VIII's reign. Although the processes of 'consultation and deliberation' were gone through on each occasion (no doubt so that recent developments in the art of war might be taken into account), the substance of the successive codes differs very little.

This can be illustrated by an examination of the corresponding articles in a series of codes. For example, one of the many provisions common to all the principal sets of regulations deals with 'havoc'. It was of fundamental importance in an age when every soldier was obsessed with the possibility of enriching himself with spoil that the whole army should be forced to go all out for victory and that there should be no thought of relaxation until the enemy had been beaten beyond hope of recovery. Only then could the commander-in-chief cry havoc – the signal that it was open to every man to forget the fighting and begin looting. Were the signal given too soon the troops' grip might be relaxed while there was still some fight left in the enemy, with disastrous results; and it was therefore essential to make the rule about havoc crystal clear in the regulations.

It changed little in the centuries before Henry VIII's time. In Richard II's regulations – framed in the latter part of the fourteenth century – havoc is dealt with as follows: 'Item, that no one be so hardy as to cry Havoc under pain of losing his head, and that he or they that shall be the beginners of the said cry shall likewise be beheaded and that their bodies likewise be hanged up by the arms.'[5] In Henry V's code the death penalty is retained for the principal offender, but those who take up the cry after him are let off rather more lightly: 'Also if any one shall be found to have in any manner begun the clamour called Havoc without our especial licence, he shall be punished with death, and his followers with arrest of body and goods and to be diligently kept in the custody of the constable and marshal, till they have fined with them for the offence.'[6] The regulation for Henry VIII's 1513 expedition follows very closely that of Henry V, except that there is no mention of a fine for the secondary offenders: 'Also that no man be so hardy to cry Havoc upon pain of him that is found beginner to die therefor and the remnant to be imprisoned and their bodies to be punished at the King's will.'[7] Finally, the code provided for Henry's second personal invasion of France in 1544 (which differs in some respects from the 1513 version) shows only verbal changes in the case of havoc, thus: 'Also, that no man presume to cry Havoc upon pain of death to the beginner thereof, and all the rest followers or partakers thereof to be imprisoned and their bodies to be punished at the King's pleasure.'[8]

There were thus at the beginning of Henry VIII's reign centuries-old precautions for military regulations. All that his advisers had to do was to satisfy themselves that the provisions of the immediately preceding code still fitted the circumstances of 1513, or make the necessary modifications, and then to ensure as far as possible that every man was aware of the regulations. The traditional practice of consulting the nobility and expert military opinion was duly followed, and it was then announced that 'his highness by the advice of such lords of his blood, captains of his army, and other folk as be of his Council hath made, ordained and established certain statutes and ordinances hereafter ensuing'. The ordinances were embodied in a royal proclamation – the longest of Henry's reign – so that they would have a wide circulation; and in addition copies were printed for the use of the principal officers. Thus:

> ... his highness hath over and above the open proclamation of the said statutes commanded and ordained by way of imprint divers and many several books containing the same statutes to be made and delivered to the captains of his host, charging them as they will avoid his great displeasure to cause the same twice, or once at the least, in every week wholly to be read in the presence of their retinue.[9]

If, in fact, this was done, it cannot have been very popular with the troops, for it must have taken well over half an hour, even reading at a brisk pace, to get through the ordinances.

The 1513 code made no provision for the common soldier to take an oath of obedience, as was customary later in the century. For example, the code provided for the force which the Earl of Leicester took to the Low Countries in 1585 began by requiring that every man who received pay should 'solemnly swear and by corporal oath be bound to perform the underwritten articles'.[10] In practice, any token of loyalty to the Crown, or to the army, was less necessary, as the great majority of the troops came into the army under the wing of their civilian overlord, and the duty they owed to him would continue in the field. Further, it may have been presumed that a royal proclamation, even if it was not read out twice a week, was in itself an authority that would not be lightly disobeyed, and that it was superfluous to require the private to swear to obey regulations which he knew were issued in the name of his sovereign. It was well understood that the private must obey orders unquestioningly, whether or not he had taken an oath. There was a duty on all mortals to obey the law of God, and as the sovereign derived his authority from God, anyone speaking in his name must also be implicitly obeyed. Even though 'the precept be contrary to the mind of some soldiers who be not worthy to know the secrets of the officers in authority, yet must they in all points obey them by the laws of God and the prince though the things be both painful and perilous'.[11]

In Thomas Audley's treatise, which was based on his experience of military affairs in the second quarter of the century, the soldier's oath features prominently, which suggests that the need was perhaps beginning to be felt for a tighter control of individual loyalty. It is envisaged that the regulations will be read out to the assembled troops – as had been the practice from time immemorial, and indeed it is claimed that unless a regulation has been read out it 'cannot be admitted as a law'. The company captain was expected to swear in his men one by one. The private placed his hand on the company standard and swore that by the faith he bore to God and the king he would truly obey the martial laws or statutes governing the expeditionary force, or else be accounted a forsworn vile person, meet to be punished at the discretion of the commander-in-chief.[12]

Audley distinguishes between the regulations made effective by virtue of the soldier's oath and those which were 'penal statutes' issued by the commander-in-chief. The former, which may be regarded as covering fundamental military duties, included the soldier's obedience to the king, commander-in-chief, senior officers, his captain, and company officers right down to the 'vintener', or corporal. Secondly, the soldier swore to follow, support and defend the company standard at all times – in battle, assault, skirmish, and watch and ward; to report to the place of assembly with all possible speed, and take his place in battle formation when ordered to do so; and finally, to ensure that when the company was dismissed the standard was suitably accompanied back to the captain's tent with drum, fife and a guard of halberdiers. The so-called 'penal statutes' forbade the robbing of victuallers, making an affray, causing a nuisance by slaughtering animals within the camp and leaving their carcasses lying about, making a disturbance after the 'watch piece' had been fired, keeping a woman in the camp, drinking to excess and gambling.[13]

Henry's 1513 code, however, does not make this sort of distinction. It is simply a mixed bag providing procedural instructions (for example, as to the taking of musters, payment of wages, keeping of watch and ward, ransom of prisoners and so on); the definition of offences against pure military discipline (for example, absence without leave, attempting to assault a fortress without due authority from the higher command, and going into battle without wearing the cross of St George and the badge of the company captain); and the appropriate penalties for these offences. In short, the regulations contained something each of the drill book, organization and method, pure discipline and the moral behaviour expected of the private soldier.

The first of Henry's ordinances defined the relationship between the rank and file and the most senior officers. Everybody in the army, 'of what nation, estate, or condition they be', was to show obedience to the king, or run the risk of execution by drawing, hanging and quartering. Further, all men, except the commanders of the fore-ward and the rear-ward and the king's deputy in the middle-ward, were also to obey the high marshal. (In practice, of course, the king's deputy and the high marshal were one and the same person.) The ward commanders were responsible, not to the marshal, but direct to the king.

The marshal had the task of administering justice generally, in addition to his other duties in connection with victualling and guarding the camp. In earlier times his post had been associated with that of the lord high constable, and indeed the functions of these two royal household offices were almost indistinguishable.[14] In the disciplinary codes over a long period down to the time of Henry VIII they are mentioned together. Offenders were, for example, to be kept in the custody of the 'constable and marshal' and fines were payable to them. The importance of the constable's post had declined, however, and at the beginning of the sixteenth century its military significance had completely disappeared. For all practical purposes the office vanished with the execution of the holder, Edward Stafford, third Duke of Buckingham, in 1521; but when Buckingham joined the 1513 expedition it was simply as a 'captain' with 500 retainers, and his household office gave him no special position in the army. The process which was to separate the household and military offices of high marshal was also under way, but in 1513 the marshal of the household was still considered to be the first choice for second-in-command of the army, given that the king was commander-in-chief.

Each ward had an under-marshal to whom the provost marshal and his staff reported – the deputy provost marshal, tipstaves to arrest offenders and keep them in custody, the 'ghostly father' (the priest whose job it was to comfort and confess the condemned) and the executioner. The ultimate authority was, of course, the high marshal, but as a rule decisions would be taken by the under-marshal serving in the ward; and indeed this was inevitable when the wards were marching independently, as they did at the beginning of the 1513 expedition.

Offenders were tried in the high marshal's court, probably with only the marshal or his deputy sitting on the bench for minor offences, but with several senior officers, and perhaps the whole council of war, in the case of a more serious offence. The 1513 disciplinary code does not describe how cases were to be tried, but when the army got to Thérouanne there seems to have been an extension of the normal arrangements. It was announced that if anyone considered that he had a grievance in a sphere with which the high marshal was concerned – the issue of rations, for example – it was open to him to bring his case to the marshal's court, which met three times a week, on Mondays, Wednesdays and Fridays. The troops were given an assurance that any who took advantage of this facility might rest assured that they would see justice done.[15] If, however, the grievance was over a question of pay the matter had to be referred to the treasurer-at-war.

A separate procedure applied to the establishment of the master of the ordnance, no doubt because it consisted largely of civilians – cannoneers and their assistants, carters, smiths, carpenters, wheelwrights and so on. It was laid down that all offences within the ordnance establishment (but not offences committed by members of that establishment against outsiders) should be judged and punished by the master of the ordnance, either on his own, or with the help of any other officers he chose to call in. It was, however, open to those sentenced in the ordnance court (which was empowered to try even cases of murder) to appeal 'at all seasons and for all causes' to the high marshal, whose judgement was final.[16]

There was a clear understanding that the senior officers and captains were under an obligation to guarantee the good behaviour of the men under their charge as far as was humanly possible. This point was covered in the contracts under which individuals supplied men for Henry VII's expeditionary force to France in 1492. The contracts specifically subordinated the suppliers to the statutes and ordinances of war approved by the king for the expedition; and they also obliged them to do their best to see that any offender in their retinue duly appeared in the marshal's court to answer the charges against him. So that there might be no misunderstanding about this, all those under contract with the king were given a copy of the statutes.[17] This was repeated in 1513, when every lord, captain and petty-captain 'having any retinue great or small' was required to look to 'the good rule and guiding of his people at his parcel and charge, as he will answer for them to the King'.[18]

Authority to arrest was vested in the provost marshal and his staff, and also in king's sergeants, porters and others. Resisting arrest was in itself an offence punishable by imprisonment; and if the offender maimed an officer seeking to arrest him he was liable to the death penalty.

The punishments prescribed in the 1513 code ranged from fines and stoppages of pay to execution, usually by hanging, but in the case of disobedience to the king himself by the more drastic drawing (on a hurdle to the place of execution), followed by hanging and quartering. (A distinction was made between disobedience to the king and to one of the subordinate commanders. The latter merited only death by hanging.) If a man left the position assigned to him on the march, without the authority of his superior officer, he was deprived of his arms and equipment, and of his horse, if he was a cavalryman, and imprisoned until such time as he had paid a fine and given a satisfactory guarantee about his future behaviour. The penalty for having a woman in the camp was the loss of a month's wages and imprisonment. If the alarm was raised irresponsibly either by day or night the offender was liable to suffer the death penalty; and the informer who had him convicted was given 'forty shillings for his labour' by the high marshal. Men convicted of gambling forfeited their winnings and were imprisoned for eight days on the first offence; and on the second the penalty was a month in gaol and the loss of a month's wages – half to the Crown and half to the informer; and on the third offence he was imprisoned at the king's pleasure, and suffered whatever other punishment the king decreed.

It is interesting to note that death accompanied by torture, which was provided for in some of the later codes (for example, the code governing the English troops in the Earl of Leicester's expedition to the Netherlands in 1585, for the offence of betraying the watchword), does not feature in Henry's regulations. They are on the whole a relatively mild set of rules, and perhaps reflect the confidence of the central authority that it had its troops well under control.

That this confidence was justified seems to be supported by the small number of offences recorded in the course of the expedition. It is true that the presence of the king with the army and the consequent reduction of the flow of communications between army headquarters and London has probably reduced the volume of evidence on this subject. It may be argued that had the commanding officers been under an obligation to send regular dispatches home for the information of the king and his Council they would probably have revealed cases of indiscipline of which there is now no record. Against this there is the undoubted fact that the quality of the English troops was high, and that it may well be that the few cases of indiscipline mentioned by those who accompanied them – Dr John Taylor, for example, whose diary records even quite unimportant happenings – represent the sum total; and if this is true the standard of discipline was very high indeed.

The few more serious offences recorded were largely the fault of the German troops. There was a general feeling that however useful they might be on the day of battle they were likely to cause serious trouble at other times, and it was no doubt for this reason that the disciplinary code stressed that men of *all* nations would show obedience to the king. On 15 August there was a riot in which English troops and their German allies fought each other. Taylor tells us in his diary that many were killed on both sides.[19] The chronicler Hall provides a more detailed account of this episode, which took place while the army was encamped near Aire-sur-Lys. No one knew what started the trouble, but suddenly there was a great altercation between the Germans attached to the king's ward and the English troops next to them, and before the argument could be settled fighting broke out and many were killed. The Germans then proceeded to take over the heavy guns of the middle-ward and trained them on their allies. Some English archers, 'greatly fumed with this matter', went for the Germans with their bows at the ready, and met a wall of German pikes. It was only the vigorous intervention of the senior officers that prevented a disastrous conflict. Maximilian arrived in the middle of the affair and was much impressed with the way the officers managed to bring the troops under control again.[20]

Almost the only other offence worthy of record occurred when the army was in the neighbourhood of Aire after the capture of Thérouanne. Four English soldiers – two pairs of brothers – went into the town and became involved in a disturbance. One pair was sent back to the army, but an example was made of the other two brothers, who were hanged.[19]

All contemporary observers agree that Henry's army of 1513 was a fine body of men. Not only were they physically first-rate but their moral standards were also high. After they had returned to England Nicolo di Favri wrote home to Venice in admiration: 'They did not take wenches with them and they are not profane swearers like our soldiers. Indeed there were few who failed daily to recite the office and Our Lady's Rosary.'[21] This may have been pitching it rather high, but di Favri's report does suggest a good level of discipline, and in particular that the law about camp followers was obeyed. It was laid down that 'no man bring with him any manner of woman over the sea' and that 'no man hold no woman within his lodging beyond the sea'. The former offence cost forfeiture of goods and imprisonment, and the latter imprisonment and the loss of a month's wages. If a 'common woman' presumed to come within three miles of the army she was branded on the cheek for the first offence. For the second she was imprisoned and given such further punishment as the marshal 'thought convenient'.[22]

These rules seem to have been effective, but things were very different in Henry's second personal venture into France. The regulations were so openly flouted that the Lord Mayor of London and the civic authorities of the other ports in the south-east of England were instructed to take steps to stop the flood of women crossing the Channel to join the army.[23] Elis Gruffudd tells us that at this time:

. . . the captains of Boulogne kept expensive tables with plenty of the dainties that could be procured from Flanders and England, for the King allowed every great captain a large sum of money every day to keep a table and give food and drink to the poor soldiers. But none of these were ever invited, except some of the petty-captains who were proud foul-mouthed tyrants full of every ungodly vice . . . . Numbers of shameless prostitutes came at every tide from England, when there was great rejoicing at the freedom to sin without fear of retribution.[24]

There was none of this in 1513, however. There was not yet the disenchantment with military adventures in Europe which was to manifest itself later in the century. Both officers and men seem to have been eager to get on with the job of beating the French in celibate dedication.

8 Battle

There was no pitched battle of any consequence in Henry's 1513 campaign in France, certainly nothing remotely approaching the magnitude of the engagement with the Scots at Flodden. It seems likely, however, that Henry's men would have acquitted themselves well in a full-scale battle, given competent generalship. Their discipline was admirable, while the French for their part were weakened by the absence of many of their troops in Italy; but a head-on collision would no doubt have caused heavy casualties on both sides without giving England any tangible benefit, even had her army been victorious. Had Henry seriously planned to extend his dominion in France beyond the boundaries of the Calais pale he would have had first to shatter the French in a pitched battle, however great the cost in terms of English lives; but as he was engaged in no more than a chivalric excursion there was no need for him to risk his troops, or himself, in a straightforward trial of strength. He might well have returned to England without a single battle honour to his name.

As it turned out, however, he enjoyed a large slice of beginner's luck. The French presented him with a resounding victory in a contest that hardly deserves the name of battle but which at the time was regarded, especially by Henry, as a memorable triumph, ranking with Poitiers and Agincourt. The battle of Bomy, a sleepy village a few miles south-west of Thérouanne, is better known as the Battle of the Spurs, not because Henry won his there, but because of the speed with which the French fled from the English cavalry in joyous pursuit. Henry had invaded France in search of glory, and it was heaped upon his army by chance, almost without effort on his part.

*   *   *

It is fairly easy to discover the extent to which practice coincided with theory in most branches of early sixteenth-century army organization; but battle presents some difficulty. Every theorist had his own idea about the deployment of troops on the field of battle, the proportions in which the various arms should be used, the relationship between cavalry and infantry, and so on, although these ideas were circumscribed by the rather narrow framework laid down by precedent, and also by the nature of the troops which the existing military obligation happened to bring into the field. For example, there was no point in evolving a theoretical battle plan that called for a great preponderance of light cavalry, if the natural product of the recruiting arrangements was an army composed mainly of archers and billmen.

This, however, is only half the difficulty. Accurate contemporary accounts of battles are rare as a rule, and the sixteenth century is no exception. The vanquished are seldom in a position to commit to paper a reliable version of what has gone wrong, even if they know; and the victors are usually more concerned with the fact of their success and its consequences than with the manner of its achievement. This means that the student is compelled to speculate a good deal in his attempt to arrive at the truth. Finally, fighting is a chancy business. Luck often plays a vital part, as it did at the battle of the Spurs, and it may make nonsense of theories. Unforeseeable circumstances may transform an act of dire folly into a stroke of military genius. The beaten general may deserve praise and the victor condemnation, unless the only measure of ability is victory.

It was not until the second half of the sixteenth century that English military theorists began to publish books on their subject, but some treatises based on experience in Henry VIII's reign survive in manuscript. Although they contain much that is medieval and chivalrous they do show that some men were beginning to think scientifically about warfare in general and battle in particular. Probably the outstanding example is Thomas Audley's *A.B.C. for the wars*, commissioned, it is true, for the instruction of the young King Edward VI, but based on the author's practical experience in the time of Henry VIII. Audley is becomingly modest in his preface. He is flattered by the confidence which has been placed in him, but he must point out to the king that he has never yet met a soldier who is expert in all the branches of the art of war, 'wherefore it is good to hear divers men's opinions and to consider them together and to take the best'.[1]

Having said this, Audley proceeds to set down his own opinions. He considers that by far the most important thing is to get the balance between the various weapons just right. If you have too many of one kind and too few of another you are bound to land in trouble; and the way to achieve the correct over-all proportion is to ensure that each company 'be like appointed to so many shot, so many pikes, so many bills'. If the proportion in the individual campanies is right, 'then you shall have a good order for the battle throughout your whole army'. This may at first sight seem to be a statement of a self-evident truth, but it was not quite so obvious at the time when Audley was writing.

In the reign of Henry VII, when soldiers were still recruited largely through the remnant of the feudal obligation, especially for service overseas, magnates brought with them retinues which differed considerably both in size and composition. This meant that the army was the sum total of many mixed bags and its suitability for the particular tasks assigned to it was therefore a matter of luck. For the invasion of France in 1492, for example, Sir Reginald Bray (the architect of Henry VII's Chapel in Westminster Abbey) supplied 12 men-at-arms, each with his attendant and page, 24 demi-lances (light cavalrymen), 77 mounted archers, and 231 archers and billmen on foot – a total of 368 men; and at the other end of the scale Thomas Brian, one of the squires of the king's body, provided no more than himself, 18 archers and 2 billmen.[2] The term 'company' 'did not signify a standard unit, rather a body of indefinite size commanded by a captain. These companies were likely to vary in composition as well as size for it does not appear that men in the train of one knight were told off to form balanced units in the field.'[3]

The position had not changed much by 1513, although there were now some

The meeting of Henry VIII and the Emperor Maximilian from a painting at Hampton Court

A detail from a painting at Hampton Court showing the city of Thérouanne and part of the city of Tournai (left) in the background, with the battle of the Spurs in the foreground

signs of an attempt to move towards standard companies. The great magnates still had their large haphazard contingents (the Earl of Essex 469, Sir Henry Marney 818, Lord Abergavenny 511, and so on), but a number of captains were allocated 100 men or thereabouts; and the records suggest that the higher command may have tried to reduce some of the larger groups to companies of 100, at least for the purpose of marching, although smaller groups were not amalgamated to bring them up to 100. Thomas Dalby and Thomas Lucy showed 20 and 66 men respectively when the middle-ward was first mustered, and when the ward marched from Calais they still commanded exactly these numbers.[4]

So long as recruitment for service overseas was largely carried on through the agency of the nobility and landed gentry – and it was by this means that the great majority of the troops were found for the 1513 expedition – it was impossible to introduce universal standardization of either the size of the company or the weapons it carried. If the Crown raised troops through the magnates it had to take what they were in a position to offer; and it was not until virtually the whole of the army was recruited from the population at large through the militia system that the central authority was able to regulate the size and composition of companies with any degree of accuracy. The commissioners of musters in the shires could be instructed as to how many men they were to recruit, and this made it possible to put into the field a battle formation in which the balance of weapons conformed to the theories of the day. The change from contingents of varying size, weaponed at random, to uniform companies, uniformly armed, constituted a major step towards scientific warfare, and ultimately, in the latter part of Elizabeth I's reign, facilitated the all-important substitution of hand-guns for bows.

In the war with France in 1522–3 a good many companies were of 100 men commanded by a captain and petty-captain, although there were still numerous exceptions;[5] and by the time Audley was committing his experience to paper in the middle of the century it was generally accepted that where there was a choice the company should contain 100 men, and that it should have for its officers in addition to the captain and petty-captain a standard-bearer, a sergeant, and four vinteners, each of whom was given responsibility for looking after 25 privates. The company in the French army at this period also contained 100 men as a rule (except for that commanded by the constable – the equivalent of the high marshal in the English army – who was allowed 400); but as a signal honour the king might authorize a captain to command 200.[6] Audley considers that there is much to be said for the company of 200, on administrative rather than on tactical grounds. The captain's wage of 4s. a day is barely enough to allow him to live honestly, and may force him to pocket some of his men's pay, which of course passes through his hands. It is certainly not enough to enable him to provide the occasional extra comforts which the conscientious captain wants his men to have – wagons to carry the sick and wounded, for example. Therefore, why not put the captain in charge of 200 men with a wage of 8s. a day, so that he can live reasonably well himself and also look after his men better? Audley has it in mind that there should be only one lieutenant, one standard-bearer, and one sergeant in the enlarged company, whose pay would not be increased: and the sums saved are to be put at the disposal of the captain 'to bestow upon some young gentleman or some worthy soldier of his own band'.[7] This proposal foreshadows the formal 'dead-pay' scheme of the latter part of the century, which increased the pay of the company officers, including the captain, and also provided something for the 'gentlemen volunteers', who were not on the company strength. This later scheme, however, was not financed by increasing the size of the company, but by reducing it to 90 men and issuing pay for 100.

After making the point that companies should be uniform in size and composition, and perhaps thereby showing that he was ahead of his time, Audley provides a formula for the 'division of weapons'. The bigger the army, the smaller should be the proportion of shot, which for this purpose means a blend of archers, and hand-gunners, who should be stationed three, four or five deep round the battle proper – the solid block of infantrymen carrying bills, halberds, or pikes. If they are four deep, there should be two archers and two harquebusiers; but if they are five deep, there should be three archers to two harquebusiers. It is not clear why Audley makes the odd man an archer. It may be on technical grounds, because he considers the bow to be marginally more efficient than the contemporary hand-guns, which it probably was in the hands of the average man; or it may have been on grounds of economy, as the hand-gun cost a great deal more than the bow. Perhaps with Crécy and Agincourt in mind, he observes that battles have been won by the use of shot alone; but there is always the danger, especially in these times when the pike is becoming a weapon of greater importance, that if a battle contains too many shot and too few billmen or pikemen it may find itself in serious trouble. If the shot are overrun, and it comes to the 'push of the pike', sheer weight of numbers will bring victory to the enemy. This is a danger of which the Germans are well aware.

Preparations for battle are made at a very leisurely pace. The need for speed in war, which was to be stressed by the most enlightened of the military experts

The battle of the Spurs, 1513

of Elizabeth I's reign,[8] is wholly disregarded. Audley provides 'an oration to be made unto the soldiers before the battle to animate and comfort all good subjects which must be spoken by the mouth of the king or his lieutenant', which begins 'Well-beloved subjects and servants we are like right shortly by the grace of God to join in battle with our enemies and of victory we doubt nothing by His grace and your good manlike behaviour, wherefore I pray you generally to bear yourselves manfully and nobly', and goes on to promise 'great wealth and proportional honour' to those that do well in the forthcoming contest. The king will not forget their service when in some future time they come to him with a reasonable request. Finally, after some reference to the importance of knightly honour and the valiant deeds of English armies in the field in bygone times, the king is to make the valid point that it is safer to win a battle than to lose it. As long as men bear their faces and manly hearts towards the enemy there is every hope and likelihood of victory; but when they turn their backs, there is no hope but death, and perpetual shame to them and their heirs for ever.[9]

The treasurer-at-war is also to say a few 'comfortable words', and it may well be that they carried more weight than the king's references to knightly honour and to benefits that might accrue in the uncertain future. He is to announce that he has enough treasure in his coffers to issue a month's pay for this one day's service, and that he will do his best to see that every man receives it. Therefore they can throw themselves whole-heartedly into the battle without worrying about losing their horse, armour or weapons, as they will have plenty of money to replace them.

The task of raising morale is finally taken over by the captains, who have been given advance warning that battle is to be joined that day. They are to cherish their men with good meat and drink, and to remind them that God, who had ordained that in a just cause men should kill rather than be killed, will welcome the soul of a man who has been slain in his prince's quarrel. 'So let us continue and proceed to the end and ye shall be sure that I will live and die with you under mine own ensign.'[10]

It seems likely that the leisurely pace of the earlier preparations continued when the 'battle' was actually being drawn up, although it is difficult to determine precisely how the individual contingents were manoeuvred into the formation favoured for the occasion. The council of war must have agreed about the shape to be used – whether it should be a 'just square' (i.e. a square), or a 'broad square' (i.e. a rectangle), or one of the more elaborate formations (e.g. the 'saw-tooth'); how the archers and hand-gunners should be placed round the perimeter; where the cavalry and artillery should be located, and so on; and the subordinate commanders must have been instructed to march their men into the agreed formation as expeditiously as possible. But the unit was the company and the troops would report to the place of assembly still in their companies, so that a most elaborate rearrangement should be needed to form the men into the chosen shape. It is uncertain whether this was done by the use of a well-defined system of commands similar to that in use in Elizabeth I's time (e.g. 'faces to the left', 'double your ranks by right line', etc.), or whether captains simply told their men in plain English of their own choosing where to go and what to do. Thomas Audley does not lay down a system of drill, and as he was writing much later than

Maximilian and Henry VIII at the battle of the Spurs

1513 it suggests that drill had not been systematized at the beginning of Henry's reign. He does, however, stress the importance of the sergeant both in training and drilling the company. On the whole it seems likely that the captain and petty-captain were mainly responsible for marching the company into 'battle'; although it may be that as early as 1513 the company sergeant's role was beginning to develop, and that the process which ultimately led to a chain of command between the general and the companies in the second half of the sixteenth century was already under way. This chain included the sergeant-major-general and the 'great sergeants', so enabling the higher command to transmit orders quickly to the whole of the rank and file through an expert channel.

One other important point is not clear. All authorities are agreed about the paramount importance of protecting the company standard. The men took their oath of loyalty on it and they were expected to defend it to the death. But if the average company was an aggregate of archers, billmen (and later, pikemen) and hand-gunners, who for the purposes of the 'battle' were posted far away from their own standard, was their immediate loyalty transferred to the nearest standard, or perhaps to that of the member of the council of war commanding the sector? This difficulty disappeared when the regiment came in, but in 1513 the regiment was still in the distant future, and it would be interesting to know precisely where the common soldier's loyalty lay in these circumstances, and how he was informed about it.

*   *   *

An attempt has been made in the preceding pages to set down the theory of battle as it was understood in the time of Henry VIII; but it must be confessed that little of it applied in the only engagement of the 1513 campaign that has been dignified with the name of battle. The encounter at Bomy was anything but a set piece in which the moves were carefully planned and executed according to current theory.

The scene for the engagement began to be set when the besiegers decided that the ring round Thérouanne must be tightened to prevent the French from putting more food into the town. This ought to have been done as soon as the king's ward joined the rest of the army and the besieging force reached maximum strength, for it was obvious that if supplies were allowed to filter steadily into the fortress it might hold out indefinitely. Hitherto the English had neglected to cover the southern wall, partly on the assumption that the River Lys, which skirted it, provided an adequate barrier (although the Lys was narrow, it was deep and branched into two separate streams just outside the main gate); and partly because it was feared that if one of the wards were isolated beyond the river it would not be able to come to the rescue of the others, were there a major sortie or were they attacked by a French field army. Fontrailles had just demonstrated that the river presented no real problem to a force determined to revictual the place, and it was decided (largely at Maximilian's insistence[11]) that the southern approaches must be sealed off.

The master of the ordnance was therefore instructed to set his carpenters to work. In the course of a single night they constructed five bridges, no doubt making use of the 'seasoned timber' they had carried with them from England, which enabled the middle-ward to cross at dawn, taking with them their artillery. As soon as they were established south of the river a rumour that the French were preparing another attempt to get food into the town was confirmed. Sir John Neville, who had been scouting with a troop of cavalry, hurried back to the king to say that he had spotted the enemy assembling in the neighbourhood of Enguingate; and while Neville was making his report Essex and Sir John Peachy stumbled on the same company. They took a prisoner and, by promising to

Armour made for Henry VIII by Italian or Flemish craftsman working in England, c. 1515. The matching horse-armour was made in Flanders and then decorated in England, c. 1514–19

waive his ransom, elicited the information that a powerful force was on the march from Blangy, a few miles further south; and also that a second, smaller, force was to make an attack from the north. Sir Rees ap Thomas, who had also been scouring the countryside, returned at this point to report that the French were indeed approaching from the south.

Thus the middle-ward found itself in a position to frustrate a well-planned French enterprise in which the enemy leaders may have assumed that they still had a clear field south of the Lys. The advantage of surprise was on the English side, although Henry did his best to lose it. He became involved in an argument with his council of war as to whether his tents should be left up or not. His advisers thought that this would be asking for trouble, but the king had to have his way. He told the council that he wanted the field 'to be made and set in as royal wise as may be, and all my rich tents set up', which was accepted,[12] perhaps after much head-shaking by the senior officers. Lord Darcy was told off to guard the tents, and the treasure wagons, which he refused to do, as he wanted to be in the middle of the fighting, until he received a direct order from the king.

Eventually the men were called to the standard and moved south to meet the enemy, who were reported to be advancing steadily. Just as they were leaving, Maximilian appeared and began to tell Henry how to make his dispositions. He and his bodyguard of thirty men were all wearing the red cross of St George as a compliment to the English troops; and indeed at this particular moment they

PLATE VI

A complete fluted or crested harness for man and horse, c. 1510–15 (23152.c.3. plate VI.)

were English troops – at least, they were being paid by Henry. The emperor suggested that a number of light guns should be planted along the top of a low hill to provide protection for mounted scouts, and Henry readily agreed, as he seems always to have done to Maximilian's suggestions. The English cavalry rode out first and Henry and the emperor came with the infantry about a mile behind, each surrounded by his bodyguard, which in Henry's case consisted of mounted archers. Hall says that Henry was eager to go ahead with the cavalry and meet the enemy face to face, and remained behind only because the council of war insisted.

The best account of the engagement as seen through French eyes is in the *Histoire du bon Chevalier*.(1) Louis had ordered de Piennes to revictual Thérouanne, whatever the cost, although it was accepted to be a highly dangerous enterprise. The plan was that a number of cavalrymen should be loaded up with sides of bacon (Fleuranges has it that the bacon, 'which is a wonderous thing in a city', was carried on a great many carts),[13] and that (probably using the route successfully exploited by Fontrailles) they should make a quick dash to throw them near the wall, where they could be collected by the garrison under cover of darkness. A detachment of cavalry was to support them from behind, and a second was to occupy the attention of the English army north of the river. According to the *Histoire*, however, Henry knew all about the French plan through his spies.[14] It is true that the English were well informed about the intentions of the enemy through both spies and scouts, and it is natural that the French should deduce that the sudden appearance of the middle-ward in their path must be the result of foreknowledge of the victualling project. It seems more likely, however, that the decision to move the middle-ward south of the

The Emperor Maximilian I, 1508
(23152.d.13.)

river was taken to tighten the blockade in general, and that it was simply a coincidence that it was in position at exactly the right moment to meet de Piennes' forces.

Whatever the reasons, the gendarmerie were suddenly confronted by the cavalry of the middle-ward. On their flank were the light guns placed there on Maximilian's advice, and a line of archers sheltering behind a hedge. There was nothing for it but to halt, and the archers made the most of a stationary target before the French cavalry turned on their heels, their horses maddened by the pain of the arrows, and rode into their comrades coming on from behind. The confusion was increased by the sudden return of the troops carrying the bacon to the garrison, who reckoned that their task was hopeless, and came headlong into the middle of the chaos.

The French saw that they were in imminent danger of being outflanked and completely encircled, which would have led to a frightful carnage. The only hope of salvation lay in flight before the ring closed round them. The author of the *Histoire* excuses the apparently ignominious conduct of his fellow country-men by pointing out that Louis had made it abundantly clear that there was to be no question of a major engagement with the English. The captains had all impressed on their men that their objective was simply to succour Thérouanne. If they encountered a large body of English troops they were to withdraw at a walking-pace, trot or gallop, as circumstances might dictate. In the event not only was a gallop necessary, but it was a gallop in which the Frenchmen jettisoned their arms and threw away their horses' defensive armour.

Their officers tried to rally them and to get them to turn and face the enemy,

An armoured knight, 1512 (Arch. Antiq. A.II.4.)

which was the safest way to retreat – this was one of the more important of Thomas Audley's precepts – but it was no use. All were desperate to get back to the protection of their artillery and infantry in the camp, devil take the hindmost. Bayard with fourteen or fifteen men-at-arms, however, retired more correctly, 'although it was not in the chevalier's nature to retreat', and maintained contact with the English in a series of small engagements which made headlong flight unnecessary. His little band found themselves on a bridge over a great ditch full of water which drove a water-mill some distance away. No more than two horsemen could cross it abreast, and he decided to make a stand there. He told his companions that they could hold the bridge for an hour and ordered one of his archers to report to headquarters and suggest that the main French force might return in battle array and take the enemy on. But his stand was no more than a delaying action which gave his comrades more time to get back to the safety of the camp. When the English troops found that they could not drive him from the bridge they rode to the mill and crossed there. The chevalier and his handful of men were completely encircled and had to surrender.

The *coup de grâce* to the routed French was provided by the Burgundian contingent in the English army, who had remained aloof in the early stages of the encounter, but hastened to join in when they saw how things were turning out. Hall says that when the French were clearly defeated 'then up pranced the Burgundians and followed the chase', mainly to get their hands on as many prisoners as possible – whom they kept to themselves in defiance of the regulations.

While the battle of the Spurs was in progress the attack against the north side of the town, which ceased to have much point after the victualling party was routed, was also something of a fiasco. Sir Rees ap Thomas and the light cavalry spent the greater part of the day skirmishing with the French diversionary forces, and succeeded in preventing them from making contact with the fore-ward and rear-ward, which waited for them in full battle array; and numerous sorties from the town 'proudly issued out on the Lord Herbert and skirmished with his people very valiantly'.[15]

Thus the battle of the Spurs was not a classic encounter between great masses of men ranged in roughly corresponding shapes and conducting themselves according to similar sets of rules. It was simply an attempt to get supplies into Thérouanne that failed. Nevertheless, it was a notable encounter for a number of reaons. Although there was no vast slaughter as there had been at Agincourt, it was the English archers that started the rout. Secondly, the speed with which the French panicked and fled suggests that there may have been a good deal in the contemporary belief that they had an innate fear of the English. Thirdly, it seems clear that Henry, either because of the wishes of his advisers, or in the interests of his personal safety, led his army from behind; and there is no satisfactory evidence that he even joined in the chase, although Oman does credit him with 'the glorious experience of chasing the chivalry of France'.[16]

The failure to revictual Thérouanne and the defeat of the French army at Bomy removed the garrison's last hope of survival, and on 22 August their leaders asked for a parley, at which terms of surrender were agreed. It was only

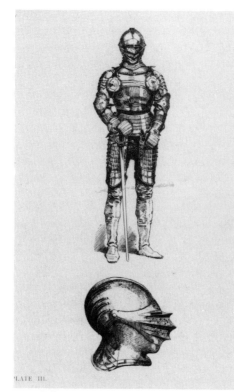

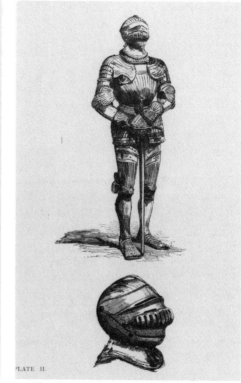

A three-quarter suit of crested armour for fighting on foot, c. 1510 (23152.c.3. plate III.)

Fluted cap-a-pie suit plus helmet, c. 1510 (23152.c.3. plate II.)

lack of provisions, according to Fleuranges, that compelled them to give in, for 'there were brave men there who knew their business well';[17] and the garrison believed themselves to be in a strong enough position to drive a hard bargain with the besiegers. They undertook to hand the fortress over at 9 a.m. on 23 August, provided that they were allowed to leave with bag and baggage, standards furled, helmets on head, and lances on thigh; and further that they should be allowed to rejoin the main body of the French army unmolested. All this was agreed, and the garrison duly left. Four thousand of them marched through the English camp, 'such soldiers as any prince would wish to have', watched by Henry and Maximilian. First came the cavalry, and then the infantry in full armour, with pikes on shoulder. It was also agreed that any pioneers and victuallers who wanted to transfer their loyalty to Henry were free to do so, and that they would be regarded as his subjects.[18]

Next day Henry and Maximilian went together to inspect the captured fortress and to discuss its fate. There were no buildings of any note, apart from the cathedral, and the civilian population was relatively small. Had Henry decided to retain possession of the town he would have had to install a large force – perhaps 5,000 men – which would have drastically reduced the size of the army at his disposal for further operations; and even if he *had* left a garrison, sooner or later it would have had to face up to a siege. It was far simpler to destroy the place, a decision which met with Maximilian's cordial approval, for Thérouanne had been a thorn in his side, and he was delighted to think that it was to be eliminated. One authority, however, claims that the reason for the destruction of the place was that Henry and Maximilian could not agree as to which of them should have it, and that the only way out of this impasse was to remove it from the map so that neither should have it.[19] Whatever the reasons, for the next fortnight Henry's pioneers and artillery, helped by Maximilian's troops, filled the enormous ditches, brought down the walls and towers, and finally burned all the buildings except the cathedral and the houses of the clergy adjoining it.[20]

The king's success was enthusiastically received in England, particularly by the queen. In a letter to Wolsey of 25 August she said: 'The victory hath been so great that I think none such hath been seen before. All England hath cause to thank God for it, and I specially, seeing that the King beginneth so well.'[21] A month later she wrote to Henry forwarding a detailed account of the battle of Flodden, and observing tactlessly that 'this battle hath been to your grace and all your realm the greatest honour that could be, and more than ye should win the Crown of France, thanken be God for it'.[22] Henry must have realized with irritation that *his* battle hardly compared with Flodden, for which he could take no credit; and his irritation cannot have been assuaged by his wife's suggestion that the tremendous victory there was worth more than the crown of France.

NOTE

(1)   Oman ascribes 'curious errors' to this account, but himself errs in blaming the author for recording the loss of St John the Evangelist on this day. In fact, the *Histoire* (cited as Bayard) does not misdate this episode.

9 Prisoners

The victory of the Spurs was almost bloodless. One authority suggests that no more than forty were killed in the battle, and the highest estimate is four hundred.[1] It produced an unusually large crop of prisoners of war, however, including wealthy French noblemen, who were disposed of, or at least were supposed to be disposed of, according to traditional rules dating from the time of high chivalry. Although it was progressively less easy to apply these rules as warfare became more of a science, they still held good in theory in the English army at the beginning of the sixteenth century. They were restated for the benefit of the rank and file, few of whom had experience of active service, in the royal proclamation setting out the 1513 expedition's disciplinary code, so that no soldier could plead ignorance of the law, were he caught illegally disposing of his prisoner.[2]

Not only do the rules in the proclamation governing the capture, custody and ransom of prisoners still show marked traces of the chivalric code, they also provide a reminder that chivalry and a keen business sense were not incompatible. It might be a gracious act to spare the life of a worthy adversary who had had the worst of it in a hand-to-hand fight; but there remained the hard fact that dead he would be worth no more than his personal adornments (which admittedly might be worth a substantial sum), whereas alive he might be worth a fortune in ransom.

Prisoners of the blood royal, dukes, lieutenants general, great constables, and so on belonged to the king, regardless of who had captured them; and it was a capital offence for the man who had captured a member of this exalted group to take it upon himself to ransom him or to set him at liberty. He must deliver his captive at once to the king or the commander-in-chief, which entitled him to a reasonable reward, the amount of which was not specified. Any less exalted prisoner belonged to the first soldier who had him at his mercy, provided that he yielded formally and surrendered his weapons, or gave some other token of his defeat. If these formalities were satisfactorily concluded there was, at least in theory, no need to keep the prisoner under surveillance. He was out of the game for the time being and it was assumed by the laws of chivalry that he would take no more part in it. It was also laid down that a prisoner who had thus formally yielded could not be taken subsequently by anybody else, unless he broke the rules by escaping.

If he did this, in spite of the convention that he should not (for example, by suddenly producing a hidden weapon), and was recaptured by somebody else, his second captor was entitled to a half-share in him. The second captor was also given responsibility for the custody of the prisoner – he would no doubt take rather greater care of him – and he was required to negotiate the sale or ransom and to ensure in due course that the appropriate share was paid over to the man who first took him. A similar rule applied where an enemy soldier 'borne to earth' was virtually taken prisoner, then rescued, and finally taken by another to whom he 'yielded his faith'. In these circumstances the prisoner was shared equally between 'the smiter down' and the 'taker of the faith'; and again the final captor was responsible for negotiating the ransom and ensuring that his partner received his fair share.

Any soldier who killed another man's prisoner after the victory had been won was liable to the death penalty.

Before a private could start negotiating the sale or ransom of a prisoner he had to get his captain's permission, partly to ensure that the transaction was carried out in an orderly way, but, more important, to make certain that the captain could claim the one-third of the ransom money to which he was entitled by custom. If the private tried to pocket the whole of the proceeds of a prisoner and was found out, he forfeited to the captain the whole of the ransom, and further, was imprisoned by the marshal until he came to an amicable settlement with the captain, which presumably involved the payment of some further compensation. Equally, no captain was allowed to dispose of a prisoner without the authority of the commander-in-chief or the treasurer-at-war; and any man who bought a prisoner as an investment without going through the proper procedures was liable to forfeit both the purchase money and the prisoner.

If the private properly sought permission from his captain to sell a prisoner it was not to be unreasonably withheld and the soldier was to be given a completely free hand to drive the hardest bargain he could. If, however, the captain was prepared to match the sum finally offered for the prisoner, which he would want to do only if he were satisfied that it was below the market price for a man of his standing, or if there were reason to believe that the value of the prisoner would appreciate with the passage of time (for example, if he were likely to inherit a fortune in the fairly near future), he was to be given the first refusal of the prisoner, and pay the agreed sum to the captor.

Traitors serving with the enemy were outside the normal rules. If one was captured he was immediately thrown into prison and dealt with as a traitor, and not as a prisoner of war; and irrespective of the wealth of the captured man (which was in any case forfeit to the Crown) his captor was entitled to a reward of no more than five pounds. If the captor was caught negotiating the sale of the renegade's freedom he was himself liable to execution as a traitor.

The clergy in an invaded country were also a special case. So long as a priest went about his ordinary duties he was not to be attacked or taken prisoner; but if he was found aiding or abetting the king's enemies, or possessing arms, he was to be taken into custody and brought before his captor's superior officer, who was in turn to take him to the king or high marshal, when he would be examined and suitably punished if the charges against him were proved. The man who made the initial arrest was given a reward which varied with the importance and standing of the apprehended cleric.

Regulations laid down for the garrison of Berwick show that, however out-of-date the rules about prisoners may have been, they were still widely applied. (It was, of course, much easier to observe them in a garrison town than in the field, where the army was constantly on the move and the facilities for keeping men in custody were limited.) It was envisaged in Berwick, for example, that a soldier of the garrison might be tempted to make a private bargain with his prisoner, under which the latter would obtain his freedom by paying a smaller sum than the going rate. This would give the captive his freedom more cheaply, and it put rather more money into the captor's pocket than he would have had if the transaction had been conducted according to the rules. The man who suffered in this case was the captain, who was done out of his one-third share. If a Berwick private was caught negotiating such a deal he forfeited all his possessions, including armour and weapons, and also his horse if he were a cavalryman; and his body was 'at the captain's will', which probably meant that he was detained in prison until he had paid appropriate compensation to his defrauded superior.[3]

The Berwick regulations also throw some light on the arrangements for the custody of prisoners, and suggest that although it was a far cry from the days of true chivalry a good deal of trust was still placed in the captives. It was permissible for a prisoner to move freely about the town provided he was escorted by someone 'from the great retinue', but at night he had to return to the porter's prison. If his captor allowed him to wander round the town unescorted or if he failed to get him back into prison at night, the prisoner was fair game for anyone who spotted that the regulations were being broken and claimed him for his own. The original captor then lost his rights and his carelessness was rewarded with eight days in prison.[3]

The financial arrangements for the sale and ransom of prisoners (and also for the disposal of booty) were no less complicated than the rules governing their capture. Every private was bound to pay one-third of the amount realized on a prisoner to his captain, and the captain in turn paid to the king one-third of the sums raised on his personal prisoners, plus one-third of the sums received from his subordinates. In Henry VII's time this rule was written into the indenture between the king and the magnate supplying troops: 'and as touching the paying of the third of all manner of winnings to our said sovereign lord . . . the said earl, not only for himself, but also for his said retinue and every person thereof, bindeth him to the performance and observation of the same';[4] but in 1513 the Crown relied only on the ordinances of war to ensure that the traditional share of the spoils was paid over. Even men who did not serve for wages – volunteers who had not taken the king's shilling but who simply 'lodged or hosted under the banner of a captain' as soldiers of fortune – had to pay thirds like everyone else. The captains submitted to the high marshal a daily record of prisoners taken, and he sent a consolidated list to the treasurer-at-war every eight days; the latter had to ensure that the proceeds of royal or high-ranking prisoners, and the appropriate amount of 'thirds of thirds', was being paid to the Crown.

It must have been difficult enough to ensure that the rules were effectively applied, even in the heyday of chivalry, when a battle was simply the aggregate of a number of individual hand-to-hand combats in which the better man won and had his opponent at his mercy. In the confusion and heat of an engagement there was no satisfactory way of recording what actually happened at the moment of

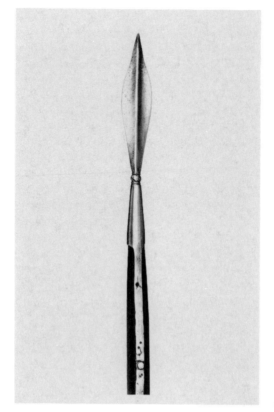

An early sixteenth-century English pike

capture of a prisoner, let alone the manner of his escape, if he contrived it, and perhaps his subsequent recapture. Even if it is assumed that the strict code of chivalry discouraged the members of the victorious army from cheating each other, which is a big assumption, witnesses would be much too busy playing their own part to be able to testify about the activities of their neighbours in the battle. Many knights must have reckoned in good faith that they were legally entitled to the proceeds of a prisoner, when, if all the facts had been known, the judicial interpretation of the rules would have awarded the man, or a share of him, to a third party.

How infinitely more difficult, then, to apply the traditional rules in warfare of a totally different nature, where hand-to-hand fighting was less important and science was beginning to take over. The use of missile weapons, at longer ranges than the bow was capable of, tended to keep combatants further and further apart; and even after the long-range exchanges, when men were within striking distance of each other, and it came to 'the push of the pike', the line of pikemen acted as a unit. Divided they were more likely to fall. The old rules about prisoners had thus lost much of their significance, as they did not apply very precisely to warfare that was becoming more of a team game and less a series of singles matches. Nevertheless, despite the fact that the rules had been originally drafted with single combats in mind, some attempt was made to pay lip service to them. Records throwing light on the taking of prisoners and the subsequent administrative processes are scanty, in the nature of things, but it is possible to get some idea about the working of the system from scattered references.

The prisoners captured in the engagement at Fort Nieulay at the beginning of August[5] were taken by the victors to Calais and there offered for sale. Hall's account provides an interesting picture of the way the market in prisoners operated. A cooper employed in the town bought one of the prisoners – unfortunately it is not recorded how much he paid, and without this figure we cannot assess his profit – and sold him his freedom for a hundred crowns, which were duly paid over. The Frenchman lived in Boulogne and asked the cooper to be good enough to see him safely out of Calais on his way home. The cooper, a simple fellow, readily agreed, and without telling his friends what he was doing escorted his late property to the end of the causeway leading across the marshes out of Calais. At this point, when they were about to say goodbye, the Frenchman overpowered the cooper, who was an old man, and led him off to Boulogne as *his* prisoner. There the unfortunate cooper was detained until he had returned the hundred crowns he had had from the Frenchman, plus a substantial sum in lieu of interest.[6]

One of the few surviving documents relating to the transfer of a prisoner of war is among the state papers in the Public Record Office. It is in the form of a receipt by Lord Abergavenny for 200 marks which he has had 'by the King's commandment of John Dauncey' (the treasurer-at-war) 'for the interest claim and demand of Étienne de Ruyaux man-at-arms unto the French King taken prisoner by Thomas Morris servant to the said Lord Abergavenny in the journey called Bomy'. Abergavenny waives all rights to the man, and acknowledges that he is 'well and truly content and paid in full contentation'. One hopes that his lordship saw that his servant Thomas Morris received at least some of the 200 marks which the king thought that Ruyaux was worth. Henry in fact made a loss on the deal, for the Frenchman escaped when the expedition was on its way back to Calais, before the king had been able to exact any ransom from him.[7] There also survives a draft undertaking by one of the French standard-bearers, who had been handed over to Lord Darcy, that he 'will be true prisoner and will not leave without ransom made or leave given'.[8] One of the prisoners from the Battle of the Spurs who escaped from custody was de la Palice. According to the Venetian ambassador to France, Marco Dandolo, he killed the two English archers in charge of him and got safely back to the French camp. Dandolo says that Henry displayed great graciousness towards the prisoners. If the appropriate ransom was, say, 4,000 ducats, the king would reduce it to 2,000 and promise the captor that he would make good the difference. Further, if a foot soldier was taken with only 20 ducats in his purse, 'that sum suffices and the King has him stripped [i.e. of his armour and weapons] and set at liberty: so that he treats all well.'[9]

The long list of distinguished prisoners was headed by Bayard and the Duc de Longueville. The *Histoire du bon Chevalier* has a detailed account of the capture of its hero and his treatment in the English camp. It suggests that, when the small group defending the bridge threw their hand in, Bayard went up to an English man-at-arms who was so exhausted that he had no energy left to look for a prisoner. The Chevalier put his sword to the astonished man's throat and demanded his surrender, and only when the Englishman had given himself up did Bayard explain that in fact *he* was surrendering – on one condition. If they came across any on the way back to the camp who wanted to kill them, he must have his sword back. In the event Bayard did claim his sword, to go to the rescue of some of his fellow countrymen who were about to be killed by their captors on the ground that they were too poor to produce a reasonable ransom.

The Chevalier then spent a few days in the English camp in the company of his captor. Inevitably Henry and Maximilian got to hear of the distinguished prisoner and summoned him to their presence. Henry asked what he had to say about the flight of the French troops at Bomy, the like of which had never been seen before, although they were pursued by only four or five hundred cavalry: to which Bayard replied that the French higher command had issued strict orders that there was to be no pitched battle with the English army, as they had no infantry and no artillery. According to the *Histoire* he then gave an account of his surrender, and Henry said that in the circumstances he could have his freedom after an interval of six weeks, to be spent touring the cities of Flanders, unarmed. Bayard agreed and off he went.[10] It is not clear if a ransom was ever required for him, although a report to Venice in October said that the sum of 1,200 ducats was paid, and that he was back in the French court.[11] It may be that Henry paid the ransom, and that this was one of the cases referred to by the Venetian ambassador.

The Duc de Longueville had more conventional treatment. He was sent to England, to remain in the royal household until peace was made with France in

Catherine of Aragon (Montagu illustration 149.)

the following year. He seems to have enjoyed his stay in England, for after he got back to Paris (having paid his ransom)[12] he asked to be remembered to the queen, and 'to all his fellows, both men and women'.[13] The queen was not too pleased about having him on her hands, and wrote to Wolsey: 'It is thought to me and my council that it should be better the said duke be as soon as he cometh conveyed to the Tower.' She was worried because she had no one who could look after him properly.[14] However, this did not deter her from congratulating Henry on his success. She added that he might have sent her a captive duke (although it was no great thing for one armed man to take another); but any day now she might be sending him a captive king.[15]

10   Negotiation

If Henry aimed at further conquest in France the sensible course would have been to turn his attention to Boulogne, St Quentin or Montreuil, which wer~ near enough to Calais to have some strategic value for England; but these objectives were of little interest to Maximilian. To him a much more attractive prize was the French city of Tournai, right on the doorstep of the Low Countries, which were ruled by Margaret of Savoy in the name of his grandson Charles; and he guessed rightly that Henry would be stupid enough to try to capture the city for him if he were asked to do so. He did not, however, bargain for the fact that Henry would also be stupid enough to hold on to his conquest regardless of the cost, although in the long run this turned out to be a blessing in disguise for Maximilian.

The civic leaders of Tournai had realized for some weeks that if the invaders

Plan of Tournai showing the town, walls, arms and fortifications, c. 1566. (Montagu illustration 191.)

succeeded in disposing of Thérouanne it might be their turn next, despite the obvious attractions to the English of other objectives; and as early as 12 July[1] (nearly a month before the garrison of Thérouanne capitulated) they had begun to prepare for a siege. The four councils – the governing body of the city, which was run on highly democratic lines – announced to their fellow citizens that a multitude of Englishmen, their ancient enemies, were besieging Thérouanne with the support of some of Tournai's neighbours, and that it now behoved everyone to show loyalty to France and to play his part in preparing their defences. All honest men who had lived in the town for more than a year and a day were required to re-affirm their adherence to Louis XII and not to leave without permission. All rogues, vagabonds and beggars were thrown out. They would not be worth the food they ate and might prove a positive threat to security should the city be beleaguered.[2]

The people of the town considered that they had a good chance of holding out, although it is difficult now to see what their optimism was founded on. They had no garrison, and if they did allow French troops into the town it would be a violation of the treaty of 1478 with the emperor, on which their commerce was based. They might find that they had preserved their political independence at the expense of their commercial prosperity. In any case, the invading army stood between them and any help that Louis might scrape together. The fortifications, which had never faced the fury of modern siege artillery, were in a state of decay. The cannon on the walls were out-of-date and fragile, as were the hand weapons available for issue to the citizens to meet a direct assault. Nevertheless, the men of Tournai prized their liberties and were eager to put up a good defensive show – which was not too difficult so long as Henry's twelve apostles were fully committed to the conversion of another town many miles distant. When asked by the central government if they would need help, they replied with a brave pun. Tournai had never turned, and never would turn; and if the English did come, they would soon find out who they were talking to.[3]

The city had endured many sieges in its long history, some of them successfully, and the civic authorities may have derived some comfort from this. They were in a serious dilemma, however. Their geographical position at the far end of a long narrow corridor running between Flanders and Hainaut meant that their natural trading partners were the cities of the Low Countries; and these were now, technically at least, their enemies. Although Tournai had acknowledged French sovereignty for three and a quarter centuries the town had led an existence largely independent of the French Crown, and it was natural that the citizens should try to solve their problems in their own way.

If there was a real danger that Tournai was next on Henry's list the obvious course was to try to negotiate a settlement which would leave unimpaired the commercial freedom which was the city's lifeblood. The problem was how to establish their neutrality without betraying the cause of Louis XII. It would take superhuman negotiating skill but the men of Tournai were businessmen first and foremost and they energetically approached the task of talking themselves out of an impossible situation, knowing that it was the only hope of maintaining their existing way of life, if Henry did in fact intend to attack them.

They had reason to believe that at least Margaret of Savoy would listen sympathetically to their case. Recently, when some of her subjects in Hainaut had used the state of war as an excuse to plunder French property, and had captured two or three wagons bound for Tournai with a consignment of wine, she had ordered them to restore the wine to its rightful owners. At the same time, probably urged on by those of the businessmen of her own community who had a vested interest in peace, she wrote that she wanted to live 'in peace and communication' with the people of Tournai, so long as they reciprocated, which led the Tournaisiens to believe that she shared their anxiety to avoid disruption of the region's commerce. This belief was strengthened at the beginning of September, when she signed an order saying that since, in spite of her proclamations, soldiers continued to molest the people of Tournai and its outlying territory, and because this was prejudicing their long-established trade with the city so much that it might wither away completely, the attacks must stop.[4]

The leading men of the town met at once to discuss Margaret's letter, with its happy implication that open hostilities might yet be averted. They decided to strike while the iron was hot by sending a deputation to express the city's gratitude for her goodwill, and to ask that commerce between Tournai and the Low Countries should continue without let or hindrance, as provided for in their treaty. The deputation, three prominent citizens, Jean Hacquart, Claude Dimanche and Michel Allegambe, was further instructed to suggest that she might try to persuade Henry and her father to recognize Tournai's neutrality – for which privilege they would be prepared to pay a reasonable sum.[4] As traders of long experience they believed that the banker's draft is mightier than either the sword or the pen, and they hoped that Henry and Maximilian might be brought round to this point of view.

Almost as soon as the mission had left for Lille, where Margaret was, their colleagues in Tournai received a sharp reminder that they were playing with fire in dealing with the enemy. A letter came in from Louis that evening confirming that it seemed likely that the invaders would next make for Tournai, and urging that the town should forthwith lay in supplies of wine, wheat and other provisions needed for a siege, and that they should see to the repair of the fortifications. This communication was immediately considered by the four councils in their separate colleges; and when they came together after their deliberations they found that all had reached the same conclusion. Loyalty to the king must come first.

This was all very well, but their representatives had just been sent to Lille to negotiate with the enemy, and if they were to avoid a charge of treason they must at once tell Louis about their dealings with Margaret. They decided to break the news gently in a letter which was taken back by the dispatch rider who had come from the king. This promised that a more detailed account of the progress of their mission would follow in due course, together with a description of the state of the fortifications, which were just about as weak as they could be. A copy of the reply to Louis was sent on to the mission in Lille, so that they would be kept fully in the picture.

Margaret received the deputation with great cordiality and listened patiently to their representations. She said she would pass them on to the emperor (who was of course still in the neighbourhood of Thérouanne) as soon as he reached Lille; and she also undertook to write to Tournai about the results of her approach – ostensibly to save the mission the trouble of waiting indefinitely in Lille, but more likely to avoid the embarrassment of having a delegation from the enemy in the town when Henry and Maximilian arrived. The three delegates accordingly went home on 4 September to report progress. Their fellow citizens were not too enamoured of the idea of leaving a matter of such vital importance to correspondence, and decided that their interests would be better served if the mission returned to Lille, where they might keep up the pressure on Margaret and continue to urge that Tournai should be allowed to remain neutral in the struggle with France; but before the delegation could leave for the second time their plans were overtaken by events.[5]

Now that they were so deeply embroiled with Margaret it was more necessary than ever to keep the record straight with Louis, and on Thursday, 8 September, two men (Claude Dimanche, who had gone with the first mission to Margaret and could therefore speak with authority about her attitude, and Jean d'Étables) set off for Amiens where the king was. Although by this time it would have been virtually impossible for a French force to get through to Tournai without clashing with the invaders, it was easy enough for a handful of well-mounted horsemen to keep out of trouble, and the deputation reached the king safely on 9 September. They duly reported that they were in touch with Margaret; further, they gave an account of the poor state of the fortifications and made clear their estimate of the city's chances of holding out, should it come to a siege. The mission had also been instructed to ask Louis to provide whatever help he could, preferably without landing them in a war with the emperor, and to seek his permission to come to some arrangement with Maximilian. There is no record of the king's reaction to these points, but it cannot have been very favourable.

Saturday, 10 September, was an eventful day. First of all Ferry Carondelet, Maximilian's ambassador, rode into Tournai and demanded an audience with the civic authorities. He told them that the King of England, who was now at Lille, had asked his master whether Tournai was to be regarded as an imperial town or not. If the town did *not* belong to the empire, Henry, the lawful King of France, intended to attack it and reduce it to obedience. On the other hand, if it were declared to be an imperial town, he would not wish to lay hands on it.

This put the citizens in an impossible position. If they agreed that they owed allegiance to the emperor, Tournai would become part of his vast domains, and that would be that. Louis would no doubt seek to bring them back into the fold at the earliest possible moment, and they would simply have exchanged one powerful enemy for another. On the other hand, to say that they owed allegiance to France would be to invite Henry to launch an attack on them. Their only course was to play for time. The problem was therefore referred to the four councils for consideration.

The councils came to an admirable conclusion. They decided that the logical next step was to arrange a further meeting – this time with the representatives of the king and the emperor. When they saw Carondelet again they proposed that he should return to the emperor and obtain a safe conduct, to enable their representatives to come and discuss the position. This piece of gamesmanship did not please the ambassador at all and he pressed for an immediate reply to his loaded question; but the townspeople stood firm and repeated their request for a safe conduct. Carondelet eventually agreed to pass on their suggestion – with all the ill-temper of a second-rate ambassador who has failed to get his way – and he warned the authorities that their attitude would certainly incur Maximilian's displeasure.

On the same Saturday the news reached Tournai that the invading army was now at Pont-à-Vendin, only thirty miles away. They had made a point of taking prisoner everyone encountered on the march, to prevent the news of their movements from being carried ahead, and their destination was still doubtful, although Carondelet's visit was a pretty clear pointer. But that night all doubts about the enemy's intentions were removed. After the watch had been set, the village curé of Wannehain appeared at the gates and demanded admission. He explained that he had been sent by one of the magnates of the district who was well-disposed towards them to say that he had learned for a fact that the invaders were committed to lay siege to the town. It now looked as if the chance of negotiating a settlement was very faint, and the authorities accordingly began to turn their attention to the problems of physical defence.

A few days earlier they had come to the conclusion that the houses and trees near the city wall could afford shelter to the guns of a besieging force. The buildings must be demolished and the trees felled. Those rendered homeless would have to come into the town, bringing with them their goods and chattels. The clearance of the area had not been tackled seriously, however, for people were reluctant to sacrifice their homes so long as there was a chance that the town might be allowed to remain neutral; but now that it was established that Tournai was the objective of the English army the civic authorities ordered that the destruction of the suburbs must be vigorously undertaken. It was too late to start the work in earnest that Saturday night, but those living outside the wall were told that they must abandon their homes to leave a clear field for the demolition squads next day; and those inside were ordered to look to their arms.[6]

After midday dinner on Sunday, 11 September, Carondelet, who had spent the night in the city, took his departure to report to Maximilian and Henry at Lille. He was still grumbling at the line the authorities were taking and saying that there was little chance that the king and the emperor would grant them the safe conduct they had asked for. The time for talking had passed, and before long they would feel the weight of the English artillery. But hardly had the ambassador disappeared through the smoke of the burning suburbs when the townspeople were again in conference about negotiating a settlement. It was known that the Vicomte of Ghent, who had often shown himself to be a good friend of the town, was at Antoign, not very far from Tournai, and it was believed that he might be persuaded to intercede with Henry and Maximilian. Adam le Grut was sent to him with a formal letter from the town, saying that they would be prepared to pay an annual sum to have their neutrality recognized; and he also carried a number of personal letters from the vicomte's friends.

While the civic authorities were thus trying to find a new ally, Margaret was doing what she could for them in Lille. When Henry and Maximilian sat down at the council table to discuss their plan of campaign, she joined them and entered a strong plea for the city, no doubt having in mind that the trade the people of Tournai were so anxious to maintain was a two-way traffic which benefited her own subjects. The others heard her out, and then Henry said:

> My very dear sister, don't speak to me, or to your father, of the Tournaisiens. Rest assured that they have broken their treaty with the Emperor; and with God's help I shall avenge the wicked things they have been saying about the rulers of the Low Countries. They are an incorrigible, ill-disposed lot, lampooning their neighbours, even making fun of *me!* So let's hear no more on the subject.

With that he stalked from the council chamber, closely followed by Maximilian.[7]

It may be that Robert Macquereau in attributing these remarks to Henry was drawing on an order made on 14 October, the day after the King finally left Tournai, to the effect that anyone who composed, sang, or uttered any defamatory song or ballad would be guilty of a criminal offence;[8] but there is little doubt that Henry's *amour propre* suffered at the hands of the wits of the town, who may well have had some fun at his expense in the weeks before the English army invested the town, when there was still time for the composition of lampoons.

Macquereau's account, if true, throws further light on the motive for Henry's campaign. The king's anger at being the butt of scurrilous ballads rather than the hero of an epic poem shows how much his primary objective was personal glory; and the fact that he insisted on going through with the siege of Tournai, when it was crystal clear that the inhabitants would rather come to terms, confirms that what he wanted above all was not the spoils of war, but the glory. So far everything had gone like clockwork. He had brought his army to France without mishap; he had routed the flower of the French forces at Bomy; he had captured the powerful fortress of Thérouanne and spectacularly destroyed it; he had led his troops deeper into France without serious loss. Even if the people of Tournai did not merit punishment for their grave *lèse-majesté* in lampooning him, to accept their surrender without firing a single cannon shot would be unsporting and unsatisfying, a disappointing anti-climax to a brilliant campaign (at least as Henry saw it). Any lingering doubt that he was on top of the world must have been removed when the news of the rout of the Scottish army at Flodden came through, as the English army was nearing Tournai. The Almighty was clearly on his side and had appointed him to be the scourge of France. Tournai might be a sitting duck, but none the less it must be bagged.

Surprisingly enough, however, the delaying tactics the town had adopted with Carondelet bore fruit. On Wednesday, 14 September, when the authorities must have been thinking of abandoning all hope of a peaceful settlement, a herald's trumpet was heard at the gates. The emperor's ambassador had returned for further discussions. Carondelet was duly admitted and he told the town's representatives that their refusal to answer the question about their allegiance had much displeased his master, adding with some satisfaction that he had, of course, warned them all along that this would happen. Nevertheless, he had been able to persuade Henry and Maximilian to issue a safe conduct, but only by assuring them that this time there would be no nonsense about giving a satisfactory answer.

It is not clear why the two monarchs continued to deal with the town in this way. They were, however, in no great hurry. They knew that French reinforcements could not get through, and as the invading army was not yet in position round the town nothing was lost by talking. Further, by acceding to the request for further discussion Henry may have felt that he was putting the townspeople in the wrong, and justifying his eventual murderous attack on a city that was virtually without defences. Again, at this time Henry was spending a few days at Lille relaxing with the ladies of Margaret's Court, and he may have taken the view that so long as he was thus engaged his lieutenants might just as well be occupying themselves at the conference table.

So on the following day a party of seven or eight, including Hacquart and Allegambe, set off with Carondelet for the town of Lannoy, a few miles to the north-west. Two or three of them made a point of riding beside the ambassador, perhaps in the hope that personal contact might win him over to their side, and make it easier for them to get their way in the talks that were to follow. The meeting with the representatives of the king and the emperor was held in the chapel of the château of Lannoy. The English team included Sir Edward Poynings, Sir Robert Wingfield, men of great experience, and John Young, Master of the Rolls.

The delegation from the town immediate. put their only card on the table. They would be prepared to pay a reasonable annual sum if they were left in peace and allowed to carry on their normal commercial activity; but this was not good enough for the other side. It was essential that Tournai should formally abandon its allegiance to France (which meant Louis) and submit either to Henry or Maximilian. If this were done the lives and property of the citizens would be safe. If they refused, there was no point in carrying the conference any further.

The town's representatives said that they had not been authorized to commit their fellow citizens; but they were prepared to clutch at any straw. They would put the proposal to them and return next day to Lannoy, or anywhere else suggested by the English, to report what progress they had made. This was accepted, apparently without protest, and the delegation at once returned to Tournai, where the four councils and leading citizens assembled to hear their report. After some discussion it was decided that the people should be told that their leaders considered that the town must be handed over to the emperor. The only alternative was to wait until it was put to fire and the sword.

The citizens were duly assembled on the morning of Friday, 16 September, to be told that there seemed to be little prospect of negotiating a settlement on their own terms. The provost, Adam le Grut, added: 'We have been talking about burning the suburbs, but surely it would be cheaper in the long run to surrender the city' – which suggests that the work of destroying the suburbs had not got very far. This line at once precipitated a crisis that had been simmering for several days. The more prosperous citizens, who stood to lose most if the city were subjected to the full rigour of a siege and assault, supported the provost; but the common people, who had little to lose, at least in the financial sense, considered that loyalty to France demanded that they should continue to resist. Their spokesman said that he completely disagreed with the provost. The suburbs must be burned and the town defended. If the provost feared for his skin he could take himself away; and in any case they no longer had any confidence in him. Le Grut tried to say something in his defence, but no one would listen: two or three hotheads made for him with drawn swords, and he escaped only by finding sanctuary in the cathedral.[9]

The mob was now completely out of hand, and one of them mounted the steps of the town hall and cried: 'Be of good cheer, my friends, we shall live or die in the King's cause!' Flags bearing the arms of France and the château of Tournai were run up at the town hall, and the alarm bells were rung. The authorities admitted defeat and allowed the guild banners to be issued as a symbol of continuing resistance. All thought of a negotiated settlement was abandoned.

11 Capitulation

The common people, by thus putting an end to their leaders' efforts to settle matters without bloodshed, were playing Henry's game. He wanted the glory of conquest, not a contract worked out at the conference table, however favourable; and when the mob refused to allow the provost to fight to the last ditch of negotiation they became Henry's allies. There was now nothing to stop him from indulging in a glorious bombardment until the walls were in ruins, and then sending his forces through the breaches against a powerless opposition.

All this time the invading army had been closing in on the town, and they could now be clearly seen from the towers in the walls. Messengers were sent to Amiens (where Dimanche and d'Étables were marooned) to plead for help from Louis, but no reply came and it was assumed that they had never got through. Indeed, from reports coming in from the outskirts it seemed that all roads were held by the English and that there was no hope that a French force could approach the town.

Before they finally took up their positions the English army was mustered before Henry in person;[1] and on the afternoon of Friday, 16 September, the bombardment began. The leaders of the besieging army had correctly taken the flags hoisted on the town hall to be a signal of defiance, and all through Friday afternoon and Saturday their guns fired without interruption. They met with no serious reply as they moved nearer to accelerate the tedious work of reducing the fortifications to rubble. The chosen sectors crumbled steadily and the shattered masonry fell on either side of the wall to form the saddles over which the final assault would be made. It seemed to be only a matter of time before the city's fate was sealed.

On Saturday, however, there was a small ray of hope for the besieged. One of the servants who had accompanied Jean d'Étables to report their plight to the king at Amiens slipped through the enemy lines with the news that his master hoped to bring 1,500 cavalry to their rescue. It was just possible that this force, which was at Harlbecque, would arrive next day and try to fight its way in to either the Brussels or the Marvis gate. The townspeople were to stand by at both gates, ready to throw them open the instant the cavalry arrived.

Some of the citizens were overjoyed at the news, particularly because the force was commanded by Robert de La Marck, sieur de Fleuranges, a soldier of great experience,(1) but most were sceptical. They refused to believe that a relatively small contingent could break through the English lines, and considered that if they did they would be caught like rats in a trap.[2] Even if food were plentiful, 1,500 soldiers, or what was left of them after a bloody engagement with the English army, could hardly be expected to hold out against a massive force equipped with the latest siege guns and ample supplies of ammunition. Rations were running short and hundreds more mouths to feed would merely accelerate the starvation of the whole population.

The problem did not have to be faced, however. The French cavalry seem to have decided that discretion was the better part of valour, for they never came face to face with the English army. The Milanese ambassador recorded on 16 September (the day before the news of the possible rescue reached the town) that the English controlled the high ground outside Tournai and were in such a commanding position that there was no danger of attack from the French.[3] A day or two later he informed the Duke of Milan that the most the French were able to do was to threaten the imperial town of Cambrai in the hope that the besieging army would be compelled to divert some of its strength.[4]

The town was now confronted with a new danger from within. The rogues and vagabonds had been thrown out earlier on, but the siege had created a new class of unemployed. Many of the inhabitants of the suburbs whose homes had been destroyed, and farmers and labourers from the surrounding district who had come into the town, were without means of support. Moreover, the siege had brought the activities of the guilds to a standstill, so that many of the city's normal population were also penniless. These unfortunates claimed that they faced starvation and asked either that they should be allowed to leave the city and take their chance of getting through the besiegers' lines, or that some special provision should be made for them. Otherwise they would take the law into their own hands and pillage the homes of the wealthier citizens. The danger was averted by persuading a number of men of substance each to take into his service twenty or thirty of the unemployed and provide them with a living wage.

Now that the citizens were cut off from the outside world their fine boast about never having turned was forgotten. Alarm and despondency began to spread,[5] and the people went to confession in droves to prepare themselves to meet their Creator. Processions were organized, prayers said, and the wealthier classes, believing that they would have little further use for them, showered their worldly possessions upon the Virgin – gowns, suits and jewellery – in the hope that she would be their advocate. All prepared to render the account to be met at the end of their days, having no hope except in Almighty God. Thus writes the diarist who has left a graphic account of the miseries endured by the city at this time. It did not help the citizens to realize that they were badly off for powder and artillery. They had no professional cannoneers, and the guns sometimes burst in the hands of the amateurs firing them, who did not know what charge of gunpowder they could safely take. On the other hand, the English cannon were now beginning to make themselves felt, and women and children had to be pressed into service to carry materials to the places where breaches were appearing.[6]

In spite of the wishes of the English council of war that Henry should keep away from danger he insisted on directing the bombardment in person. A week earlier, however, he had taken a few days off to disport himself with the ladies of Margaret's Court. He arrived in Lille on Sunday, 11 September, preceded by thirteen pages, and at the head of a company of two hundred men-at-arms, a large detachment of the yeomen of the guard and many of his nobles, having left a skeleton staff to organize the siege. The wardrobe of the robes and the armourer had risen nobly to the occasion. The king's apparel and bard(2) were of cloth of silver edged with cloth of gold and bordered with red roses; and his armour was freshly burnished and set with jewels.[7] The mounts of the leading men in his entourage had trappings of solid silver and were covered with cloth of gold on one flank, and on the other black velvet adorned with gold stripes and the fleur-de-lis.

The emperor rode out to meet his distinguished guest and escorted him back to the gates of the town, where the huge cavalcade was received with fitting ceremony. The keys of the city were presented to the king and duly returned to the provost, and a guard of honour was mounted. The streets were overflowing with the entire population, or so it seemed to Dr John Taylor. Girls offered floral crowns, sceptres and garlands to Henry; tapestries were hung from the houses; the stories of the Old and New Testaments – 'goodly pageants pleasant to behold' – were enacted along the route of the procession, which was lined with flaming torches, although it was broad daylight; and the crowds were so dense that it was almost impossible to pass.[8]

They made their way as best they could to the town hall, where Margaret and Prince Charles were waiting on the steps; and there Henry ordered that the drawn sword and maces which had been carried before him should be put away, as a token of respect. When all the ceremonial was over the king and his nobles 'were lodged and feasted according to their degree'. Henry was taken to Margaret's palace, where he was given a suite of four magnificent rooms hung with tapestries worked in gold thread. It had been intended that he should dine alone, but the dowager, accompanied by some of her ladies, 'took her plate' from her own supper table and joined the king in his banqueting chamber, where she was made most welcome. As soon as the meal was over Henry led her to the dance floor, kicked off his shoes and danced with her until dawn in his shirt sleeves; and to show his gratitude for her generous hospitality he presented her with a diamond of great value. Maximilian, whose youth was a long way behind him, and who probably needed a good night's rest, tactfully withdrew when the revelry began.[9]

Next day Henry was up betimes, in spite of his strenuous night. After Mass he received da Laude, the Milanese ambassador, and listened with commendable patience to the greeting he bore from his master the Duke of Milan; but when the ambassador tried to pin him down to the discussion of affairs of state the king said politely that they must have a talk about these matters some other time. He was in a hurry to go and dine, and afterwards to dance – in which pastime, da Laude wrote, 'he does wonders and leaps like a stag'.[9] There followed an endless round of 'banquets, plays, comedies, masques and other pastimes'.[10] These pleasures could not go on indefinitely, however.

It was with the greatest possible reluctance that the king took his leave of Margaret and returned to the camp at six o'clock in the evening of Tuesday, 13 September. Da Laude reported that Henry had in the space of a few days become so attached to Margaret's Court that he simply did not know how to leave; and he did so only after he and the noblemen in his suite had given Margaret and her damsels many beautiful rings and other jewellery worth a fortune, and after he had instructed his treasurer-at-war John Dauncey to distribute nearly five hunded pounds 'by way of reward' to the officers and servants of Margaret's household.[11] Margaret for her part had shown Henry great honour, and in da Laude's opinion could not have done more for him during his visit.[9]

The only thing that marred Henry's stay in Lille was a rumour that three men armed with hand-guns planned to assassinate him. Many suspects were arrested but nothing certain was discovered. Henry himself seems to have been little disturbed by the rumour that reached the English troops and there was much anxiety about his safety. Those left behind in the camp 'were never merry' until they saw their sovereign safe and sound. There was also a slight contretemps before the troops did see him again, for his party lost their way about a mile from Lille in thick fog. Back at the camp the master of the ordnance realized that Henry was overdue and fired several shots in an attempt to give him and his companions their bearings; but the sound of the cannon was deadened by the fog. It was only after a long and anxious wait that they met a victualler coming from the camp who was able to lead them to safety.[12]

Henry and his retinue may have let it appear that they were missing the company of women and that their brief interlude in Lille was therefore especially welcome, for the Milanese ambassador remarks upon 'one marvellous circum-stance' in the English camp. They had no women of their own, or if they had, they were so few that they could not be seen. Moreover, there was virtually no gambling in the army, except that the senior officers played with the King, who liked high stakes and saw to it that those he played with ended the game richer than they started, whatever luck they had. Da Laude said that he understood that the virtual absence of women from the English camp and the fact that there was very little gambling were due to the strict orders of the king and his Council, which suggests that the disciplinary code laid down before the expedition started was well observed.[13]

Henry had come to France to win glory on the battlefield and not on the dance floor or in the boudoir; and the problem of the beleaguered city of Tournai still remained. Not that it was much of a problem. Brian Tuke, who was to become the first master of the posts, records that there was no soldiers in Tournai, but only 'a great amount of peasantry and butchers without any commander-in-chief'. It was true that those in the city thought themselves strong enough to resist the whole world, simply because they had a great many cannon; but as they had little gunpowder, they were hardly in a strong position. Tuke, like others, was impressed by the great beauty of Tournai and he must have shared Robert Macquereau's regret that it should suffer so heavily from the English bombard-ment.[14]

Henry, however, did not allow the beauty of the city to inhibit him. On his return to the camp he did everything he could to step up the bombardment. Tuke tells us that he was unwilling 'to lose a moment of time' (perhaps because he felt that he had already spent too long enjoying himself in Lille), and that when the enemy fired a shot in his direction as he was visiting the trenches he was so incensed that he ordered all his cannon to make an all-out effort against the fortifications.[15] About this time the news of the rout of the Scots at Flodden had begun to come through, and on Saturday, 17 September, there was a service of thanksgiving in the camp. Mass was celebrated in the tent of cloth of gold, and in his sermon Edmund Birkhead, Bishop of St Asaph, gave thanks for the great victory.[16]

On Sunday, 18 September, the people of Tournai had their first direct contact with the English since their abortive meeting at Lannoy three days earlier. During a lull in the bombardment Thomas Benolt, Clarenceux King of Arms, was sent to seek an interview with some of the leading citizens. He informed them that Henry and Maximilian were much displeased at their failure to keep their promise to continue the Lannoy talks. Indeed, they regarded it as a personal insult and unless amends were made it would have the direst consequences for the town. The wretched citizens were terrified by this threatening line. They begged Clarenceux to believe that they had had every intention of fulfilling their promise, but that events in the town over which they had no control had made it impossible; and they added piteously that for God's sake the king and the emperor should not persecute them in this way. After all, they were not men of war. All they wanted was to be left in peace.

Clarenceux then revealed what appeared to be the real reason for his visit. Henry believed that an English gentleman (a relative of his) was held prisoner in the town and he was most anxious that no harm should befall him. He prayed that he should be treated as a gentleman and a prisoner of war. This mystified the authorities, as they had no reason to think that any of the besiegers had been captured. Nevertheless, to make absolutely certain, and perhaps also to gain twenty-four hours in which there might be a chance of resuming negotiations for a peaceful settlement, they promised to make inquiries and to report the result to Clarenceux the following day. When Benolt returned on Monday they assured him that there was no trace of the man Henry was worried about; and once again they threw themselves on the mercy of the king and the emperor, begging that the bombardment should cease and the besiegers depart.

Benolt then abandoned his formal approach, and spoke man to man. He said that they must not imagine for one moment that the English army would withdraw before it had captured Tournai. He personally was very sorry for them, for they had a beautiful city and it was sad to think that it should be so terribly damaged. It was perfectly obvious, however, that as they had no soldiers and as their defences were weak they had not the slightest chance of survival. He was sure that it was in their best interests to surrender without more ado. He added that he had no instructions to speak on these lines and did so simply because he was deeply sorry for them in their hopeless plight. If there was anything he could do to help he would gladly do it.

The city's representatives eagerly seized on the chance thus offered. They asked the herald to give them until eight o'clock next morning to persuade the fiery spirits who wanted to fight to the death that the situation was hopeless. The besiegers were well aware that the town was divided against itself. The Milanese ambassador reported on 18 September that the nobles and great merchants, who were on the whole well disposed towards the emperor, wanted to surrender, and were prevented only by the common people, who were loyal to France. He added that it was believed that the common people were now in control of the city, which was not far from the truth.[17]

Benolt returned punctually at the appointed hour on Tuesday morning. The town's representatives were ready for him and said that there was at least general agreement that the only course was to surrender. The bombardment (which seems to have gone on without interruption, so that the herald took his chance along with the besieged during his visits) was becoming so terrible that those who had refused to think of surrender a few days ago were beginning to lose heart. The authorities asked for a new safe conduct so that they might come to discuss terms of surrender. Benolt carried this news back to the camp, and late in the evening re-appeared with a safe conduct from Henry and the promise of a second from Maximilian next day. He would return at ten o'clock on the Wednesday to conduct them to a meeting with the representatives of the two sovereigns.

While Clarenceux King of Arms was leading the wavering inhabitants to the brink of surrender, Henry and Maximilian were preparing to administer the *coup de grâce*. Both monarchs seem to have taken a keen interest in the conduct of the bombardment, and it may well be that Henry, who considered himself as an expert in this field, thought that Maximilian was poaching on his preserves, but he seems nevertheless to have deferred to the greater experience of the older man. The three wards of the army were encamped on three sides of the town. The king's ward – the middle-ward – was to the north, the fore-ward, under the Earl of Shrewsbury, to the south, and the rear-ward, under Lord Herbert, to the west. Maximilian directed the planting of the English guns (although he went through the motions of consulting the English artillery experts), and also of his own mortars, which fired at random into the town.[18] Henry personally directed the fire of some of his apostles from a position to the west of the city. He ordered the cannoneer in charge of St Bartholomew to aim at the towers of the cathedral of Notre Dame, a building of great beauty, which in 1513 had already stood there for nearly four hundred years. Robert Macquereau tells us that he was quite near the king and heard him give the order, adding that it would do no harm if a few cannon-balls were dropped on the houses of the ecclesiastics living round about the cathedral. It might rouse them from their sleep and give them a new incentive to serve God. The very first shot carried away one of the corners of the bell-tower, and the cannon-ball and the dislodged masonry plunged on to the houses beneath, severely damaging them and killing a number of wealthy people who lived there.[19]

At times during the night of Tuesday, 20 September, the bombardment was so heavy and unrelenting that the defending cannoneers dared not remain at their places on the walls. Macquereau says that there were many casualties – too many to record, although he does mention one or two. A servant in the house of an apothecary had her foot taken off by a cannon-ball that came through the window. A married couple visiting Tournai for the annual religious procession, who had retired for the night, perhaps thinking that bed was the safest place, were killed by a single cannon-ball. The authorities later claimed that there had been few casualties, however, despite the fact that the streets were littered with cannon-balls, many of them from the emperor's mortars.

Once or twice during Tuesday night and the early hours of Wednesday the bombardment stopped, and the rumour spread that this was the signal for the assault; but the guns resumed their fire, and, paradoxically, the citizens breathed again. So long as the cannon-balls continued to smash against the walls, their lives, property and the honour of their womenfolk were relatively safe; but the knowledge that sooner or later the assault must come, and that when it did they could offer no resistance, at last had its effect on morale. When the Lille Gate fell into the hands of the besiegers the end seemed very near.[20] The common people began to exhort the 'men of substance' to come to terms with the enemy.

At a meeting of all the citizens shortly after dawn on Wednesday it was agreed that the town was doomed, and there was a unanimous vote in favour of resuming talks.[21] A committee of eight was appointed to meet the English and to 'make every effort to save the lives of the inhabitants with some of their goods'. So much for the proud boast that Tournai would never turn.

At ten o'clock the delegation met Thomas Benolt and a herald from the emperor at the St Fontaine Gate and were told that if they treated in good faith they would be honestly dealt with. They were at once joined by the English representatives, who included the Bishop of Winchester, Sir Robert Wingfield, John Young, and Thomas Wolsey. Michel Allegambe, who was again spokesman, reminded the Englishmen of Carondelet's visit to Tournai and the subsequent meeting at Lannoy, and explained that since then the town's leaders had done their best to persuade the citizens to accept the emperor as their lord and master, so that their lives and fortunes might be preserved. They had refused to see reason, however, and they had even rebelled against the city's governing body. There had been nothing for it but to await developments, in the hope that sooner or later the common people would come to their senses – which they had done only that morning. Now everyone accepted that there was no question of remaining neutral; and given the alternatives of waiting until the city was put to fire and the sword, and surrendering to the emperor, they had no hesitation in choosing the latter.

The English delegation quickly seized on the last point. There was no longer any question of surrendering to the *emperor*. Henry was the lawful King of France. Tournai was part of his dominions and must surrender to *him*. The Tournaisiens, however, were skilful debaters. Why then, they demanded, had Carondelet, who represented both king and emperor, originally asked them whether their city was French or imperial? They understood that the emperor had always regarded Tournai as his, and if the city's loyalty had to change it seemed right that it should be transferred to him.

The English replied that Benolt had been instructed to make this point quite clear. They were now dealing with Henry and not with Maximilian, and if they had the town's best interests at heart they would agree without further argument to do what Henry asked. Otherwise, they would have to take the consequences. The bombardment would continue without mercy until the city fell like a ripe plum into the hands of the besiegers. Although most of the English delegation were anxious (as Clarenceux King of Arms had been) to save the town from further bloodshed and destruction, some seem to have hoped that the city would still refuse to surrender, so that the one-sided bombardment might continue.

The town's representatives were astonished that they would not be allowed to surrender to the emperor. They withdrew for a private talk, but soon reluctantly decided that there was nothing for it but to acknowledge Henry as their new ruler. The alternative of breaking off the negotiations yet again and returning to the town to await the inevitable end was too grim to contemplate. Surrender arranged in the calm atmosphere of the conference chamber was much to be preferred to unconditional surrender after the city had been sacked. They therefore rejoined the English delegation and asked that as a first step the bombardment, which had continued unabated during their talks, and all other 'acts of war' should be suspended; and they undertook that they for their part would do the same. Lord Lisle was still reluctant to silence the guns, but it was finally agreed. Heralds were sent throughout the besieging army to instruct the cannoneers to cease fire and the captains to halt their approach to the walls; and simultaneously messengers were sent round the town to stop desultory cannon-fire, although it was hardly a menace to the besiegers.

Now that there was a truce the two sides got down to working out the details of surrender. The English agreed that no further damage would be inflicted on the city or the persons of the inhabitants, so long as it was clearly understood that Tournai was part of Henry's dominions and the citizens accepted him as their true liege lord. The town's delegation agreed to pay a contribution towards the costs of the siege, in addition to the 6,000 livres a year they paid the King of France, which would now be due to Henry. When, however, it was proposed that the English should put a garrison into the town, which even Louis had not been allowed to do, Allegambe and his companions jibbed. They held another private meeting, and then said that this must be cleared with the emperor before they could agree to it. The English delegation replied impatiently that there was not the slightest need for consultation with Maximilian, and that any agreement they reached would be automatically approved by the emperor; but Allegambe would not budge. The point must be put to Maximilian. The English representatives pointed out that it would be difficult to get hold of him as he was dining at the Château d'Antoing. Perhaps it would be enough to arrange for his nominees to join the discussion? This was not enough, however. The town must be absolutely certain that it was not committing itself to anything that would displease the emperor.

As it was nearing the dinner hour the English decided to adjourn the discussion to report progress to Henry. The town's delegates, who had gone without their usual sumptuous meals for some days, were entertained to dinner by some of the English gentlemen who remained behind while their leaders reported to the king. It seems that the English delegation now had a change of heart, for after dinner heralds came from the king and the emperor to invite the town's representatives to go to the abbey of St Martin, where both sovereigns were waiting to receive them.

They found Henry and Maximilian in the garden and knelt humbly before them. The Bishop of Westminster was also there and summarized the morning's discussion in Latin. Michel Allegambe confirmed that the bishop had accurately described the position, and added that the only question now was whether the emperor agreed that the town should be surrendered to the English. Maximilian, also speaking in Latin, said that he did. They must henceforth regard Henry, King of France, as their sovereign. Henry added that they might rest assured that he would look after their interests well, that the people and their property would not be molested, and that all their franchises and privileges would be carried on unimpaired. It remained only to commit the details of their agreement to paper.

This was provided for in a document prepared in the English camp on Friday, 23 September, which started off by blaming the townspeople for the siege – at some length. They had defied the summons to yield the town and had compelled their lawful sovereign to use force against them; but they had seen the error of their ways, and now humbly begged for mercy. The settlement they were offered was generous. They were to renounce Louis, the *soi-disant* King of France, and to receive Henry at all times with the honour and dignity due to their natural sovereign lord. They were to pay him, in addition to the £1,200 a year they had customarily paid to France, £800 a year for ten years, and a lump sum of £10,000 towards the cost of the siege. In return, all the rights and privileges they had formerly enjoyed were to continue unimpaired. Citizens who refused to recognize Henry as king were given twenty days to leave the city, taking with them their goods and chattels; and those who were away on business were given forty days to get back to take the oath of loyalty to their new sovereign. In short, the citizens found themselves in almost exactly the same relationship with Henry as they had with Louis, except that the price had substantially increased.[22]

Brian Tuke was thus able to report with satisfaction to Richard Pacey in Rome that the 'opulent, strong, fair and extensive city of Tournai' had surrendered. 'We now have the city of Thérouanne, which was called *la chambre du roi*; and Tournai, on whose walls was inscribed "*La pucelle sans reproche*" that is "the unsullied maiden". The *chambre du roi* is burned, and this maiden hath lost her maidenhood.'[23]

NOTES

(1)   One of the authorities for these events.

(2)   i.e. his horse's bard, in this case the ornamental cloth and not the protecting armour.

12 Occupation

FIRST WEEKS

Henry made his ceremonial entry into Tournai on the morning of Sunday, 25 September, through the St Fontaine Gate at the north-west corner of the city. He rode a magnificent barded courser and wore a full suit of richly decorated armour. The procession, the most splendid of the campaign, included the English nobility in their finest outfits, the henchmen carrying the king's weapons, heralds in their colourful uniforms, and even the royal minstrels, who on this occasion gave their first public performance. A group of leading citizens went to the village of Maire about half a mile out to meet the king. After appropriate speeches praising him and pledging their loyalty they led him back to the city, where a large crowd carrying torches awaited the arrival of their new sovereign and managed with some difficulty to raise a few dutiful shouts of '*Vive le Roi!*'

Six burgesses carried a silken canopy over Henry as the procession made its way along the Rue St Jacques to the cathedral. The broken masonry had been cleared from the streets, the houses were decorated with tapestries hung from the windows, and tableaux lined the route. The victors went to Mass in the cathedral – it was only a Low Mass as time was limited – and Henry, whose devout manner was remarked on by the Tournaisiens, knighted forty-nine men who had distinguished themselves in the campaign, including the treasurer-at-war, John Dauncey, and Christopher Garnishe, who had over all charge of the tents.

After midday dinner at his lodging (the residence of one of the ecclesiastics whom a day or two earlier he had been teasing with cannon-balls) he was presented by the civic authorities with a generous quantity of Beaune, which he received with gratitude. He then went to meet his new subjects in the market-place. The town was already in the hands of a strong English force, and an attempt on the king's life would have been dearly paid for; but as an additional precaution there had been a thorough house-to-house search to reveal any sign of conspiracy. Further, for what it was worth, the whole population, young and old, had been required to take an oath of loyalty in the presence of Wolsey. Henry mounted the steps of the town hall and the crowd was addressed in his name in ingratiating terms; but they listened sullenly, with downcast eyes. Not a single one showed 'an amiable countenance', not even when the king took off his bonnet and bowed graciously in all directions; and this cold reception may have contributed to Henry's decision to return to the camp to enjoy the safety and comfort of his wooden house, rather than spend the night in the town.[1]

A Saxon tournament, dated 1509 by Lucas Cranach

Undaunted by the citizen's thinly veiled hostility, Henry commanded that jousts should be held on 8 October, believing, perhaps, that an exhibition of his horsemanship would help to put the Tournaisiens in a happier frame of mind. The tent of cloth of gold, in Robert Macquereau's opinion 'the most beautiful of its kind in Christendom', was erected beside the lists in the market square to give added splendour to the occasion; but once again the king had bad luck with the weather. The Milanese ambassador, who was among the spectators, tells us that the jousts were 'honoured by a constant downpour, by no means slight'. He also provides the fashion commentary without which the sixteenth-century ambassadorial dispatch was incomplete. Henry was dressed 'in the most sumptuous manner imaginable'. He wore a tunic over his armour, which da Laude says, deprecatingly, he had worn before, although its second appearance was justified by its great beauty. In spite of the weather the programme was duly proceeded with in the presence of a great crowd of spectators, but the heavy rain 'spoiled all the sport'. The king was inevitably declared victor, and escorted in triumph round the lists 'in most honourable fashion', apparently fresher than when the jousts began. After the jousts came the complementary banquet, with a hundred dishes. Margaret of Savoy, who had been the principal spectator, was the principal guest, and once again there was dancing far into the night.[2]

While Henry was enjoying himself jousting, feasting, dancing and generally showing off, the foundation was being laid for the occupation of the city, most of the hard work on the English side being done by Thomas Wolsey. Henry, who had little inclination for business at the best of times, certainly had none for it now. When the Milanese ambassador tried once again to discuss some matters with him, 'his majesty did not choose to enlarge much, nor is it his habit; but he referred me to the Bishop of Winchester who would talk about them at more length. And so I left his majesty talking with the damsels.'[3] On one occasion when the king did take the initiative he made a first-class blunder. Shortly after he entered the city he grandly announced, apparently without discussing the point with his advisers, that all banished men were now free to return to their homes and resume their normal way of life, thanks to his clemency. Perhaps he was himself beginning to believe his oft-repeated statement that France was part of his kingdom and had therefore concluded that all who had been banished while Tournai was ruled by Louis XII must deserve his help.

The civic authorities were staggered by the proposal, and took an early opportunity of pointing out that the normal way of life of the banished had little to commend it – they were mostly murderers, incendiaries and men guilty of a long catalogue of serious crimes, including some who had escaped from the city after breaking the 'quarantine'. This was a rule of long standing that if there were a fracas it was a capital offence for a friend of one of the protagonists to attack a friend of the other during the first forty days after the quarrel began, on the assumption that after forty days tempers would have cooled off. Henry readily conceded that none of these criminals should be allowed to return under his dispensation, and to regularize the position a formal decree was issued on 1 October 1513.[4] This said that although on the king's joyful first entry into Tournai he had authorized all banished men to return, he had, of course, never meant that dangerous criminals should be allowed to avail themselves of the licence; but whoever drafted the document left it far from clear who *was* to be permitted to return. It was therefore necessary to issue a further decree a few days later which established a proper procedure for reclaiming citizenship.[5]

One administrative task that must have fallen to the king was the choice of a governor, and he selected Sir Edward Poynings, who had the right experience for the job. He had been at one time or another Warden of the Cinque Ports, Lord Deputy of Ireland, and Governor of Calais. Henry also appointed a marshal, to be second-in-command of the garrison, a treasurer, comptroller, master porter, and other officers on the pattern of Calais,[6] and, later on, a keeper of the 'seal royal of Tournai'.[7]

Even before Poynings was appointed, measures were being taken to ensure the security of the garrison. On 30 September the citizens were ordered to return to store the weapons issued to them when the siege began, for so long as they remained armed the position of the English troops was weakened. The weapons had not been of much use against the besiegers, but they might be very effective on a dark night in the narrow streets of the city. The people were given fifteen days to return the varied collection in their hands – harquebuses, cross-bows, clubs, bows and arrows, and 'other instruments of war', which in any case belonged to the town and were supposed to be kept in store, except when there was an emergency.[8] The guild banners, which had great symbolic value, were also recalled, for while they remained in the hands of the people there was the danger that they would be used to bring to the surface any latent

Target shooting with composite crossbows. An engraving by Hans Schaufflein from illustrations of the Emperor Maximilian I c. 1520

discontent with the new regime.[8] The four councils were summoned to a meeting with the English leaders on 5 October, to be told that the king had decided to leave a garrison of 1,000 cavalry and 4,000 infantry, but that it would not in any way affect their rights and privileges.

This was simply not true. Tournaisiens had enjoyed freedom from a garrison for many years, and it was also a condition written into their trading agreement with the Low Countries. If they admitted French troops they were liable to forfeit any property they held in the territories of the Archduke; but the capitulation document stipulated that the installation of a garrison by Henry or his heirs and successors would not prejudice the position of the burgesses, whatever the treaty with the Low Countries might imply to the contrary. Further, this was to be guaranteed in a letter from Maximilian.[9] The English higher command was apprehensive about the reaction of the Tournaisiens to the announcement about the garrison, for they said that, if the townspeople wanted their privileges to be increased, they had only to ask.[10] Throughout the occupation, however, the mere fact that they were saddled with a garrison, however benevolent, irked many of the citizens.

The debating skill of the Tournaisiens, which had been much in evidence while they were negotiating to save the city, was again shown during the early stages of the occupation. Every document put out by the English was closely scrutinized, lest a subtle piece of drafting should commit the city to something undesirable. For example, a legal mind among the city fathers suspected that the article in the capitulation treaty which said that those who refused to take the oath of loyalty were free to leave the town within twenty days of Henry's entry might somehow carry the implication that those who *did* take the oath did not have such freedom of movement. This point had to be spelt out in a document of 6 October which made it crystal clear that those who were loyal to Henry did in fact have as much freedom of movement as those who refused to recognize him.[11]

On Thursday, 13 October, the town's leaders were summoned to be told that Henry proposed to depart that day. The first phase of the occupation was over.

ADMINISTRATION

Sir Edward Poynings and his 5,000 troops were now on their own about a hundred miles from Calais, the nearest English territory, left to make the best they could of a difficult and potentially dangerous position. The attitude of the citizens when Henry appeared before them in the market place, and the offensive songs and lampoons that were making the rounds of the town, suggested that the new governor was not going to have the easiest of tasks in administering the place; and so it proved.

Many people abandoned their homes and went off with their goods and chattels to make their living elsewhere. It is easy to understand their apprehensions, for although they had been subject to the Crown of France for more than three hundred years, the control exercised from Paris was gentle and the citizens regarded themselves more as an independent city-state than as part of the French kingdom. This came out clearly enough when they found themselves negotiating almost like a sovereign state with Louis XII on the one hand, and Maximilian and Henry on the other. Louis was much farther away than Paris, but the representative of the English Crown, supported by a powerful military force, was now sitting in their midst; and in spite of Henry's repeated assurances that the city's privileges would be unimpaired, it was obvious that he could do as he liked with their liberties whenever he chose. This was a new situation and many found it intolerable.

The exodus began right away, and almost as soon as he was back in England Henry had to send a pained message to the town. Although it had been agreed in the treaty with the citizens that any who wanted to leave might do so, the numbers availing themselves of the right were considered to be much too great. The king was sorry to learn that people had already left, taking their possessions, and that others were going to follow suit. It seemed that they were not showing due obedience, and he hoped this was not because the governor was treating them less favourably than his subjects in other parts of the realm. He had also heard that they were spreading a rumour that he proposed to hand the city over to some other prince. This was untrue, as they would learn from the deputies they were sending to the parliament to be held at Westminster after Christmas.[13]

This is the first clue that it had been decided to extend the parliamentary system to Tournai, but the decision was almost certainly taken while Henry was still in the city, probably as part of his campaign to ingratiate himself with his victims. The four councils found it difficult to decide who should represent them. They reached no decision at a meeting on 20 December and the debate had to be resumed on the following day.[13] Deputies, one of whom was Jean le Sellier, were eventually selected, however, and they turned up at Westminster to attend the session of parliament which ran from 23 January to 4 March. It is recorded on 26 February that the representatives of Tournai have drawn attention to problems in the administration of justice in the city as a result of the substitution of the English Crown for the French, and that provision has been made for their solution. Cases which had been before the courts when the city capitulated were still awaiting judgement, and judgements which had been given just before the English attack had not been carried out. Until the constitutional position was clarified, however, those concerned felt that they could do nothing, and the situation was becoming intolerable.[14]

Henry, professing himself most anxious to ensure that his loyal subjects in Tournai did not suffer because of the transfer of their allegiance, issued a decree, with the approval of parliament, to the effect that all the suspended cases should proceed to trial in his name, and that the suspended judgements should be executed as if they had been delivered by one of his own judges. This enabled the machinery of justice to start moving again, but a further measure was necessary.

Certain cases had been customarily referred from Tournai to the *court de parlement* in Paris, but, as the French were now considered to be in rebellion against Henry, their true sovereign, this superior court had to be replaced. Litigants could hardly be expected to make the long journey to London to attend a court of appeal, so Henry established a bench of five judges – '*notables personnaiges, clercs et licenciez*' – who were to reside in Tournai and to deal with cases which had formerly gone to Paris. This court was to hear cases arising not only in Tournai and the surrounding district, but also those from Thérouanne (in spite of the fact that the town had been virtually wiped from the map) and any other French towns won by Henry in the future. It was to hold assizes once a month on the most convenient day and it was provided with a clerk and other court officers.[15]

There was more to be done, however, before the integration of Tournai with England could be regarded as complete. Although one of Henry's first administrative acts after the fall of the town had been to confirm the citizens' rights and privileges, and although the intention had been to form a 'common market' with the rest of his kingdom, English merchants had made a strenuous bid to take over the cloth trade on which Tournai's economy depended, seemingly by arrogating to themselves powers which the English Crown did not intend to take even for itself. Henry therefore issued a decree pointing out that damage to the cloth trade would have serious implications for the city as a whole and re-affirming that the people of Tournai continued to enjoy all their former rights. Further, it was completely open to them to trade in England, to acquire property there, and to export English goods, paying no more than the ordinary dues paid by the native English. In short, in matters of trade they were placed on exactly the same footing as Henry's other subjects.[16]

There was a related Act of Parliament which looked forward to a great increase in trade between England and Tournai. Henry:

> ... by his great wisdom and singular policy hath now reduced the cities and towns of Thérouanne and Tournai to due obedience, by reason whereof now shall follow and ensue great amity, familiarity, and intercourse in buying and selling of merchandises, wares, and otherwise between the citizens and inhabitants of the said cities, towns, and precincts of the same, and the King's natural subjects, inhabitants in this his realm of England.

All those who participate in this trade must have 'true and indifferent justice' and the king has therefore appointed two notaries to record contracts, which are to be sealed and kept in safe custody by the keeper of the royal seal in Tournai.

Disputes arising on duly recorded contracts may be heard before the bailiff of Tournai, or in the Court of Chancery in England. Parallel procedures are laid down. The Lord Chancellor will provide the Bailiff of Tournai with particulars of a contract which an English merchant claims has been broken. The bailiff is empowered to send a sergeant or other officer to the defaulter to require him to fulfil his part of the bargain; and if the latter claims that he is no longer bound by the contract he must pay into the court 'sufficient gage and pledge to the very value of the contents of the same', or remain in custody while the case is tried in the bailiff's court. In cases where a merchant of Tournai seeks to enforce a contract against an Englishman the procedures apply the other way around, the Court of Chancery taking the initiative on a complaint from the aggrieved Tournaisien. Finally, for good measure, contracts and bargains registered before the 'mayor of the staple' in Calais are brought into these arrangements.[17]

An Act of the English parliament did not apply automatically in Tournai, even though the members for the city had been present in the parliament that passed it, and steps had to be taken to make it effective there. This was done by means of an 'inspeximus', a device normally used for authenticating a charter or similar document. The Act was translated into French and provided with an additional Latin preamble in Henry's name, which says that the king has examined ('inspeximus') the Act, the provisions of which apply equally to his subjects in Tournai and in England. There is also a Latin tailpiece which refers to the 'humble petition and present request of the citizens of the aforesaid city of Tournai' (suggesting that the measure was introduced at their request), and adds that it is the king's firm belief that the Act will be for the mutual benefit of his Tournaisien and English subjects. The document, which is under the Great Seal, is dated 4 March 1514, the last day of the parliamentary session, and it must have been drafted very quickly after the royal assent was given to the bill.[18]

The surviving records are not conclusive, but it seems likely that the representation of Tournai in the English parliament was a precedent for Calais (or at least that it came first), despite the fact that Calais had been English for nearly 200 years, rather than the other way round. The vast statute of 1536, which has already been referred to,[19] and which was designed to improve the administration of Calais, also provides for the return of two burgesses to the English parliament, one by the governor and his council, and one by the mayor, burgesses, and freemen. There is no reference in this Act to any existing or previous arrangement for representation, and the drafting suggests that the proposal is new. The names of Calais representatives are recorded only from 1547, but there is evidence of unnamed representatives in 1542. There are no general records for the earlier parliaments of Henry VIII, and there may, therefore, have been members for Calais in 1514 and even before that. It seems more likely, however, that Calais was not represented before 1542, and that Tournai did in fact provide the first 'overseas' members of the English parliament.

In addition to the measures described above, others of lesser importance (for example, the restoration of the arrangement whereby the city was entitled to requisition one-sixth of the grain entering by the River Scheldt to be used as a stockpile,[20] and the cancellation of certain payments due by the citizens of Tournai to people resident in territories hostile to England)[21] were promulgated during the session or shortly after it ended, and the members for Tournai (whose numbers are not clear from the records, except that there were more than one) must almost certainly have been consulted on all of them.

The complicated municipal government seems to have been carried on virtually unchanged, and, indeed, to make any significant changes would have been quite contrary to Henry's policy of leaving rights and privileges unimpaired as far as possible. In any case, the constitution of the four councils was so elaborate – one had 2 *prévôts* and 18 *jurés*, the second 2 mayors and 28 *eswardeurs*, the third 2 mayors and 12 *échevins*, and the fourth 36 deans and 36 sub-deans of the guilds – that to make even a small change would have upset the whole balance of the machine. There was, however, one important new feature. The English governor was also the bailiff, so that the lines of civil and military authority culminated in one man. Decrees promulgated in London could be addressed to the governor in the knowledge that they would be applied to the civilian population through him in his capacity of bailiff. The security of the town was, of course, in the hands of the military authorities, but the day-to-day administration of the city and the large volume of commercial business were looked after in the ordinary way by the four councils. One development, however, was that a branch of the royal mint, which had already set up an outpost in Calais, was established in the city.[22]

Thus within six months of the capture of Tournai three fundamental steps had been taken towards administrative unification with England, and indeed also with Calais. Allegiance to the English Crown, which had been exacted from the people by force of arms, was now supplemented by the extension of the English parliamentary system to Tournai and its satellite territories; a common market was established in which Tournaisiens had equal trading rights with the English merchants; and provision was made for justice in the highly important field of commercial law to be dispensed on the same principles in Tournai, Calais and England – remarkable first steps towards not a colonial empire but the extension of the kingdom of England. It seems that it was Wolsey's hand that guided these far-reaching moves, although there is little in the records to support this conclusion. Henry had had the fun of his continental excursion and his sole continuing interest in Tournai lay in improving the fortifications. He had no real concern for the administration of the place in the wider sense, despite the fulsome language of the measures to which he put his signature. Wolsey, on the other hand, had his eye on the immensely rich bishopric of Tournai, which may have inspired first the idea that the town should be occupied by an English force (as Macquereau suggests), and later that it should be integrated with England, on the assumption that the bishopric was more likely to fall into his lap if the city were English. Whatever the reasons, by the middle of 1514 Tournai was well on the way to becoming part of England.

In spite of all that was done to make things easy for the Tournaisiens few of them accepted English sovereignty with enthusiasm. Most were prepared to tolerate the occupation because they had not the courage to oppose it actively, and perhaps also because they knew that it would not last for ever. A handful, including Jean le Sellier, were prepared to collaborate, not because they approved of the new regime, but because they were well rewarded for their services. Sir Richard Jerningham neatly summed up le Sellier by saying 'he is the best Englishman there and hated accordingly' by his fellow Tournaisiens.[23]

Most of the citizens, however, remained secretly loyal to France. The lengthy argument about sending members to the English parliament may well have been concerned, not with the actual choice of representatives, but with the question as to whether anyone should go at all. On 21 December 1513 the governor had to remonstrate with the civic authorities about the fact that the guild banners which were supposed to have been recalled when Henry was in the town were still in the hands of the citizens. They bore the arms of France and it was dangerous to leave such symbols of French power with the guilds.[24] Shortly afterwards when the municipal elections were being held many of the city fathers refused to offer themselves for re-election. In November 1514 Poynings had to complain that there were still a number of citizens who had not taken the oath of loyalty to the English Crown, which was supposed to be done once a quarter.[25] In 1515 an anonymous report said that 'the people of Tournai complain that they are treated like dogs and will revenge themselves by some trick if not well watched';[26] and at the beginning of 1516 Jerningham reported to Wolsey that the leading merchants had moved their headquarters to Ghent and Bruges. They refused to live in Tournai so long as it was English.[27]

Not all, however, were prepared to settle for passive resistance. Some were willing neither to collaborate nor to make their homes elsewhere, and formed an underground movement to recapture the city for France at the earliest moment.

The ringleader was Jean d'Étables, who had played a prominent part in the affairs of the city before the capitulation. The details of the plot, which was nipped in the bud, are scanty. In September 1514 Sir Edward Poynings reported to Wolsey that two friars who had been concerned in an enterprise against the town had been taken prisoner;[28] and shortly afterwards he wrote to Margaret of Savoy telling her he had imprisoned several citizens of Tournai, who had attempted to take the town for France, with the intention of using it as a base against her. The leaders had escaped to Lille and other towns in Hainaut, and Poynings asked her to have them arrested.[29] Eventually the principal conspirators, Jean d'Étables and Jean de Malines, were declared traitors and their property was confiscated.[30] Those who had followed them were considered by Mountjoy to have been misled; and he sought Henry's authority for a general pardon, which was granted.[31] While Henry was still in Tournai it had been suggested that he should take 200 hostages to ensure the town's loyalty; and he may have regretted that his 'great kindness' (da Laude's words) prevented him from acting on this advice.[32]

This seems to have been the only important occasion when a group of citizens openly defied the occupying power. The great majority of the Tournaisiens were content to wait patiently for the inevitable withdrawal of the English. A dozen conquerors and would-be conquerors had come and gone in the last 1,400 years (starting with the Germans in AD 182 and finishing with Edward III of England in 1340), and no doubt sooner or later Henry's men would follow them in their turn.

Margaret of France c. 1545, from a drawing of the Clouet School at Chantilly (236985.e.10.)

GARRISON

The English government's attitude towards Tournai was singularly enlightened, although it faced a hopeless task in attempting to integrate the city with the kingdom of England. Tournai was not prepared to become English at any price. The government's attitude towards its own troops, however, was anything but enlightened.

Two main themes run through the five-year period of the occupation. There was a consistent effort to reduce the cost of the garrison by reducing its size; and an equally consistent failure to provide adequate funds for the maintenance even of the diminishing forces. It very soon became apparent that it was going to be enormously expensive to maintain the initial 5,000, and there was constant pressure on the governor in office to agree to drastic reductions. Calais, where admittedly the problem was different (it was nearer home and reinforcements could be moved across the Channel under the protection of the royal navy), was able to get by with 700 or 800, which made the 5,000 left by Henry in Tournai seem quite disproportionate; and in any case, as tension with France eased after the peace treaty of April 1515, the need for a huge occupying force became less.

The damage was really done, however, with the original decision to leave 5,000 troops for garrison duty. Tournai was now an English city, and many of the original occupying force must have believed that they would make their career there. They were part of a permanent military establishment that was by far the biggest in the history of England. Pay was adequate at first, promotion prospects were good, conditions of service not too rigorous. The Tournaisiens enjoyed a high standard of living – probably higher than most of the English soldiers were accustomed to at home – and there was no reason to suppose that the occupying force would be any worse off than the natives. In the beginning the troops must have thought that their prospects were excellent.

The bright future faded rapidly. None of the factors that had kept morale high during the 1513 campaign applied during the occupation. The king was not present with his troops as commander-in-chief. Eagerness for the fray and the blood of the traditional enemy was no longer a moving force. The spice of danger which had kept them on the alert in camp and on the march was replaced by the tedium of garrison life in a strange country where English was not spoken. Money had been plentiful in 1513, but the pay of the occupying force was constantly in arrear, and the soldiers found it difficult to make ends meet.

There were three governors during the five-year occupation. Poynings, an able administrator, who kept things well under control from the date of his appointment until the beginning of 1515, when he was appointed ambassador to the Low Countries; Lord Mountjoy, who ran into trouble as soon as he arrived, and never got out of it; and finally, Sir Richard Jerningham, who had been treasurer during the latter part of Mountjoy's stewardship.

Mountjoy was appointed in January 1515 and arrived in Tournai on 5 February. He brought with him a new marshal, Sir Sampson Norton, who had been master of the ordnance since 1511, and a new treasurer, Sir Edward Bensted, so that there was a change in all the three senior posts. He also brought unpalatable instructions. The great cost of the garrison was beginning to worry the Privy Council seriously, and Mountjoy was commanded to explore the possibility of reducing its size. He was also to arrange for the payment of wages in arrear, a sensible move, for if soldiers were paid in advance it was more difficult to control them, and they could easily desert without financial loss to themselves.

These two proposals caused immediate discontent. As soon as he arrived Sir Sampson Norton discussed with his colleagues ways and means of reducing the number of troops, and it was suggested that 'the worst and most misruled men might depart, and the best and tallest men to tarry'. Rumours of this reached the ears of the soldiers 'and every man was in fear to lose his room'. In the morning, when they made their daily call at the governor's residence to collect the keys of the town gates, the porters swore that no gate would be opened that day unless they were paid under the old arrangements; and in the evening, when the marshal was foolish enough to accept the under-marshal's invitation to inspect the watch, they found the market-place in a turmoil. According to Norton's own account, written from Lille after he had fled from Tournai, they all cried out at once 'Money! Money! Money!' He told them that they could have their money and that it was even then being counted out; but this was not good enough. The men were out for his blood and cried 'Down with Sir Sampson!' One voice made itself heard above the others, shouting 'Thou art come to hang us all – go set gallows round about the market-place. If thou hangest one, thou shalt hang us all!'[33]

Mountjoy said that they would have killed the marshal had he not been given sanctuary in his house and later spirited from the town. The governor and his fellow councillors decided that they had no alternative but to give in to the demands of the mutineers; and, in reporting this regrettable fact to Henry, Mountjoy asked that a replacement should be sent for Norton (who was now clearly unacceptable as marshal) and also that his own commission should be revised to give him greater powers. Lancaster Herald was sent off post-haste with these requests and a long list of other matters for the consideration of the Privy Council, including a declaration that the town could not be defended with fewer than the original military establishment. In particular, it said, there must be no question of dispensing with the cavalry, who were vital for 'scouring the country and keeping it clear of thieves'. If the king insisted that the garrison must be reduced, then Mountjoy was not prepared to remain in charge of the town. He also repeated the request for wider financial powers that he had made direct to the king. He must have authority to make payments without the prior approval of the treasurer, when he considered that they were necessary for the security of the town.[34]

The governor wrote separately to Wolsey complaining about the lack of ready money and suggesting that the town could not be kept secure without it. In this letter he gave a graphic description of some of the problems the occupying force was up against:

> We see the city great and large, much people therein, and there must be four gates for the most part daily open, which must have strong wards. Many strangers resort daily hither. Amongst them of the town is very much weapon and harness. Many

cankered stomachs, which some hath not let to show both afore my coming and
since. And some stark traitors of the which we have some in hold. Many of our
soldiers be rude and but small be trusted with them in the town.[35]

Mountjoy's plea for more liberal instructions was written on 16 February –
ten days after the riot – but in spite of the urgency of the matter Henry did not
reply until 22 March, showing how painfully slow decision and communication
could be. The king said that those who had made the attempt on Sir Sampson
Norton's life must be punished, to which Mountjoy replied that it was out of the
question, as far too many were implicated. It would be more to the point if
money were sent, for after the garrison's next pay the treasury would be empty,
and then 'all things will be in hazard'. In fact, nothing seems to have been done
about the mutineers for several months. In the middle of August it was
suggested from Tournai that there should be a general pardon for the men who
had rioted on Mountjoy's arrival, and in September Mountjoy was still seeking
authority to pardon the rioters. He was afraid that many of them, both English
and Welsh, would go over to the enemy (presumably he meant the French,
although technically there was peace with France) if they were not pardoned;
and once again he argued against reducing the size of the garrison. At last, at the
end of September, Henry said that he was now content that a pardon should be
granted to all those engaged in 'the late rebellion'.[36]

Hardly had the decision to allow a general pardon been taken when there was
fresh trouble. Sir Richard Wingfield reported to Wolsey from Calais on
24 October that he had just heard news of a 'great disorder' among the soldiers
of Tournai.[37] This time, however, there was no question of a general pardon.
There was a commission in the city to make recommendations about strength-
ening the fortifications, headed by the Earl of Worcester, and it may be that the
tougher line against the rebels was urged by him, for he was a stronger man than
Mountjoy. Six of the offenders were executed in December, for 'seditiously
exhorting the people, spreading rumours, being in harness [armour] on the day
of the rebellion', and a number of others were banished from the garrison for
'maintaining rebellious opinions' and consorting with the more dangerous
rebels.[38] One of those executed was found guilty of 'exhorting and advising of
the persons out of wages at St Martin's' not to take 'the King's reward to bring
them home', but to remain in Tournai in hope of better things – a direct attack
on the government's policy of reducing the garrison; and two who were banished
had taken 'the King's reward' to get them back to England, and had then
returned to Tournai. Mountjoy said that he hoped that the severity that had
been used would have a salutary effect, and that the king would show mercy to
those who had not suffered the extreme penalty. He added that several of those
who had been sentenced to death had on the day of execution exhorted their
comrades to beware of rebellion, 'so that every man thinketh it came more of the
devil than by any other'.[39]

Sir Richard Whethill, who had taken the place of the unfortunate Norton as
marshal, also gives some idea of the difficulties facing the garrison in a letter to
Wolsey. In the first place, there were more like 20,000 people in the city than the
10,000 Wolsey had been assuming in his calculations for running down the

garrison. The main danger came not from the citizens themselves but 'by treason from without', which might, however, lead to the disaffection of large numbers of the inhabitants. There was no way of legislating against this, however. Another problem was the difficulty of assembling the soldiers, 'who are quartered in different lodgings', at short notice in an emergency. The perimeter of the city was three miles, with seven gates set in the walls, two great sluices (at the points where the River Scheldt entered and left the town), and ninety-nine towers. This meant that the proposed reduction in the size of the garrison would leave scarcely twenty men between one tower and the next – implying the Wolsey wanted to reduce the numbers to about 2,000 men. Whethill was against any reduction by decree, but suggested that as members of the garrison left for one reason or another their places should not be filled – which on the face of it seems illogical, as any reduction, whether ordered from London or the result of natural wastage, must have had the same effect on the ability of the garrison to defend itself. The marshal considered that the townspeople were delighted to see the English element in their midst diminishing, as they still hoped that one day they would return to France.[40]

Nevertheless, the policy of steadily reducing the size of the garrison continued, until at the beginning of 1517 it was down to a mere 1,000.[41] The reduction in the complement must have contributed to the poor morale of the men, for there is little incentive in any organization if promotion prospects become poorer year by year; and lack of pay, which was to bedevil the English army for the rest of the sixteenth century, became a chronic ailment. Matters were not helped by suppliers of food and other essentials who found that they were able to hold the private soldiers to ransom; but perhaps the most serious weakness during the greater part of the occupation was the absence of inspiring leadership. Mountjoy seems to have found the post too much for him, and during the latter part of his governorship devoted almost as much energy to trying to persuade Henry to recall him as he did to the job.

Nor was it only Mountjoy who found life in the garrison town uncongenial. Some of his colleagues also did what they could to escape from their posts. Sir Richard Whethill told Wolsey that he was unable to save a penny in Tournai and in fact had to draw on his private means. He suggested that he would be better able to serve the king in Calais, where 'that little God hath sent me lieth'. He had been born in Calais, 'wherefore my mind is most there; and also the King's subjects there would be glad I were amongst them, for lightly our contrymen desireth most another, if they be kind people . . . howbeit a servant is always at the commandment of his master'. Whethill said that if he were lucky enough to be given the post of his choice, he would like authority to 'leave twenty of my retinue in wages in the citadel [in Tournai] so that else I shall not well wot how to shake hands of them for the service they have done to the King here and elsewhere under me'.[42]

The cost of living troubled the garrison through the whole of the occupation and was particularly worrying in 1517. A new decree from London was considered to be the last straw. This was that, as part of the economy drive, pay, which had been issued quarterly, should now be issued half-yearly – the argument, of course, being that the longer the interval between pays, the more the Crown would save in wages to men who died or were dismissed from the forces. The English gentlemen in the garrison – sixteen of them, who corresponded to the 'gentlemen volunteers' of Elizabeth I's reign, in that they served as supernumeraries hoping to qualify for a commission and the perquisites that went with it – submitted a petition to London pointing out that 'sixpence now goeth not so far nor is not so good nor profitable as fivepence was wont to be', implying a 20 per cent fall in the value of money, which had not been compensated for by an increase in the rate of wages. The gentlemen also pointed out that in the king's garrisons elsewhere 'the householders be all of our nation and willing to help. Here it is the contrary.'[43]

The gentlemen's protest was echoed by the yeomen in the guard serving in the garrison and the 'vinteners of the castle', who also claimed that Tournai was a special case. They must always be ready to stand a siege: English victuallers were unpopular with the Tournaisiens, and had to pay excise duty on wines and beer, which was not done in other garrisons: and the king's money was worth less than its face value.[44] The governor himself agreed with the line taken by the troops. He thought that the longer interval between pays would lead to greater hardship – and things were bad enough as it was. Even as he wrote his dispatch some victuallers came to him to complain that the soldiers had just taken supplies from them by force, without payment, excusing themselves by saying that they had no money and could get no credit, and without meat and drink they could not live.[45] The council in Tournai took the same line. It was impossible to adopt half-yearly payments 'for every manner of victuals and other necessaries is so dear that there is neither baker, brewer, nor butcher that will trust or lend his victuals unless he have ready money'; and the credit of the garrison as a whole was so bad that the council was forced to pay an imprest to the victuallers to provide some food for the troops and save them from starving to death.[46]

The strategic case for the steady reduction in the size of the garrison was the rebuilding of the fortifications, and the addition of a citadel, which would make it possible to defend the town with a much smaller number of soldiers. This was a costly investment that showed no saving in the short term, although it might well have paid for itself in ten or twenty years. As it turned out Henry had the worst of both worlds. The absence of a powerful citadel for the greater part of the occupation meant that a very large garrison had to be maintained; and just when the citadel was virtually completed – at enormous cost, and after great organizational difficulties – it was decided to return the city to the French. Much of the great effort that had gone into the rebuilding was wasted, for the sum paid for them by the French represented a good deal less than their true cost.

THE KING'S WORKS

Although there was not the shadow of an argument for the English occupation of Tournai, there was a strong case for rebuilding the fortifications, given the decision that English troops were to remain there. Tournai was completely surrounded by a wall studded with nearly a hundred towers and a moat fed from the River Scheldt; but there had been little effort to maintain its defences. They were certainly not in the same class as those of Thérouanne, and by the time the siege ended Henry's guns had done a good deal of damage. The occupying force's first task was therefore to ensure that the breaches were repaired (which the citizens paid for), lest the French should find it possible to lay siege to the city in their turn.

There was more to be done, however. The château in the north-west quarter of the city had no real defensive value, and, above all, accommodated only a handful of troops. If the defences were to be made satisfactory a citadel had to be provided to take a substantial number of men. At first the English soldiers had been billeted on the citizens, and also 'outside the town in places hard by in order not to straiten the food supply of the city too much'[47] – an unsatisfactory arrangement. It was dangerous, for so long as the troops were scattered they might prove easy victims if the citizens rebelled; and it was unpopular with the householders on whom the troops were billeted. A new citadel would diminish the friction between the soldiers and the townspeople; it would enable the former to sleep more securely, and to act quickly as a body in an emergency; and it would make it possible safely to reduce the numbers in the garrison. The king and Privy Council considered that 'the garrison that was kept there was chargeable and therefore it was determined that there should be built a castle to chastise the city if they rebelled and to minish the garrison'.[48] The last point was important, for to maintain indefinitely the whole of the 5,000 men originally left would have been an intolerable burden. In any case, whatever the practical advantages of concentrating the troops in a smaller area, fortification was one of Henry's passions, and it was natural that he should want to improve the defences of his new city, which were manifestly inadequate.[49]

It was not until the middle of 1515, nearly eighteen months after the fall of Tournai, that the plans got properly under way. The idea was that part of the north-west quarter (about one-twelfth of the total area of the city), the southern boundary of which was made by the River Scheldt, should be walled off separately, and that a large castle should be built within the confines of this subsidiary wall. Needless to say, the citizens opposed the idea, not only because it meant demolishing a number of private houses. When the Earl of Worcester, one of the commissioners sent from London to examine the proposals generally, invited a group of them to dinner they 'complained that their city, hitherto a place of trade, was being converted into a city of war'. They asked that the plan to build a citadel should be deferred, and put up alternative proposals for safeguarding the town.[50] They were overruled, however, and the scheme went ahead. William Pawne was appointed 'commissioner for making of the King's citadel at his city of Tournai';[51] and was given to serve under him a huge number of artificers – masons, mortar-makers, carpenters, sawyers, rockyers, hewers, and labourers (some of the last being 'cranemen' employed in winding the fifteen 'gins' which lifted stone from boats in the Scheldt).[52] His establishment was reduced in the winter, when the weather was not suitable for building, but for most of the year it exceeded 2,000.

Although it was quite clear that Henry's proposals would be implemented, the citizens' opposition continued. At the beginning of 1516 a memorandum prepared by the four councils pleaded that they should not be required to contribute to the building of the citadel. They had been impoverished by the late siege, they had been burdened with paying Henry £10,000, which they had had to borrow (as their representatives had stated in the English parliament), repairs to the town walls had cost nearly £2,000, many thousands of citizens had died of the plague and so on.[53]

A year later a deputation went to England to lay the city's case before Henry himself, and received no encouragement. It was pointed out to them that the garrison and the new citadel were for the common good and that their cost should therefore be shared. Even those whose houses had been demolished to make way for the new works were given little hope of early compensation. They were simply told to 'make application to the form prescribed'. It was 'right agreeable to law and reason that all and singular inhabitants by a common contribution should make recompense'. This was what was normally done in London, and what Tournai itself had done to compensate those whose houses had been burned when the English army was approaching in 1513.[54] The city's plea of poverty was considered to be ill-founded, although it was admitted that its wealth had been reduced by the departure of some of the leading burgesses;[55] but the citizens were prepared to argue indefinitely if they thought that it might save them a few pence.

The king's works gave rise to trouble, both technical and administrative, right from the start. The chosen site was very difficult, especially near the river, where water seeped into the excavations for the foundations and slowed progress. The commissioner was constantly in trouble over his accounts and his relationship with Mountjoy. In a memorandum of March 1516 (in which he says that he has served the king and the king's father for thirty-four years 'without incurring any rebuke', and asks to be relieved of his duties in Tournai) he listed a number of proposals by the governor deemed to be either purposeless or contrary to the wishes of the king;[56] while in December of the same year Mountjoy told Henry that Pawne had been 'guilty of misdemeanours'.[57]

The governor in turn had difficulty over *his* relationships with London. Henry took a close personal interest in the progress of his works, and it seems that many decisions that ideally would have been taken on the spot, in the light of local conditions, had to be referred to him for approval. For example, should the towers be vaulted with brick, stone, or timber, and how many lofts should they have?[58] At least on one occasion Henry accused Mountjoy of departing from the plans he had approved, and elicited an angry reply. Only minor changes had been made; and in any case it had proved impossible to get answers from London on important matters and decisions therefore had to be taken on the spot.[59]

Henry's interest in the fortifications is also illustrated by instructions he sent in 1517 to Sir Richard Jerningham, after he had considered the recommendations made by the Earl of Worcester. He had come to the conclusion that they contained many things 'superfluous and more than needeth', and that he would be landed in enormous expense, not only because of the 'sumptuousness of the works', but because of the consequential need to maintain a large garrison until the more elaborate fortifications were completed, which would take a long time. Henry then went on to indicate which works should be completed as soon as possible, and which should be deferred, and ordered that the citadel should be in a position to take all the artillery by May Day, when he considered that a further 500 men could be discharged. At this point the cavalry in the garrison would be reduced to a mere 100, of which 50 were to be English, and 50 'strangers'. He also set a limit of 2,000 on the number of artificers and labourers to be employed, but when the citadel was completed that number should be reduced to 500 or 600.

An interesting feature of this memorandum (which laid down the height and thickness of the walls, among other things) is a reference to English money, which presumably included the coins produced by the royal mint in Tournai. Henry is aware of 'the crying down of the English money in Flanders (which would inevitably have an effect on its value in Tournai, given the close trading relationship between Tournai and the Low Countries), and the memorandum goes on to say that the king 'trusting in the perfect fidelity of his said deputy [Sir Richard Jerningham] doth remit the ordering of his issuing of English money to his wisdom for the King's most profit and advantage'; and in the meantime he will get in touch with his ambassador in the Low Countries to see what can be done about the position.[60]

The Earl of Worcester also provided suggestions for regulating the conduct of the artificers and labourers engaged in building the fortifications. It was proposed that the governor should make a proclamation in both French and English that soldiers must not 'intermeddle' in the king's works 'nor keep no communication with none artificer nor labourer' working on them. Further, none of the townspeople were to allow the artificers and labourers 'to sit drinking within their houses, nor in none other wise to loiter within them at such times and hours as they should be at their work'. None of the workmen were to play dice, cards, or any other unlawful game, either by day or by night; and finally, no one was to be so hardy as to steal any of the king's tools in the possession of the workmen.[61]

Two 'comptrollers' were appointed to supervise the activities of the commissioner of works – Jean le Sellier, who had represented Tournai in parliament, and Thomas Hart – and according to Pawne they 'misconducted themselves'. On the other hand, there were allegations against Pawne which seem to have been not proven, as he remained in office until the end of the occupation and was given the job of disposing of the surplus stores remaining when the English force finally withdrew. He was, however, a difficult character. He wrote to Wolsey: 'Your grace hath been informed on my behalf that I am fumous, that no man can have no rule with me. I assure your grace that I was never fumous but as I have been always sharp in my prince's causes; and my said fumes hurted never no man so much as myself.'[62]

In spite of all the wrangling and inefficiency the citadel was eventually built, or at least enough of it to provide a residence for the governor and barracks for the troops. On Tuesday, 29 September 1517, Sir Richard Jerningham informed the councils that he intended shortly to order all his troops into the citadel; henceforward it would be up to the civic authorities to provide men for guard duties as they had done in former times. The councils took careful note of the proposal and said that such an important matter must be put before the subsidiary civic bodies – an admirable delaying tactic which had been successfully used in the negotiations before the siege began in 1513.[63] They managed to keep the matter under discussion for the next three months, for in January Wolsey was expressing the hope to Jerningham that not only would the civic authorities resume the function of watching and warding, but that they would employ many discharged English troops for the purpose.[64] The town, however, refused to engage Englishmen, and Jerningham had with Henry's approval to continue to use 200 of his troops for general guard duties in the city;[65] the governor was nevertheless instructed to use every possible argument to get the townspeople to look after their own security.[66] In March 1518 the citadel seems to have been usable, although not finally completed, and Jerningham was able to look seriously at the practical problems which would arise when the troops finally occupied it, which do not seem to have been understood in London. He said to Wolsey:

> . . . it shall be necessary to devise some substantial way for the discharging of the garrison and labourers at the entering of the castle when it is at defence. I write not this for no jeopardy of us that shall be in the castle, but for the danger and spoiling of the town; for if we follow the commandments of the King's letters at that day we must discharge at one time of soldiers and labourers the number of 1,700 or 1,800 which shall be no small danger for the town, without good provision and order may be taken for the same.

He promised to send by the next post his council's 'poor opinions' as to how the problem should be tackled.[67]

At the end of May, however, there was still a good deal of work to be done; for Jerningham, in informing Wolsey of rumours of a possible attack to be led by Richard de la Pole (brother of the Earl of Suffolk, who was executed just before the 1513 expedition left England),[68] said that he was sorry that Wolsey and the Privy Council 'hath not given credence to our oft writings for the advancement of such works as should have been great and most necessary for the surety of this the King's citadel'. If only the governor's advice had been followed there would be no danger now.[69]

Even when the town was handed back to the French nearly a year later the new works were still unfinished; and it was left to the commissioner, William Pawne, to drive the best bargain he could with the French for the materials he had bought, and which had not yet been used. It is impossible to work out anything like an accurate profit-and-loss account in respect of the works at Tournai. Under the treaty the French contracted to pay about £80,000(1) for the still incomplete citadel; but it seems likely that during the four years that building was in progress much greater sums were expended in wages and in the acquisition of materials for the construction of a fortress that Henry's yeomen used for only a few short months.

RESTORATION

The restoration of Tournai to France was being mooted within two years of its capture. Henry saw it as a bargaining counter in his negotiations with the new

French King, Francis I; and Francis for his part urged Wolsey to procure the return of the city. It was not until September 1518, however, that an embassy came from Paris to negotiate a general settlement in which the surrender of Tournai was to be one of the elements. According to Polydore Vergil it was really Wolsey who took the decision to restore the city 'under the pretence of a marriage alliance'. He first persuaded Henry to agree and then had little difficulty in getting the Council to follow suit.[70] The French embassy was more like an invasion than a diplomatic mission, 1,200 strong, 'which was thought to be too many for an ambassade. These gentlemen of France were very fresh.'[72] The leaders, the Lord Admiral, William Bonnivet, and the Bishop of Paris brought in their train: 600 horses, 70 mules and 7 baggage wagons. The Venetian ambassador, Sebastian Giustiniani, in reporting this to the Doge, said that the like had never been seen before.[72] After the triumphal progress from Dover the French delegation were put up in the Tailors' Hall and in the neighbouring merchants' houses.

As soon as the ambassadors were safely out of the way at the peace talks the hangers-on, who included 'a great number of rascals and pedlars and jewellers', opened the parcels of goods they had brought in duty-free – 'hats and caps and divers merchandise' – and offered them for sale in the Tailors' Hall, so that it looked more like a market than the administrative headquarters of one of London's leading livery companies. Many merchants complained about this unfair competition, 'but it availed not'; and it would have comforted the aggrieved traders little to know that this was neither the first nor the last time that diplomatic privilege was to be exploited.[73]

After some bargaining, which was hardly necessary as Henry and Francis had already agreed the general line of settlement, four separate treaties were signed. The two most important were one which provided for the return of Tournai to France, and one which provided for the marriage of Henry's daughter Mary,

The Westminster Tournament Roll showing Henry VIII

then two years old, to the dauphin, who was still a babe in arms. Under the former the French were to pay £120,000, in addition to the £80,000 for the fortifications built during the occupation; and under the latter Mary's dowry was fixed at £66,000. France also agreed to pay any sums that the citizens still owed to England. On Sunday, 2 October, after Mass had been celebrated in St Paul's Cathedral by Cardinal Wolsey, in a ceremony which the French mission told Francis was 'too magnificent for description', Henry and the French delegates swore to abide by the treaties.[74]

In the next few days there followed a round of splendid banquets, starting with a dinner given by the Bishop of London after the service in St Paul's. This was followed later in the day by a supper at Wolsey's residence, more sumptuous, according to Giustiniani, than any given by Cleopatra or Caligula. 'Countless dishes of confections and other delicacies' were served; there was a performance by twenty-four masked dancers, whose leaders turned out to be Henry and his sister Mary, the dowager Queen of France; dice and bowls of money were handed round to the guests, so that all could gamble at no cost to themselves; and finally the tables were cleared from the banqueting hall and there was dancing into the small hours. The festive occasions, which included jousting and elaborately-staged pageants 'of such a sort as are rarely seen in England' and a banquet at which there was no gilt plate, everything being of solid gold, culminated in a 'costly dinner' given at the Goldsmiths' Hall by the Lord Mayor, which the French singled out for special praise.[75]

The arrangements for handing over Tournai, ensuring the orderly disbandment of the garrison, and bringing back the artillery to England were committed to Charles Somerset, Earl of Worcester, the Bishop of Ely, Sir Edward Belknap, and several others, most of whom knew the city well either because they had served in the garrison there or had been present when it capitulated. They had to visit Paris *en route* to tie up some loose ends in the treaties, but were held up for a fortnight in Calais (after what the Bishop of Ely describes as 'the sickest passage that ever I had') while their ships returned to Dover to pick up their horses and baggage. The journey to Paris was slow because of the 'very deep and foul roads', and the commissioners were further held up by a request from Francis that they should delay their arrival until Saturday, 11 December, as he was away on a hunting trip.[76]

They had their first audience with him on the following day, although in fact they suspected that he had been one of a group of masked horsemen who had ridden among them and scrutinized them very closely as they passed through the suburbs. It soon became obvious that Francis was anxious to keep up with Henry in matters of pomp and hospitality, and indeed he later admitted as much to Worcester. He told him that he had heard from his ambassador in London that the English delegates had been sending home glowing reports of French hospitality, and added that Henry 'in honouring and royally entertaining his folk' had set a good example, and all that was being done for Henry's ambassadors in Paris could not countervail half of what Henry had done for *his* ambassadors in England.[77] Francis was in fact entering on the second round of the showmanship and hospitality contest that ended in a dead heat at the Field of the Cloth-of-Gold two years later.

Cardinal Thomas Wolsey

The mission was formally received by the king in the great chamber of the royal palace decorated with blue hangings ornamented with the fleur de lis. He sat on a throne covered with cloth of gold, beneath a canopy of gold brocade, and with a cushion of cloth-of-gold at his feet. His robe was of cloth-of-silver embroidered with a floral design, and lined with Spanish herons' feathers. Over it he wore a doublet of exceptionally rich cloth-of-gold and on his head was 'his usual cloth cap'. The English team were hardly less magnificent, and had ample opportunity to show off their finery as they went through the diplomatic routine before the entire Court, including the ladies, who were seated at one end of the hall, except for the queen and her ladies-in-waiting, who peeped at the ceremony from behind a screen. Shortly afterwards the ambassadors 'in pompous array' and all wearing massive gold chains accompanied the king to Mass in the cathedral of Notre Dame, where he took the oath that Henry had taken in St Paul's two months earlier – that he would loyally observe the articles of the treaty signed in London.[78]

Francis' contribution to the social programme was a banquet in the courtyard of the Bastille, where a floor had been laid and three wooden galleries erected one above the other. Overhead, 80 ft up, an awning of blue canvas (thoroughly waxed to keep the rain out) represented the night sky, and from it hung golden stars that glittered in the 'marvellous blaze of light' from myriads of candles and torches. The members of the two delegations, who were provided with partners, danced to the music of trumpets and fifes until three o'clock in the morning, then ate their way through a nine-course supper in which 'the viands appeared on large dishes emitting fire and flames', each course being announced with a flourish of trumpets. Masques followed, and after 'a collation of confections' served by the ladies of the Court 'by degrees the company dispersed'. On another occasion the Bastille was the scene of a tournament in which Francis took part; and he also arranged stag and boar hunts, which had not featured on the programme in England. It is difficult to decide which country won this round in the international hospitality contest; but perhaps we may award the palm to England, if only because there is no evidence that the members of her mission tried to make something on the side by trading under their diplomatic immunities.[79]

Between the festive occasions, however, the business of state had to be attended to. In particular two impediments to the final ratification of the treaties had to be removed. The quality of the hostages to be handed over by France had been written into the agreement about Tournai – they were to be nobles from good well-to-do families and were to be approved by Henry – but their number was not settled, although it had been discussed round the conference table. In Wolsey's view the matter of the hostages was of critical importance and it had to be satisfactorily settled before there was any question of surrendering the city.

Secondly, the future of the castle and town of Mortagne, which went with Tournai in spite of being several miles distant to the south, was in some doubt. Henry had given them to Antoine de Ligne, Count of Faulconberg, in token of his help on the 1513 campaign, on the understanding that they would be handed back on demand; but de Ligne made it clear that he had every intention of retaining them and their revenues until further notice, whatever Henry and Francis might do about it.

Henry VIII and Francis I meet on the Field of the Cloth-of-Gold

The Field of the Cloth-of-Gold, showing the meeting of Henry VIII and Francis I

The English delegation reported to Wolsey on 18 December that they were having great difficulty in getting the French to name more than four hostages, but they were confident that an acceptable solution would be found.[80] Some weeks later Henry grumbled that only one of the four men nominated had been a member of the French king's Privy Chamber, and that as Francis had no great affection for any of them their value as hostages must be slight.[81] One solution, advocated by the Bishop of Paris, was that instead of hostages 'ye should have banks bound in London for such a great sum as ye would desire'; but the Bishop of Ely refused to entertain this proposition, on the ground that Henry meant 'to have everything according to the treaty and none otherwise'.[82] Eventually, however, Worcester was able to report to the king that after long debating of the matter . . . with divers stormy conversations' the business of the hostages had been satisfactorily completed.[83] It was agreed that the men nominated by Francis should be accepted; and on 22 January they turned up at Calais on their way to England, to the surprise of the governor.[84]

This left only the recalcitrant de Ligne to be dealt with, but as he had a long list of grievances he might well prove to be difficult. In a letter to Wolsey in 1513 he had claimed that he was winning the campaign single-handed. He had been responsible for recapturing the English cannon lost to the French, settled the fight between the English soldiers and their German allies, and played a major part in the battle of the Spurs. One of his men had captured the Duc de Longueville, but never had a penny for him, and so on. He was convinced that, in spite of all this, Henry detested him. He knew 'by the face the King showed him' when he was in his presence that he had no regard for him.[85] There was little room for argument about his rights, however, as he had clearly contracted to restore Mortagne when asked to do so; but perhaps here was a chance to get his own back for all the imagined insults he had suffered at the hands of the English five years ago. Moreover, he had found his tenancy profitable and was naturally reluctant to see it ended.

The fact that he had strengthened the fortifications of the castle may have encouraged him at first to take a firm stand. He let it be known that he would have to be torn by wild horses before he left the place.[86] This caused some consternation among the English delegation and in London, for it seemed conceivable that one frustrated and reckless man might jeopardize all the hard work of the last four months. Henry had sworn to hand Mortagne over to Francis, and if he were compelled to break his oath, not only would it be almost shameful thing but it would give the French king grounds for wriggling out of the treaties if it happened to suit his book.

Some of the English delegation felt that they must try to avoid the humiliation of admitting that they had no control over one of the elements in their package deal with Francis,[87] but the solution of mounting an attack on Mortagne from Tournai had little to commend it. They therefore proposed that France should take the castle and town by force, with England's blessing; and on 14 January Worcester was able to report thankfully to Henry that he had induced Francis 'to take upon himself the recovery of Mortagne at his proper charge and cost and utterly discharge your grace of your oath and promise made in that behalf'. All that Henry was committed to was to summon de Ligne to surrender, to help

Francis with words and letters as a 'friend is bound to do to another', and finally to keep their agreement secret, as knowledge of it might stiffen de Ligne's resistance.[88]

Worcester reached Tournai on 30 January and, no doubt to the great relief of the English commissioners, de Ligne promptly threw his hand in. He must have realized that he had no hope of resisting the combined strength of France and England. He made an effort to save his face by surrendering the castle to Jean de Hesdin, as agent for Margaret of Savoy, pleading that sickness and other reasons prevented him from travelling to England and handing it over to ›Henry personally as he had been asked to do; and he also tried to protect his financial position by proposing that Henry should compensate him for losing the revenues of Mortagne. The English delegation, however, said that they could make no promises, which was hardly surprising in view of de Ligne's intransigence during the preceding weeks. They simply accepted the documents from de Hesdin, and in due course the Bishop of Ely transferred them to Francis' representative. Henry's honour was safe, at least in so far as the treaty provisions about Mortagne had put it at risk.[89]

The main job of the English commissioners was, of course, to hand over the town, but there were other things to be done. The fortifications built during the occupation had already been sold to the French, but the quantities of stone, timber and other building materials had to be disposed of. The governor, Sir Richard Jerningham, thought that the stone would fetch very little, as it was 'hewn at a scantling', being intended for the further extension of the castle. It seemed probable that the French authorities would try to get it for a song, knowing that it was of little use to a private buyer because it had already been cut to a particular shape. On the other hand there would be no difficulty in realizing a good price on the timber. It was decided that William Pawne, who had been in charge of the work on the fortifications, should remain behind after the garrison had left to negotiate the best prices he could.[90]

The treaty allowed Henry to remove the artillery he had installed in Tournai and also the stocks of gunpowder and cannon-balls, not an easy task in the middle of winter when even an unencumbered rider found the roads difficult. Indeed, it was considered quite impracticable to send the guns overland at that season, but as the Scheldt flowed conveniently through the middle of the city water transport provided a simple alternative, provided that satisfactory safe conducts could be obtained. There was some difficulty about this, but eventually the necessary authority was received by William Knight, the English ambassador at Brussels, and the convoy set off down the Scheldt some hours before dawn on Thursday, 8 February.[90]

The final task, apart from the formal surrender of the town, was the orderly removal of the garrison. It was feared that rogues and vagabonds might take advantage of the vacuum created between the withdrawal of the English troops and the arrival of the French to pillage the town; and Jerningham had therefore ordered that all known idle persons should be ejected some weeks before the hand-over was due. It was also feared that there might be trouble with the troops themselves. Most of them had been with the garrison for four or five years, and many who now had wives and children 'proposing to have ended their days in the

King's service' in Tournai were, to say the least of it, unenthusiastic about this upheaval in their way of life. It had been originally proposed that they should be given a month's wages over and above their due. Jerningham pointed out, however, that it had been the practice to give men who left the garrison of their own free will a month's extra pay to get them back to England, and that it therefore seemed rather mean to give no more than this to men 'discharged against their wills', many of whom were married and who would find it a costly business to get their wives, children and household effects across the Channel. This was reinforced by Worcester, who said that many of the soldiers were so heavily in debt that unless they were generously treated there might be trouble when they left. It was proposed that free passages should be provided to Dover or Sandwich, and also that the Council should consider giving the discharged men protection from actions to recover debts for a year after their return. All in all, a good deal of thought went into the arrangements for disbanding the garrison, and it seems that they worked well. Less satisfactory were the arrangements for receiving the troops in England and resettling them. Hall tells us that many of the garrison were reluctant to leave Tournai (and indeed a handful did remain behind). 'Then began the captains and the soldiers to mourn knowing that the town should be yielded to the French King and many a young gentleman and many a tall yeoman wished that they had not spent their time there.'[91] When they got back to England many of the yeomen found that they could not settle down to civilian life again, and turned instead to a life of crime. Of the soldiers who had married in Tournai only four decided to remain there with their families.[92]

The commissioners' final act – the formal handing over of the town – produced a blazing row with their French opposite numbers, which effectively dissipated all the good will engendered by the wining, dining, and hunting they had enjoyed in Paris, and provided a splendid climax to the five years of occupation. Gaspard de Coligny, the representative of the French king, who had taken part in the festivities in the capital, arrived on 8 February (the day the English artillery left) with 1,200 cavalry and 500 infantry to take possession of the town. Sir Edward Belknap met him outside the wall to collect the money which Francis had contracted to pay under the treaty, but de Coligny refused to hand it over until some of his men were inside Tournai. Belknap then demanded to see his commission to receive the town, so that he might take it to the Earl of Worcester, but de Coligny refused to part with it, although he allowed Belknap to read it.

The Englishman, warming to his task, said that he must have the commission, as the King of England would certainly want to see it. Further, he must have a certificate to the effect that Tournai was being handed over as a gift, and not taken as a conquest. 'Otherwise,' he added firmly, 'be you sure that the city shall not be delivered.' De Coligny was furious at this rebuff, and for four days there was an acrimonious exchange of correspondence with the English commissioners, who steadfastly refused to allow the French troops to enter the town until the king's commission was safely in their possession. De Coligny was equally adamant that he would not part with it, and so the deadlock remained until the day originally agreed for the departure of the English troops arrived.

Then de Coligny 'caused his trumpets to be blown and displayed his own banners and the Duke of Vendôme's', and set his troops and artillery in battle array. The Bishop of Ely was sent to protest, and told him that he was behaving more like a conqueror than one who was taking over a town by treaty: to which de Coligny, angrier than ever, said that he knew how to enter a town better than the bishop. This development was reported to Worcester, who immediately sent Clarenceux herald to inform the marshal that there could be no question of his entering the town in warlike array.

This finally brought the Frenchman down to earth. He saw that there was nothing for it but to hand over his commission and to furnish the certificate that the city was accepted as a gift; and, no doubt with the worst possible grace, he did so. But the row was not yet over. The Englishmen still had a card up their sleeve.

De Coligny led his men towards the city with banners displayed, which promptly brought the Bishop of Ely back into the fray. He pointed out that as Tournai had not been 'yielded or gotten' it was quite out of order to enter it with banners unfurled. This was the last straw for the unfortunate Frenchman, but Worcester and his colleagues, no doubt enjoying their mastery of the situation, could not be moved. The French troops 'had no remedy but to roll up their standards and banners'. They were kept waiting at the gates of the city while the commission and the certificate that the town was a gift were read out for all to hear. Then, and only then, were they allowed to enter, with drums beating – the sole demonstration allowed by protocol as interpreted by the English commissioners; and, to keep the record quite straight, Worcester made a point of riding abreast of de Coligny as he passed through the gates. The squabble was over. Tournai was French again.[93]

NOTE

(1) 400,000 crowns.

CONCLUSION

The 1513 campaign ended with the capture of Tournai. No new objective suggested itself, and even the king was beginning to be shaken by the mounting costs of the expedition. In any case, the campaigning season was virtually over and there was little point in keeping the army in France. Henry told the Pope, however, that he intended to return with another powerful army; and he modestly attributed his victories to God, who had given him the strength of a Saul or a David.[1] Rapin-Thoyras wrote that he returned home after 'a glorious campaign', but quickly added 'I call it glorious if one looks only at his military success'. Henry had been the dupe of the Pope, the Emperor and Ferdinand of Aragon, who had loaded the whole burden of the war on him. The only tangible benefits went to the emperor, when Thérouanne was put out of action and Tournai was occupied by a friendly power; and to Wolsey, who won the bishopric of Tournai.[2]

John Taylor and Brian Tuke provide contemporary assessments of the expedition. The former was mainly impressed by the way the emperor played second fiddle to Henry throughout the campaign, by the fine weather the army enjoyed on the march, and by the great storms at night 'when the camp stood still'.[3] Tuke echoes Taylor's comments on the weather and adds that in spite of the different nationalities composing it the army was free of dissension – which was certainly not true. Further, he reckons that a force of that size was lucky to escape a serious epidemic, and observes that provisions were so plentiful that the men lived more cheaply abroad in time of war than they did in peace at home. They gained 'victories hitherto unparalleled, being always against many', a proof of divine assistance.[4]

In fact, the most that can be said about the campaign is that Henry achieved his personal objective. He had captured two important French towns, destroying one and occupying the other. He had won the Battle of the Spurs and taken prisoner some of the leading noblemen and captains of France. Honour was satisfied – at a staggering price.

It was not only the costs of the army that had to be brought into the account, although they were heavy enough – the Venetian Lorenzo Pasqualigo told his brothers that the sums spent on 'artillery and other camp furniture' alone would fill a well of gold.[5] Henry's expenditure on himself and the members of the royal household who accompanied him was lavish and it seems that he wanted to impress Europe with his wealth as much as with his military prowess. Antonio Bavarino reported to his business colleagues in Venice that the king took with him fourteen wagons laden with gold and four with silver coin – 'facts which sound like tales of romance but are nevertheless true'.[6] On one occasion Henry and the emperor talked at dinner about jewellery and the king showed off some fine pieces brought from the Jewel House. He offered the emperor one in the form of an eagle studded with diamonds and a single great pearl. 'The Emperor acted like a good physician, who will not take money from a sick friend, but at last he allowed himself to be persuaded.'[7] On his two visits to Lille Henry gave 'money by way of reward' to Margaret's household servants amounting to nearly £1,000;[8] and the day before he sailed home from Calais he bestowed rewards on his allies and his own subjects who had served him well on the campaign totalling just under £3,000.[9] Even his personal wardrobe cost a fortune. He took several wagon-loads of clothes with him and also made supplementary purchases of large quantities of materials *en route*, including cloth of gold at between £2 and £3 an ell, and velvet 'gowns' trimmed with ermine, which cost anything up to £17 a skin.[10] These were all paid for from army funds and not by the office of the wardrobe. Some idea of their real cost may be gathered from the facts that the standard 'coat money' allowance for a private was a mere 2s., and *his* coat had to last him for the whole campaign; and that the sum paid for one good-quality fur skin would have kept a soldier in wages for nearly two years.

If the invasion had had political or commercial benefit as its primary objective, rather than the blooding of Henry, and if the campaign had been planned sensibly, the army would have tried to capture Boulogne; and at first they did make for this town. It is difficult to see why Thérouanne was substituted, but, as has been suggested above,[11] it was probably the result of pressure from Maximilian. If Henry was simply flexing the muscles of virile youth, it mattered little where the display took place.

The political consequences of the expedition were little short of disastrous for England, even if it is reckoned a success in purely military terms. The main result was to saddle her with a troublesome outpost, absorbing scarce financial and administrative resources that would have been much better devoted to Calais. A strong Calais had many advantages – naval, commercial and political – none of which was provided by the distant unhappy island of Tournai; and had England's five years of painful effort there been devoted instead to the Channel port, it might not have fallen to the French fifty years later.

*　*　*

It cannot even be argued that the 1513 campaign helped the development of the English forces. So long as there was no standing army and no war department the lessons learned in one campaign were likely to be forgotten long before the next; but none of the Tudors would tolerate a permanent force. The feudal military system had left too much power with the barons, and was therefore dangerous; but a standing army (also controlled by the nobility, as it was inconceivable that anyone else could have commanded it at this stage in the development of the society) would have been more efficient than the feudal array, and therefore an even greater potential threat to the Crown.

There were, of course, some 'regular' troops that made up a permanent military establishment, but they were not a standing army in the accepted sense. They included the yeomen of the guard, the 'King's Spears', and garrison troops in strong points throughout the country. The yeomen bodyguard had been created by Henry VII, and consisted of a handful of stalwarts selected 'for the safeguard and preservation of his own body'.[12] The seed showed signs of germinating when his son increased the corps to 600 for the invasion of France in 1513, but thereafter the establishment was reduced as an economy measure. The yeomen continued on military duties – for example as garrison troops, and even as naval officers[13] – but their primary function was to act as a royal guard. They were still a semi-military body in 1669, when the Privy Council fixed their establishment at 100, plus officers, but after 1760 they ceased to have any military function.[14]

Secondly, from 1510 to 1515 there were the 'King's Spears', men of noble blood who were established as a well-born bodyguard. There were 50 of them, each with three supporters – an archer, a light cavalryman, and a mounted attendant – making a total force of 200. A similar body, the 'gentlemen pensioners', was set up in 1539, and survives as the Corps of Gentlemen-at-Arms.[15] Their purpose was also to protect the person of the sovereign, and they complemented the yeomen. The latter were an 'other ranks' bodyguard, but the 'spears' were officers and gentlemen.

The garrison troops throughout the country were much nearer to being a standing army. Berwick, Dover and Calais had the biggest establishments (if Tournai is left on one side as being a special case), but there were over a hundred castles and fortresses, each with a handful of soldiers and gunners. The total strength of this scattered force must have been between 2,000 and 3,000 men, but they could not be safely used as the nucleus of a foreign expedition or of a force to suppress rebellion at home. It was just when the country faced an emergency that these troops were most needed at their posts. They did, however, provide at least a slender thread of continuity in military affairs.

England's progress towards a permanent professional army may have been hindered by accidents of genetics. For nearly sixty years the sovereign was disqualified from acting as commander-in-chief in the field, first by age, in the case of Edward VI, and then by sex, in the case of Mary Tudor and Elizabeth I (the presence of the last with her forces at Tilbury in 1588 hardly weakens this point). During these sixty years the monarch had no personal professional interest in developing a standing army; but there were other reasons for relying on the traditional forms of military obligation. It was cheaper to assemble men when they were needed and to disband them when their job was done. It took time to recruit an army, but if an overseas expedition was contemplated it could be planned at leisure in the winter. A defensive war against the Scots or the suppression of rebellion at home needed quicker action, but in practice the existing arrangements proved adequate, although once or twice it was touch and go. Henry VII was nearly caught out in 1486, when he just managed to nip Lovell's rebellion in the bud by throwing in his own retinue, including the yeomen of the guard, wearing home-made leather uniform.[16]

There were, of course, strong arguments against living from hand to mouth in military affairs, as the Tudors did. A contemporary Spanish memorandum claims that a force formed at short notice will be expensive, because the scarcity of men of 'warlike habits' has to be compensated for by recruiting greater total numbers;[17] but this is less valid if a country is engaged in war only at long intervals. Of the 118 years of the Tudor dynasty, perhaps 77 were reckoned 'peaceful', so that for nearly two-thirds of the period a standing army would have been thought an unnecessary expense; and even in the war years the army would often have eaten its head off in the winter months when campaigning was suspended – although it is arguable that the mere existence of a permanent force would have minimized rebellion and deterred foreign aggression.

Henry VIII backed the navy, and he was right on strategic, economic and technical grounds. Nature dictated that ships must provide the first line of England's defences, except on the northern border. So long as the navy kept enemy troops off her beaches, the citizen army would never have to face the supreme test. The fate of an English force invading the Continent was unimportant. It was physically impossible to carry more than a fraction of the potential military strength of the country overseas, so that even if a force were completely wiped out its loss would have little effect on the country's defences – although the loss of its trained leaders would certainly be serious.

Military opinion, however, was beginning very gently to question the wisdom of rejecting the idea of a standing army; and on at least two occasions in the first half of the sixteenth century the government did consider the establishment of a permanent force. The first of these was in 1518 when the king wrote to a number of 'able captains', including Sir Henry Willoughby, saying that although the country was now at peace it was nevertheless sound policy 'to provide and foresee remedies against war when the same shall fortune'.[18] It was therefore proposed to appoint a number of men experienced in the wars to retain companies of soldiers, and to put them 'in a readiness conveniently horsed and harnessed, to do unto us service as well within this our realm as elsewhere at our wages whensoever and as often as we shall require and command them so to do without danger or penalty of any statutes or ordinances heretofore made against retainers'. The king's letter commands Willoughby to say how many men he can retain under these arrangements, whereupon he will be licensed to engage them.

The only other document that throws light on this system of licensed retainers is a draft of the certificate which was to be issued to the chosen captains.[19] This starts in much the same way as the letter quoted above. In spite of the fact that the country is at peace (thanks to 'our great study, labour, costs and policy') both at home and abroad, it is nevertheless prudent to provide for a possible future emergency, particularly because of the mutual-assistance pact which has just been entered into with 'other right mighty princes', and the need in such an emergency to send 'a crew' at short notice to reinforce the garrison of Calais, 'after the old manner in time of need'. The chosen captains are authorized to retain a specified number of men, whose names are to be submitted to the central authority, and whom they will personally lead to the wars when the king so commands. The men are to have a suit of almain armour, a jacket of the royal colours (green and white), the king's badge and the badge of the man retaining them, and to be ready to serve at reasonable notice. They are to be mustered at least 'once or twice' a year, but are to be provided with horses only when they are called to the colours; and it is only then that they will enter into the king's wages. If the licensee engages a greater number of retainers than the licence stipulates he is at the mercy of statutes against retainers, but only in respect of the excess number. It is impossible to say how extensive the scheme was intended to be, but there is no evidence that it came to anything.

The second important government initiative was in 1551, when the Privy Council discussed at length 'whether it were convenient the King's majesty should have a number of men-of-arms in ordinary, as well for the surety of his majesty's person as for the stay of the unquiet subjects and for other services in all events', and finally agreed to adopt the proposal. A number of men were appointed to command companies of cavalry from among their own dependants and were paid substantial imprests for this purpose.[20] It has been suggested that this force was no more than 'a thinly-veiled device for subsidizing the principal members of the Council',[21] and it is true that all the captains appointed were members of the Council. Another authority sees it as an army created by the Duke of Northumberland 'to enforce his revolutionary policies, to dominate his rivals, and to crush the rebellious peasantry'.[22] It was, however, disbanded, as an economy measure, less than two years after it had been set up.[23]

Thus on neither of the occasions when the government made a serious move towards a standing army did they get very far. Both schemes had the disadvantage that they relied on armed retainers, while the second also involved substantial payments to the chosen men in time of peace. (The merit of the 1518 scheme was that, although it encouraged the maintenance of large numbers of retainers, the danger of which was recognized in the statutes against this practice, it would have been a charge on the government only when the force was required for service.)

In spite of the Crown's refusal to introduce a permanent force, private individuals still ventured to put forward their own proposals. One is in the form of a draft Act of Parliament prepared about 1537,[24] and although it does not reflect official thinking[25] it is interesting on two counts. It confirms that there were some who wanted a standing army and sets down how it might be run. The king was to appoint the commander, who was responsible for all other appointments. The force was to have both cavalry and infantry in companies of 100, headed by a captain and petty-captain; and groups of ten companies were to be under 'grand captains' – forerunners of the regiment and the colonel. It was to be stationed throughout the country, but its administrative headquarters were to be at Coventry, partly because it was in the middle of England, and partly to put some life into the depressed economy of the town. Pay was to come from the revenues of the remaining monasteries, the larger of which were to be used as old soldier's homes.

An even more ambitious scheme to re-organize the militia, and perhaps to make some progress towards a standing army, came in Edward VI's reign. A group of gentlemen, including Sir Thomas Wyatt the younger and Leonard Digges the mathematician (who took a scientific interest in military affairs), formed themselves into a working party to study military reform. Their proposals form a substantial document,[26] and make a good case on technical grounds for introducing a greater element of permanency into the forces. Special attention was to be paid to the quality of the recruits. The commissioners of array were to muster only those who were personable and active and showed themselves eager to serve their prince – a qualification which would have ruled out nearly the entire male population towards the end of Elizabeth I's reign. They were to reject men with young families, or with land worth more than 20s. a year. After a few weeks of the travail and peril of army life these people became painfully aware of the difference between sleeping under a hedge in all weathers and in a bed with their wives at home. Such hollow men as wished themselves back in their smoky houses encouraged better types to follow their example. Therefore, leave them out. It is not clear how permanent the rank and file were intended to be, but at least it seems that the selected men were to train together more regularly than the ordinary militia. The captain's post was to be filled annually by a succession of eligible men, so that there would be a pool of experienced officers available in each country.

The memorandum throws light on the fears held by some that a standing army might be politically dangerous, and tries to prove them groundless. There are those who consider that to put weapons into the hands of all men must be tempting Providence – if you put fire and tow together, you will, peradventure, fire the whole house; but strife can develop between two factions just as easily if they are unarmed as if they are armed. Varying conclusions can be drawn from this section of the report. The working party may have taken the view (as Thomas Audley did) that the Statute of Winchester was now a dead letter, and that people no longer possessed arms on the scale required – else why worry about the dangers of arming the nation? Or they may have had in mind the new weapons of fire, which raised new problems of control. Or they may simply have regarded 'arming' the nation as the setting up of a permanent force, the loyalty of which might become divided on religious grounds.

There was much good sense in their conclusions, but their report, like many another, was firmly pigeon-holed. It had been intended to put the document to the Privy Council and then to the sovereign, from whom 'the whole business should receive life and motion'. The new army was to be managed by a permanent council of war on which would sit some of the king's 'most grave, sober, skilled, and best experienced subjects both for matters military and for knowledge and observation of the course in like cases in other governments' – in effect, a separate department of state was to be set up. There was a good deal of support for the scheme, but it was not proceeded with, 'either for the newness of the thing, or that it was not at that season thought convenient to have the subjects armed whereof the greater number were evil-affected to the religion they professed', or simply because there was a majority in the Privy Council who did not like it. So the King's Militia, or Ordinance of Soldiers, never got beyond the paper stage.

At least in the eyes of Sir Thomas More the French precedent for a standing army was not encouraging. He suggests that it is bad enough to have to put up with discarded retainers who have taken to thieving for a living; but how much worse it is in France, where the whole realm is full of hired soldiers in time of peace – if indeed you can call it peace. The French have ever to be looking for war so that their professional soldiers can be kept at the peak of efficiency; and they have found by bitter experience how pernicious and pestilent a thing it is to maintain such beasts, who are not much use as soldiers in any case. They have seldom succeeded in getting the upper hand even of untrained levies.[27]

These thoughts are repeated in a paper in the Lansdowne manuscripts which summarizes the dangers to a kingdom 'that maintaineth soldiers that use war for an art'. The author examines the objections to both a state-financed army and one run by private enterprise. In time of war the latter would have to resort to 'rapine, murder, and theft' on a grand scale in order to provide for themselves in time of peace; and in peace they might have to fend for themselves by violent means. Think, for example, of the plight of the vintners of England if the importation of wines from the Continent were banned by government decree, and the measures they might be driven to in their dire extremity. Soldiers brought up in the wars, with no other trade to live by, must fall into like extremity in time of peace, with disastrous consequences for the realm. Even as there can be no fellowship or agreement between light and darkness, even so there can be no consenting or union between peace and war. Having thus disposed of the improbable case where a government tolerated a 'free-enterprise' army, the author enumerates the objections to a state-financed permanent army. If the king maintains garrisons on the scale needed to meet any possible attack by his enemies the financial burden will be crippling. It will have to be borne either by the king, 'a thing very inconvenient', or by the citizens, who will find it 'displeasing to their condition and most intolerable'; and in any case the advantages of a permanent force will in no wise 'countervail the mischiefs that thereby might grow'.[28]

* * *

In the absence of a standing army Henry had to rely on the two existing military obligations, and on the hiring of mercenaries on the Continent – 'Almains' and 'Burgundians'. By the end of the fifteenth century the classical feudal obligation had already been replaced by the use of contracts under which the nobility agreed to provide so many soldiers for a given period in return for payment – a change which helped the Crown in that it now paid the piper and was therefore in a better position to call the tune. The other obligation – to serve with the county militia, the 'fyrd', which existed as early as the seventh century – was overshadowed by the feudal obligation introduced by William from the Continent, but it was kept going and became potentially more important as society developed. The growth of the economy and the expansion of the middle class increased the proportion of men in the community liable for militia service and moderated the influence of the barons in military affairs. The fyrd, however, also had its limitations. It was primarily intended to defend the county against invasion and it was statutorily exempt from serving outside the county boundary, although in practice this exemption was usually ignored.

It has been suggested by Dr J.J. Goring that although the two different obligations were clearly understood by contemporary observers some recent historians have confused them, with the result that they have dated the Elizabethan practice (in which recruitment by commissioners predominated) back to the beginning of the century.[29] That there were two distinct systems in use is demonstrated by the fact that there could be conflict between them. When the commissioners of array in Hertfordshire tried to recruit the tenants of Sir

John Mordant, whom he had been instructed to levy himself, it was ruled that the tenants should serve under Mordant and not with the militia.[30] Part of the confusion about the two sorts of obligation may have arisen from the fact that 'commissioners' were involved in both, although with a different function. The commissioners of array selected recruits for the county forces, whereas the commissioners concerned with the 'feudal' levy were simply muster-masters appointed to ensure that the troops brought into the field by a magnate conformed with his agreement with the Crown.

For his overseas expeditions Henry VII made contracts with certain of his subjects to supply soldiers to serve in all such 'places, rooms, commissions, and feats of war' as it might please him to command. They ran for a year and specified how many of each type of soldier were to be supplied – good and able persons, armed and equipped in all respects according to the custom of war.[31] When dealing with rebels at home Henry drew on the militia, which was constitutionally correct; but he also made some use of the retinues of lords and gentlemen for this purpose. Further, he used armed retainers for garrison duty. Lord Darcy, the governor of Berwick, was instructed to put 1000 of his retainers in the garrison, and was given a licence exempting him and the men from the provisions of the laws against retainers.[32] The militia, however, played a negligible part in his overseas campaigns. Even if he had contemplated relying solely on the county forces:

> ... privately raised contingents, dangerous though their existence may have been, were too valuable to be dispensed with ... The machinery of the militia, especially if the handling of it were left to the sheriffs [as it was when there was no time to issue commissions of array], was clumsy and inefficient, and a better force could be assembled in a shorter time by ordering the leading magnates to levy their dependants.[33]

The instruments on which Henry VIII had to rely for his military operations – the county militia, and the force created out of the remnant of the feudal obligation – were thus quite distinct in their constitutional basis and in the nature of the performance that could be legally required of them in the field. In the early years of his reign Henry did make contracts for the supply of men, but they were rather different from those of his father. One that survives is an agreement with Sir Henry Willoughby to supply 830 men for the Guienne expedition in 1512,[34] but this is really more concerned with appointing him as master of the ordnance than with the provision of men, which is left to the end of the document: 'And the said Sir Henry covenanteth and promiseth to have in his retinue for the doing of the said service of war 830 able men defensibly arrayed for the war, himself accounted for one of the said number.' The main purpose of the indenture is to ensure that Willoughby is 'retained towards our said sovereign lord to be the master of the ordnance and artillery which his highness sendeth at this time with the said army ... and the said Sir Henry promiseth, covenanteth, and agreeth to the best of his wit and power to cause the said ordnance and artillery safely and surely to be kept', and so on. There is little resemblance between this indenture and the contracts entered into by Henry VII and his subjects twenty years earlier, and Henry VIII's usual practice was simply to send instructions to a magnate of his choice in a letter, the terms of which would in practice be followed no less closely than those of a formal indenture. By far the greater part of the troops for the 1513 expedition was found in this way.

By the beginning of the sixteenth century, however, the practical difference between the two sorts of troops did not go beyond the matter of obligation to give military service. Once a man had accepted this obligation (or had it thrust upon him), once he had taken the soldier's oath, he became a unit in a single force, loyal to a single commander-in-chief. The two separate obligations in earlier centuries had created two physically separate armies, which might even find themselves fighting each other; but by the time of the first Tudors there was virtually no distinction between them in the field. It is true, of course, that in some respects the different origins of the rank and file may have affected the handling of the army they composed. Orders to men recruited as 'feudal' retainers would go down through their overlord, whereas the same orders would be transmitted to the militia through their captains. Again, for part of the lifetime of the army – when it was on the march, for example, or in camp – groups of men would tend to segregate themselves according to their origin. The county levies would stick together and the retinue of a baron would regard themselves as a group with a strong element of loyalty towards their overlord. That there were two types of recruit was recognized in the Act 'against such captains as abridge their soldiers of their pay'[35] which was passed as part of the preparatory work for the 1513 expedition. It provides that wages must be paid to the individual soldier within six days 'after the said captain, petty-captain, or other shall have received their wages of the king or of the treasurer of his wars or of their lords or masters'. That is to say, bulk pay was issued direct to the captain in the case of the militia, and through the overlord in the case of the retinues.

Warfare, however, was now less of a chivalrous game in which a magnate could deploy his own retinue as the spirit moved him, and more of a scientific exercise in which all units were manipulated according to an agreed plan of campaign. The peculiar requirements of honour were beginning to fade, blurring the distinction between the retinues with their chivalric origin, and the militiamen with their more humdrum background. A billman was a billman whether he was recruited as part of a magnate's retinue or as an able-bodied man selected by the commissioners of array in a county levy; and all billmen might find themselves fighting shoulder to shoulder, whatever the nature of their obligation to fight. The sum total of the rank and file – militiamen and 'feudal' retainers – found themselves coalescing in a great melting-pot. All were citizens of England, soldiers of the king, and all had to do his bidding.

*   *   *

Although 'honour' no longer played a significant part in warfare it did make an appearance from time to time. The formal flourishes which were customary before a siege began and the honourable behaviour expected from prisoners of war have already been mentioned,[36] but there were other examples. After the capitulation of Thérouanne one report had it that it was the law of arms that kept the English army in the vicinity of the captured fortress. The king had removed to Enguingate, 'where he yet remains, according to the law of arms, for in case any man would bid battle for the besieging and getting of any city or town, then the winner to give battle, and to abide for the same certain days'.[37] In other words, the French army must be given a chance to win back the fortress, simply because it was dishonourable to win a town and then run away.

In 1543 an expedition set out from the pale of Calais to harry the countryside and found itself beneath the walls of Thérouanne, which had been rebuilt within two or three years of their destruction in 1513. Sir John Wallop, who was in command of the marauding force, sent a letter to the captain of the garrison 'requiring him that six men of arms, being gentlemen, might run with six gentlemen of our army for life and death', to which it was replied that next morning six French knights would accept the challenge, accompanied by ten armed men – no doubt to ensure fair play. The teams 'ran with one another two courses and brake their staves valiantly'. One of the Englishmen was wounded, but 'he brake two spears on him that hurt him in the head to the death'.[38]

There was another example in the following year when the Privy Council were considering how the army that had captured Boulogne should be withdrawn. The council of war expressed the opinion that the most honourable way to retire was via St Omer, for if that route were chosen the enemy would not be able to say 'that we durst not go near them'. On this occasion, however, honour may have been a secondary consideration, although it was the first point mentioned by the council of war. They pointed out that if the army went by the proposed route it would avoid using up badly needed forage in the neighbourhood of Boulogne, Calais, and Guines, and it would also minimize the risk of infecting the last two places with the plague which had been raging at Boulogne.[39]

There were isolated examples of this sort of thing during the whole of the century, but they were of no great importance. Victory by fair means or foul was becoming the order of the day. Science and cunning were taking the place of nobility and the lance dedicated to 'truth and honour, freedom and courtesy'.

* * *

It has already been suggested that the absence of a standing army meant that the lessons of a single perhaps isolated campaign were not necessarily carried into the planning of the next. It would have been difficult enough to provide for the orderly development of military administration, organization and supply, even had the sovereign and Privy Council been prepared to devise and implement a long-term plan, for the rest of Europe was undergoing a change in 'the art of war' and England's geographical isolation would have made it difficult to keep even a regular force abreast of developments. As it was, there was no real attempt on the part of the government to plan, and every time a new army was assembled many of the lessons had to be learned all over again.

Nevertheless, there were changes throughout the Tudor period, although they may have been slower than elsewhere in Europe. In the matter of obligation to serve, which has just been discussed, it is possible to observe a steady progress (a 'natural' progress in the sense that it was not consciously planned) from

Henry VII's detailed contracts with the barons to supply retainers, through the reign of Henry VIII, when the nobility still provided the bulk of the forces on the strength of letters from the king, although the militia gradually played a bigger part, to the middle years of the century, when the militia began to come into their own. Shortly after the accession of Elizabeth I the process of change accelerated. The nobility were still called upon – for example, when the Earl of Leicester took a force to the Low Countries in 1585 it contained a large number of his followers – but from this time onwards the counties found men in their thousands for the foreign expeditions, in spite of the statutory exemption from foreign service which they were supposed to enjoy, and in spite of some ill-advised protests by private individuals about sending the militia abroad. When England was committed to war in Ireland, France, the Low Countries and even the mainland of Spain towards the end of the century (necessary war which makes Henry's jaunt of 1513 seem even more pointless), war weariness set in among the people and the net had to be spread wider, whatever the constitutional position might be. All sections of the community were required to make their contribution – the towns and the shires; the faithful clergy as a token of their loyalty, and the recusants (men who did not recognize the Established Church), in cash, as a punishment for their disloyalty; the lawyers, who could well afford to provide light cavalry, and the lawless who were transferred from the cells to the ranks; tall yeomen, whose loss was a blow, and sturdy rogues and vagabonds, who were a good riddance. The dominating force in the army had moved from one end of the social scale to the other.

*   *   *

The Tudor century also saw a fundamental change in the organization of the English army. At the beginning it was still organized in great 'battles', amorphous groups difficult to control and manoeuvre. The organizational pyramid must have been relatively flat, with a correspondingly short chain of command, and it is difficult to see clearly how orders were transmitted. The decisions of the council of war in the field must have been passed on to a relatively small number of 'captains', who were then faced, possibly in the heat of battle, with transmitting them to a very large number of men, which cannot have been easy. In the absence of an efficient chain of command it was left to the senior officers to do the best they could with their men, once the general plan had been settled, with the risk of taking decisions that might conflict with those taken by their colleagues elsewhere.

That companies should have 100 men under 'centeniers' seems to have been accepted in the middle of the fifteenth century, and possibly earlier, no doubt following the Roman precedent; but in practice in the fifty years before 1513 the 'captain' might be anything from a great magnate with hundreds of retainers to a man selected by a borough to lead their contribution of perhaps 100 citizens or fewer, or a gentleman with a mere handful of followers. The term 'lieutenant' meant the king's deputy and not the second-in-command of a company, who was still the petty-captain; and the vinteners, later to be called corporals, had not yet begun to play a significant part in the organization of the company.

The position at the end of the century was very different. The haphazard agglomerations of archers, billmen and men-at-arms, the proportions of which depended largely on chance, were replaced with smaller, better-balanced, armies. Men – who were now pikemen, hand-gunners and light cavalry – were recruited as far as possible in the proportions required by current theory. They were divided into small readily deployed companies, headed by a captain and a lieutenant supported by a company sergeant and corporals, who constituted an efficient chain of command linked with the council of war through a colonel commanding a regiment of perhaps ten companies.

* * *

Pay, which was the root cause of most of the troubles in the later sixteenth-century army, presented no problems in 1513. There were two main reasons. In the first place, Henry's treasure-wagons were filled to overflowing; and in the second place, the method of pay was on the whole satisfactory, having regard to the way in which the army was made up. It dated from the time of Henry VII, who laid down in his contracts with the nobility in 1492 that they should receive conduct money for their retinues at the rate of 6d. for every twenty miles they had travelled from their homes, which, together with a month's wages in advance, was to be paid to the magnate for issue to his men as soon as they were safely on board ship. The fact that the men were to be paid in advance meant that they were able right from the start of the expedition to provide themselves with victuals, which were, of course, a charge on their pay; and the fact that the overlord was their immediate paymaster meant that there was a good chance that justice would be done to the individual soldier. The magnate was by definition a man of substance and did not have the militia captain's incentive to cheat his men out of their wages. On the contrary, the service of the men under him in the army was merely an extension of their peace-time relationship, which was very different from the relationship between a greedy captain and a company of militiamen with whom he had no previous connection, and who had no connection with each other, except that they came from the same county. ('Retinue' could mean simply 'company', especially as the sixteenth century wore on, but in the fifteenth and early sixteenth centuries it meant as a rule a band of 'retainers' in the technical sense, men who did owe loyalty to the magnate.)

The normal relationship between the magnate and his retainers was tightened by his contract with the king. It made him responsible for issuing pay to the men within six days of his receiving it; it put him under an obligation to ensure that they were thoroughly familiar with the disciplinary code (of which he was given his own copy); and it made him responsible for their conduct, and for bringing to justice any who offended. As lack of pay was the commonest cause of indiscipline, it was unlikely that he would dare to break his bargain with the king and thereby encourage his men to break the regulations, when he had sworn to guarantee their good behaviour.

In spite of the fact that there were strong incentives to behave honestly, malpractices were not unknown. Parliament passed an Act[40] on the eve of the

Henry VIII (Ekt. Pr. 231).

1513 expedition referring to the 'inordinate coveteousness' of captains who failed to carry out their bargains with princes, and did not have the agreed number of men in their retinues; but this was a word-for-word repetition of a clause in an Act of Henry VII,[41] and was perhaps intended to be no more than a safeguarding of the Crown's position. The relevant clause in the same sort of legislation in the reign of Edward VI seems to be inspired much more by actual cases of malpractice.[42]

Given that the issue of pay could be exploited by some unscrupulous magnates, notwithstanding the ties with the Crown and with their men referred to above, how much more dangerous was the position when magnates and retainers were replaced by captains and the county militia, and the bonds between the leader and the king and the leader and his men no longer existed! Had it been the policy of the Privy Council to plan the re-organization of the army they might have been prescient enough to see the trouble that the continuance of the old system would bring; but in the absence of any plan to put the army on a new footing the system of retainers changed unobtrusively to a militia system. By the time the evils of the method of pay had manifested themselves it was too late to do anything about it. The captains had the companies firmly in their grasp, and nothing could stop them from bleeding them dry.

It might have been possible to save the day in Mary Tudor's Militia Act of 1558, which in the words of one authority caused 'an upheaval in the military',[43] and of another introduced 'the most important change that had occurred for two centuries in the military system of the country'.[44] In fact neither of these statements is true. Mary's Act did no more than provide a restatement and re-assessment of the individual's liability to keep arms which dated from the Statute of Winchester of 1285. Its real interest lies not in what it did, which was hardly anything, but in what it failed to do at a moment when there was still time to save the English army from the organizational mess into which it drifted in the second half of the sixteenth century.

* * *

The 1513 expedition was outstanding in two respects. It was equipped with the best artillery that money could buy, handled by the best gunners that Henry could engage from the Low Countries. Although the twelve apostles caught the imagination of contemporary observers, there were many other notable guns. The army was perhaps less well provided with hand-guns, but here again more enterprise was shown than later in the century, when there was great reluctance to equip the forces with the new 'weapons of fire' because of the danger that they might be used in the pursuit of game in the royal preserves, or for robbery.

But perhaps the most remarkable feature of Henry's first venture into Europe was the quality of the men he led, and the excellence of their discipline. They might well have been devoted to a better cause. It is true that the evidence about discipline is to some extent negative. It has been pointed out above[45] that since the king accompanied his army the volume of material about the conduct of the campaign was greatly diminished. Had he remained in London there would have been a much greater volume of correspondence with the higher command: instructions from him and the Privy Council, dispatches from the general, memoranda from the council of war, letters home from senior officers determined to safeguard their position at Court, complaints from captains about the victualling arrangements, lack of pay and so on – a stream of communications illuminating the conduct of the campaign and the personalities of those taking part in it. But if the king was there himself much of the stream became unnecessary. The deliberations of the council of war were less important, as the king could choose to act without their advice. There was less need to record their decisons. Those who might want a minority point of view put on paper and sent home to the king, to clear themselves if the majority decision led to disaster, knew that the highest authority was already aware of their advice. Nevertheless, when due allowance is made for the limited amount of evidence, it still seems clear that the morale of the troops was higher than at any other point in the century. Contemporary opinion was certainly very favourable. Antonio Bavarino said that 'choicer troops in more perfect order had not been seen for many years'.[46] Robert Macquereau recorded that both the men and their equipment were superb.[47] Fleuranges considered that the enemy had 'une merveilleusement belle armée, tant de gens de pied que de cheval'.[48]

The standard of discipline in Calais and the other strong points in the pale also seems to have been at a peak never reached again. In 1513 Calais was well run, but by 1527 'the houses and mansions and habitations' in the town had been allowed 'for lack of repairs to fall in extreme ruin, decay, and desolation',[49] and a royal proclamation demanded that something should be done about it.

This was not enough to put the town on its feet, however, and nine years later a new attempt was made through the great Statute which has been mentioned above.[50] This may have had a temporary beneficial effect, but by the end of Henry's reign standards had fallen to a deplorable level. In 1544 the council in Calais reported to the Privy Council that fifteen or sixteen soldiers were dying each day, 'and no marvel for they lie so sluttishly and do all things so sluttishly in the midst of the streets that men were almost as good pass through a jakes(1) as any street in this town'. Nor was it only Calais that was affected. It was just as bad in Guines, which 'is like a swine stye, so filthy and so full of ordure that when the men be come thither that be appointed we fear the like death will ensue there'.[51] Apart from reporting in vivid detail the shocking state of the territory for which they were responsible the council in Calais seem to have done nothing to improve the situation.

It was inevitable that Calais should revert to France sooner or later. It seems equally certain, however, that, if Henry had been man enough to control his thirst for glory and had simply followed his father's level-headed lead in political affairs, the vast military effort he dissipated so futilely in 1513 – and the vast fortune that went with it – would have been conserved for an occasion when they were really needed. They could have been put to better use in maintaining

Maximilian I as Tuteur de Holland
(Montagu illustration 90.)

Calais as an impregnable fortress (at a fraction of the sums poured into Tournai), and had this been done England's position would have been materially strengthened in the mortal struggle with Spain at the end of the century. But the young king could not wait to flesh his sword, cost what it might.

He had set out to prove himself master of the art of war, but in the end of the day he did no more than reveal himself as a rank amateur with money to burn, who was clay in Maximilian's cunning hands, and who was much too taken up with the pomp and splendour of his own position as commander-in-chief to suspect that he was being exploited.

Maximilian and Wolsey were the real victors in the 1513 campaign. It led the king's almoner, who had personally directed all the preparatory work, to the lucrative bishopric of Tournai; and although in the event he made little out of it (the revenues continued to go to the French bishop elect) at least he received a substantial pension from Francis I in return for the surrender of his rights at the end of the occupation. It allowed the emperor to use Henry and his 'army royal' to keep the French on the defensive for a whole campaigning season, and to destroy Thérouanne. It neutralized Tournai for more than five years. These were invaluable services, for which he might well have paid handsomely; but the full measure of Henry's political innocence is revealed by the fact that it was *he* who paid Maximilian – £20,000, plus a living allowance of £20 a day – for his relatively small contribution to their joint effort. It is hardly surprising that 'during this whole journey the Emperor showed the greatest condescension, declaring publicly that he came to be of use to the king of England, and calling the king at one time his son, at another his king, and at another his brother'. Dr John Taylor also tells us that on triumphal occasions Maximilian made a point of allowing Henry to precede him, 'that he might not detract from the King of England's glory'.[52] Alas, Taylor could not read the emperor's thoughts on these occasions, but surely they must have been dominated by amused contempt for the handsome young innocent parading before him, who was fighting his battles, and paying him heavily for the privilege.

NOTE

(1) A privy (*OED*).

LIST OF ABBREVIATIONS

MANUSCRIPT SOURCES

British Museum

Add. MS	Additional Manuscript.
Ar. MS	Arundel Manuscript.
BM Loan 15	Wyatt MS. no. 17; loaned by the Earl of Romney.
Cott. MS	Cottonian Manuscript.
Harl. MS	Harleian Manuscript.
La. MS	Lansdowne Manuscript.
R.MS	Royal Manuscript.
St. MS	Stowe Manuscript.

Public Record Office

PRO 31/8	Transcripts for a new edition of Rymer's *Foedera*.
PRO E 36	Exchequer, Treasury of Receipt. Miscellaneous Books.
PRO E 101	Exchequer, King's Remembrancer. Various Accounts.
SPH	State Papers, Henry VIII.

Bodleian Library

Ash. MS	Ashmolean Manuscript.
Rawl. MS	Rawlinson Manuscript.
Tan. MS	Tanner Manuscript.

Other Collections

CUL MS	Cambridge University Library Manuscript.
Heralds' MS	College of Arms Manuscript.
LJ	City of London Journals.
Lo. MS	Losely Manuscript (Guildford).
Mid. MS	Middleton Manuscript (University of Nottingham).

PRINTED SOURCES

Source Collections

APC	*Acts of the Privy Council of England*, N.S. (London, 1890–1907).

Ellis	Sir Henry Ellis, *Original letters illustrative of English history* (London, 1824; 1827; 1846).
HMC	Historical Manuscripts Commission Reports.
Hocquet	A. Hocquet, *Tournai et l'occupation anglaise* (Tournai, 1900).
LP	*Letters and papers, foreign and domestic, of the reign of Henry VIII* (London, 1862–1910; 1920; 1929–32).
MC	*Calendar of state papers, Milan (1385–1618)* (London, 1912).
Rymer	Thomas Rymer, *Foedera, etc.* (London, 1704–32).
SC	*Calendar of state papers, Spanish (1485–1558)* (London, 1862–1954).
TRP	*Tudor royal proclamations*, eds P.L. Hughes and J.F. Larkin (New Haven and London, 1964).
VC	*Calendar of state papers Venetian (1202–1603)* (London, 1864–98).
YCR	*York civic records* (Yorks. Arch. Soc., 1939–53).

Chronicles and Contemporary Books

Bayard	*Mémoires du Chevalier Bayard dit le Chevalier sans peur et sans reproche: Mémoires particuliers relatifs à l'histoire de France*, xv (London and Paris, 1786).
Chronicle	*The chronicle of Calais in the reigns of Henry VII and Henry VIII, to the year 1540*, ed. J.G. Nichols (Camden Soc., no. xxxv, 1846).
du Bellay	*Mémoires de messire Martin du Bellay, seigneur de Langey: Mémoires particuliers relatifs à l'histoire de France*, xvii (London and Paris, 1786).
Fleuranges	*Mémoires mis en escript par Robert de la Marck, seigneur de Fleuranges et de Sedan et Maréchal de France dit le jeune advantureux: Mémoires particuliers relatifs à l'histoire de France*, xvi (London and Paris, 1786).
Gruffudd (i)	'Suffolk's expedition to Montdidier, 1523', by Elis Gruffudd, trans. by M.B. Davies, *Bulletin of the Faculty of Arts*, Fouad I University, vii (1944).
Gruffudd (ii)	*The enterprises of Paris and Boulogne*, by Elis Gruffudd, trans. by M.B. Davies, ibid., xi (1949).
Gruffudd (iii)	*Boulogne and Calais from 1545 to 1550*, by Elis Gruffudd, trans by M.B. Davies, ibid., xii (1950).
Hall	Edward Hall, *The union of the two noble and illustre famelies of Lancastre and Yorke* (London, 1542). References are to edition of 1809.
Italian relations	*A relation, or rather a true account, of the island of England* (Camden Soc., no. xxxvii, 1847).
Macquereau	Robert Macquereau, *Chronique de la maison de Bourgoigne* (Paris, 1838).
Morison	Sir R. Morison, *The strategemes, sleyghtes, and policies of warre* (London, 1539).

Polydore	Polydore Vergil, *Histoire Anglicae*, trans. and ed. Denys Hay (Camden Soc., 3rd Ser., no. lxxiv, 1950).
Sutcliffe	Matthew Sutcliffe, *The practice, proceedings and lawes of armes* (London, 1593).

Later Works

Arch.	*Archaeologia; or miscellaneous tracts relating to antiquity* (London, 1770 ff.).
BIHR	*Bulletin of the Institute of Historical Research.*
Chettle	H.F. Chettle, 'The burgesses for Calais 1536–1558', *English Historical Review*, 1 (1935), 492–501.
Chotin	A.G. Chotin, *Histoire de Tournai* (Tournai, 1840).
Davies	C.S.L. Davies, 'Supply services of the English armed forces, 1509–50' (unpublished Oxford D.Phil. thesis, 1963).
Fortescue	Sir John Fortescue, *A History of the British Army* (London, 1899).
Goring	Jeremy Goring, 'The military obligations of the English people, 1511–1558' (unpublished London Ph.D. thesis, 1955).
Grose	Francis Grose, *Military antiquities* (London, 1786–8).
Hennell	Sir R. Hennell, *The king's bodyguard of the Yeomen of the Guard* (Westminster, 1904).
Hooker	J.R. Hooker, 'The organization and supply of the Tudor military under Henry VII', *Huntington Library Quarterly*, vol. 23.
Lupton	J.H. Lupton, *A life of John Colet* (London, 1887).
MacGregory	J. MacGregory, *Geography and history of Tournai* (Harleian Miscellany, no. ii, 1809).
More	Sir Thomas More, *Utopia*, ed. J.H. Lupton (Oxford, 1895).
Noyes	A.H. Noyes, *The military obligation in Mediaeval England* (Columbus, 1930).
Oman	Sir Charles Oman, *A history of the art of war in the sixteenth century* (London, 1937).
Pickthorn	K.W.M. Pickthorn, *Early Tudor government: Henry VII* (Cambridge, 1934).
Rapin	Paul de Rapin-Thoyras, *Histoire d'Angleterre* (La Haye, 1724–36).
Stone	Lawrence Stone, *The crisis of the aristocracy, 1558–1641* (Oxford, 1965).
Stubbs	W. Stubbs, *The constitutional history of England* (Oxford, 1891).
Tytler	P.F. Tytler, *Life of King Henry VIII* (Edinburgh, 1837).
Woodworth	Allegra Woodworth, 'Purveyance for the royal household in the reign of Queen Elizabeth' (*Transactions of the American Philosophical Society*, N.S. 35, pt. I, 1945).

SOURCES

1 Objective

1. Gruffudd (i), p. 8.
2. CUL MS. Ff 2. 10, f. 19.
3. SPH 3, f. 199b.
4. Hall, p. 708.
5. Ibid., p. 674.
6. Hall, p. 521.
7. Ibid., p. 529.
8. *Italian Relation*, p. 23.
9. *VC*, ii, no. 185.
10. *MC*, no. 638.
11. *VC*, ii, no. 203.
12. Ibid., nos. 211, 215.
13. Lupton, pp. 189–91.
14. Polydore, p. 197.
15. Polydore, p. 203; Ash. MS. 1143, f. 44.
16. Polydore, p. 197.
17. *SC*, ii, no. 72.
18. Ash. MS. 1143, f. 44.
19. Ash. MS. 1116, f. 120.
20. Gruffudd (i), p. 2.
21. Ibid., pp. 3–4.
22. Polydore, p. 299.
23. 7 H. VII, c. II.
24. *Italian Relation*, p. 52.
25. Polydore, pp. 91–3, 109.
26. Pickthorn, p. 23.
27. 4 H. VIII, c. 19.
28. Polydore, p. 203.
29. *TRP*, i. 94–9.
30. 7 H. VII, c. I.
31. 3 H. VIII, c. 5.

2 Beach-head

1. La. MS. 818, f. 6.
2. *LP*, i, pt. 2. no. 2483: *MC*, no. 660.
3. *LP*, i, pt. 2. no. 2391.
4. Hall, p. 539.
5. *LP*, i, pt. I, no. 190 (39); pt. 2, nos. 1890, 1908.
6. Ibid., nos. 1815, 1853.
7. Ibid., nos. 1865, 1901.
8. Hall, p. 539; *Chronicle*, pp. xxvii–xxviii.
9. Hall, pp. 539–40.
10. *LP*, xix, pt. I, no. 271.
11. *LP*, i, pt. 2, no. 1834.
12. Ibid., no. 1948 (64).
13. Ibid., nos. 1904, 1948 (69); *TRP*, i., 105.
14. SPH 229, f. 204.
15. Chettle, p. 493.
16. Polydore, p. 119.
17. *Italian Relation*, p. 45.
18. 27 H. VIII, c. 63.

19. Harl. MS. 283, f. 154; *Chronicle*, pp. xxx–xxxii.
20. *Chronicle*, p. xxiv.
21. 19 H. VII, c. 27; 7 H. VIII, c. 10.
22. Cott. MS. Faustina E VII, ff. 89–102b. (printed in *Chronicle*, pp. 140–62). Cott MS. Caligula B I, f. 355, deals with the watch arrangements at Berwick.
23. Harl. MS. 289, no. 20.

3 Movement

1. Fleuranges, p. 142.
2. St. MS 146.
3. La. MS 818, f. 6.
4. *LP*, i, pt. 2, no. 2391.
5. La. MS 818, ff. 6b, 12.
6. Polydore, p. 211.
7. *Chronicle*, p. 13.
8. *LP* i, pt. 2, no. 2391.
9. St. MS. 146, f. 82; *Italian Relation*, p. 45.
10. SPH 3, f. 198.
11. *Chronicle*, p. 12; Hall, p. 538.
12. Add. MS. 5758, ff. 197–8.
13. *LP*, i, pt. 2, no. 2053 (2).
14. *TRP*, i. 109, 110–13.
15. La. MS 818, ff. 1–3; Cott. MS Caligula E I, ff. 7b–8; SPH 3. f. 159.
16. *SC*, ii, no. 151.
17. *TRP*, i. 121.
18. PRO, E 101/62/31; *TRP* i. 112.
19. *Chronicle*, p. 13.
20. *LP*, i, pt. 2, no. 2391; Cott. MS Caligula E I, f. 7b.
21. St. MS. 146, f. 88.
22. Hall, p. 541.
23. La. MS 818, f. 7.
24. *YCR*, iv. 83.
25. Add. MS 23971, ff. 13–14.
26. p. 32.
27. *LP*, i, pt. 2, no. 2391.
28. *Chronicle*, p. 13; Fleuranges, p. 143.
29. Hall, p. 542.
30. Tytler, p. 57.
31. *LP*, i, pt. 2, no. 2391.
32. Polydore, p. 211.
33. Bayard, pp. 342–3.
34. e.g. *VC*, ii, no. 255.
35. Macquereau, p. 31.
36. *LP*, i, pt. 2, no. 2391.

4 Camp

1. *LP*, xix, pt. I, no. 271.
2. Gruffudd (i), pp. 8–9.

3. PRO, E 36/3, ff. 72–82; *LP*, i, pt. 2, no. 3091.
4. Lo. MS 1300, no. 48.
5. p. 48.
6. Lo. MS 15, 20, 22 (I), 1300 (48).
7. *LP*, i, pt. 2, App., no. 25.
8. *LP*, i, pt. 2, no. 2053.
9. Rawl. MS 146, f. 198.
10. Hall, p. 543.
11. *Arch*. iii, 251.
12. Rawl. MS D 363, ff. 15, 19b.
13. Rawl. MS D 363, f. 19b.
14. Cott. MS Julius F, v, f. 23.
15. Ibid., Augustus III, f. 39.
16. Cott. MS Julius F, v, f. 23b; Rawl. MS D 363, f. 20.
17. *TRP*, i., 114.
18. *TRP*, i., 121.
19. Gruffudd (ii), p. 23.
20. Cott. MS Augustus III, f. 39.
21. Cott. MS Julius F v, f. 24.
22. Rawl. MS D 363, f. 22.
23. Cott. MS Julius F v, f. 23b.
24. Cott. MS Julius F v, f. 24; *TRP*, i., III.

5 Supply

1. *APC*, i. 299.
2. Gruffudd (iii), pp. 21–2.
3. *Italian Relation*, pp. 9–10.
4. *LP*, i, pt. 2, no. 1864.
5. PRO, E 101/56/23.
6. Hall, p. 538.
7. Davies, p. 168.
8. Polydore, p. 209.
9. *LP*, i, pt. 2, no. 2391.
10. Hall, p. 538.
11. Polydore, p. 209.
12. *LP*, i, pt. 2, no. 2391.
13. *Chronicle*, p. 12.
14. *VC*, ii, no. 263.
15. Hall, pp. 543–4.
16. *Chronicle*, p. 14.
17. *TRP*, i, 13.
18. PRO, E 101/72/3, no. 1068.
19. PRO, E 101/72/2, no. 1064.
20. *APC*, xxx, 623–33.
21. Woodworth, pp. 14–15.
22. HMC, *Salisbury*, i, 293.
23. *TRP*, i, 99–100; *LP*, i, pt. I, no. 1524 (30).
24. *LP*, i, pt. I, no. 1662 (35).
25. Ibid., (54).
26. Ibid., no. 1804 (22) (i).
27. Ibid., (ii).
28. *VC*, ii, no. 168.
29. Ibid., no. 219.
30. SPH, 224, ff. 205–8.
31. Grose, ii. 57.
32. Cott. MS Julius F, v, f. 17b.
33. *TRP*, i, III, 115.
34. PRO, E 36/2, p. 173.
35. PRO, E 101/62/16.
36. *LP*, xix, pt. 2, nos. 187, 195.

37. PRO, E 36/2, pp. 173–5.
38. SPH, 7, f. 51.
39. PRO, E 36/2, pp. 115–75.
40. SPH, 3, f. 160; PRO, E 101/62/16 and PRO, E 101/62/31.
41. PRO, E 36/2, pp. 91–5; Davies, p. 211.
42. R. MS 7 F XIV, ff. 72–72b.
43. *LP*, xix, pt. I, no. 272 (9).
44. Ibid., (12).
45. 'Treat roughly' (*OED*).
46. Morison, Sig. a 5.
47. *VC*, ii, no. 219.
48. Lo. MS 1086, p. 5.
49. Above, pp. 47–9.
50. St. MS 146, f. 107.
51. Above, p. 37.
52. du Bellay, p. 8.
53. *LP* i, pt. 2, no. 2391.
54. PRO, E 101/62/16.
55. SPH 7, f. 51.
56. PRO, E 36/2, pp. 197, 241.
57. These figures must be treated with caution, as the various estimates of the number and size of the guns in the three wards differ a good deal from each other.
58. Add. MS 23971, ff. 35–7.
59. St. MS 146, ff. 60, 61, 62, 65, 68.
60. PRO, E 101/62/31.
61. CUL MS Ff. 2. 10, f. 24.
62. Ibid., f. 21b.
63. 3 H. VIII, c. 3.
64. LJ, 15, f. 79b.
65. *TRP*, i, 372–3; 33 H. VIII, c. 6.

6 Siege

1. Harl MS 847, f. 59b.
2. Harl. MS. 6064, f. 70; Ar. MS. 26, f. 57b.
3. Macquereau, p. 27.
4. Ibid., p. 28.
5. SPH 3, f. 198.
6. *VC*, ii, no. 274.
7. *LP*, i, pt. 2, no. 2092.
8. HMC, *Lloyd*, p. 446.
9. *VC*, ii, nos. 262, 269.
10. 'Le siege estant devant la ville, sachies que les habitans et gens de guerre estoient moult esbahis' (Macquereau, p. 27).
11. *VC*, ii, no. 274.
12. Ibid., no. 283; *Arch*. xxvii. 424.
13. Hall, p. 538.
14. *Arch*, xxvii. 477–8.
15. HMC *Lloyd*, pp. 446–7.
16. Hall, p. 540.
17. *LP*, i, pt. 2, no. 2391.
18. *VC*, ii, no. 269; Hall, p. 543; HMC *Lloyd*, pp. 446–7.
19. Hall, p. 538.
20. HMC *Lloyd*, pp. 446–7.
21. *VC*, ii, no. 290.
22. Ibid., no. 279.
23. *VC*, ii, no. 291.

24. Hall, p. 544.
25. *LP*, i, pt. 2, App. no. 25; *VC* ii, no. 33; *Chronicle*, p. 14.
26. *LP*, i, pt. 2, App. no. 25.
27. Ibid., no. 2166.
28. *LP*, i, pt. 2, no. 2098.
29. Ibid., no. 2120.
30. Ibid., no. 2318.
31. Ellis, i, 82–4.

7   Discipline

1. Above, pp. 58–9.
2. Above, p. 4.
3. Grose, ii, 66.
4. Ibid., p. 59.
5. Grose, ii, 62.
6. Ibid., p. 72.
7. *TRP*, i. 114.
8. *Statutes and ordynances for the warre*, sig. B ii b.
9. *TRP*, i, 120.
10. Add. MS 30170, f. 35.
11. Rawl. MS D 363, f. 6; Cott. MS Julius F v, f. II.
12. Tan. MS 103, f. 45b; Add. MS 23971, ff. 3b–4.
13. Tan. MS 103, ff. 46–7.
14. Stubbs, i, 383.
15. *TRP*, i, 121.
16. Ibid. 116.
16. Rymer, xii. 479.
17. *TRP*, i, 121.
18. *LP*, i, pt. 2, no. 2391.
19. *LP*, i, pt. 2, no. 2391.
20. Hall, p. 549.
21. *VC*, ii, no. 333.
22. *TRP*, i, 113.
23. *LP*, xix, pt. 2, nos. 187, 195.
24. Gruffudd (iii), p. 13.

8   Battle

1. Add. MS 23971, f. I. (Other versions of Audley's tract are in Tan. MS 103, Rawl. MS D 363, Harl. MS 309, Cott. MS Titus B v; and CUL MS Ff 2. 10.)
2. Rymer, xii, 479–80.
3. Hooker, pp. 29–30.
4. *LP*, i, pt. 2. no. 2053.
5. SPH, 8, ff. 194–6; 28, ff. 283–93b.
6. Fleuranges, p. 143.
7. Add. MS, 23971, f. 12b.
8. Sutcliffe, p. 159.
9. Add. MS 23971, ff. 25b–27; CUL MS ff 2. 10, f. 25.
10. CUL MS Ff. 2. 10, f. 24.
11. Polydore, p. 213.
12. Hall, p. 549.
13. Fleuranges, p. 145.
14. 'par quelques espies, dont assez s'en trouve parmy les armees; et y en avoit alors de doubles qui feignoient estre bons Francois, et

ilz estoient du contraire party' (Bayard, p. 344).
15. Hall, p. 550.
16. Oman, p. 287.
17. Fleuranges, p. 150; *Chronicle*, p. 14.
18. *LP*, i, pt. 2, nos. 2186, 2391.
19. Chotin, ii. 84.
20. du Bellay, p. 24.
21. Cott. MS Caligula D VI, f. 94.
22. Cott. MS Vespasian F III, f. 15.

9   Prisoners

1. *LP*, i, pt. 2, no. 2254.
2. *TRP*, i, 106–20.
3. Harl. MS 289, no. 20.
4. Rymer, xii 478–9.
5. Above, p. 59.
6. Hall, p. 544.
7. *LP*, i, pt. 2, no. 2391.
8. Ibid., no. 2172.
9. *VC*, ii, no. 288. A ducat was worth about 4s. 6d.
10. Bayard, p. 353.
11. *LP*, i, pt. 2, no. 2396.
12. Hall, p. 569.
13. *LP*, i, pt. 2, no. 3387.
14. Ellis, i. 152–4.
15. *VC*, ii, no. 328.

10   Negotiations

1. *LP*, i, pt. 2, 2294 (ii), 2391.
2. Hocquet, Preuve, ii.
3. Fleuranges, p. 151.
4. Hocquet, Preuve, v.
5. Hocquet, Preuve, v.
6. Hocquet, Preuve, vii.
7. Macquereau, p. 40.
8. Hocquet, Preuve, xxv.
9. Macquereau, pp. 40–1.

11   Capitulation

1. Heralds' MS M. 16, f. 38.
2. Hocquet, Preuve, v.
3. *MC*, no. 656.
4. Ibid., no. 657.
5. 'de plus en plus croissoit la craincte et deso-lation' (Hocquet, Preuve, v).
6. Ibid., Preuve, xii.
7. Hall, p. 553.
8. *LP*, i, pt. 2, no. 2391.
9. *MC*, no. 654.
10. Hall, p. 553.
11. St. MS 146, ff. 96–96b.
12. Hall, p. 554.
13. *MC*, no. 657.
14. *MC*, no. 660; Macquereau, p. 41.
15. *MC*, no. 660.
16. *LP*, i, pt. 2, no. 2391.
17. *MC*, no. 657.

18. Ibid.
19. Macquereau, p. 43.
20. *MC*, no. 660.
21. Hocquet, Preuve, xvi.
22. PRO, 31 8/144, ff. 286–7b.
23. *VC*, ii, no. 316. (*La chambre du roi* is translated in the *Calendar* as 'the King's treasury'; but it seems more likely that Tuke meant 'the King's bedchamber': see p. 86 above, and the suggestion that Thérouanne was 'one of the few pillows on which the King of France could sleep in peace'.)

12   Occupation

1. Hall, p. 566; *Arch.* xxviii, 258–60; Macquereau, p. 49.
2. *MC*, no. 669; St. MS 146, f. 101.
3. *MC*, no. 671.
4. PRO, 31 8/144, f. 225.
5. Ibid., ff. 227–227b.
6. *Chronicle*, p. 15; PRO, 31 8/144, f. 251.
7. Cott. MS Caligula D VI, f. 98.
8. Hocquet, Preuve, xix.
9. PRO, 31 8/144, f. 268.
10. Ibid., f. 223.
11. Ibid., f. 229.
12. Hocquet, Preuve, xxvii.
13. Ibid., Preuve, xxviii.
14. Hocquet, Preuve, xxix.
15. Ibid., Preuve, xxx.
16. Ibid., Preuve, xxxii.
17. 5 H. VIII, c. I.
18. PRO, 31 8/144, ff. 241–2.
19. Above, p. 17.
20. PRO, 31 8/144, f. 266.
21. Ibid., f. 245.
22. *LP*, i, pt. 2 no. 2788; SPH 230, f. 144.
23. *LP*, ii, pt. I, no. 1499.
24. Hocquet, Preuve, xxviii.
25. Ibid., Preuve, xxxvi; SPH 230, f. 65.
26. *LP*, ii, pt. I, no. 399.
27. Ibid., no. 1498.
28. *LP*, i, pt. ii, no. 3247.
29. Ibid., no. 3258.
30. *LP*, ii, pt. no. 554.
31. *LP*, ii. pt. I, nos. 825, 978; Rymer, xiii. 519.
32. *MC*, no. 671.
33. SPH 10, f. 59.
34. *LP*, ii, pt. V, no. 148.
35. SPH 10, ff. 56–7.
36. *LP*, ii, pt. I, nos. 325, 824, 890, 964.
37. Ibid., no. 1059.
38. SPH 12, f. 9.
39. *LP*, ii, pt. I, no. 1259.
40. Ibid., no. 1664.
41. Ibid., pt. 2, no. 2972.
42. SPH 13, ff. 281–2.
43. Cott. MS Caligula E I, ff. 158–60b.
44. *LP*, ii, pt. 2, no. 3321.
45. Ibid., no. 3320.
46. SPH 15, f. 38.

47. *MC*, no. 671.
48. Hall, p. 585.
49. MacGregory, p. 236.
50. *LP*, ii, pt. I, no. 820.
51. Ibid., no. 1082.
52. Cott. MS Caligula D VI, ff. 96–7.
53. *LP*, ii, pt. I, no. 1607; Hocquet, Preuve xiii.
54. SPH 15, ff. 36–7.
55. *LP*, ii, pt. 2, no. 2858.
56. Ibid., no. 1656.
57. Ibid., no. 2622.
58. Ibid., no. 1403.
59. Ibid., no. 2236.
60. SPH 15, ff. 16–18.
61. SPH 14, ff. 205–10.
62. SPH 16, ff. 75–6.
63. Hocquet, Preuve, xliv.
64. *LP*, ii, pt. 2, no. 3886.
65. SPH 16, ff. 123–4.
66. *LP*, ii, pt. no. 3912.
67. SPH 16, ff. 168–9.
68. Above, p. 7.
69. *LP*, ii, pt. 2, no. 4201.
70. Polydore, p. 249.
71. Hall, p. 593.
72. *LP*, ii, pt. 2, no. 4453.
73. Hall, p. 594.
74. *LP*, ii, pt. 2, no. 4479.
75. Ibid., nos. 4481, 4491.
76. *LP*, ii, pt. 2, nos. 4582, 4594, 4613, 4638.
77. Cott. MS Caligula D VII, f. 91.
78. *LP*, ii, pt. 2, no. 4661.
79. Ibid., no. 4674.
80. *LP*, ii, pt. 2, no. 4663.
81. *LP*, iii, pt. I, no. 14.
82. Cott. MS Caligula D VII, f. 62b.
83. Ibid., f. 83.
84. *LP*, iii, pt. I, nos. 23, 37.
85. *LP*, i, pt. 2, no. 2249.
86. *LP*, ii, pt. 2, no. 4582.
87. Ibid., no. 4639.
88. Cott. MS Caligula D VII, f. 83.
89. *LP*, iii, pt. I, no. 58.
90. Cott. MS Caligula D VII, f. 41.
91. Hall, p. 596.
92. Cott. MS Caligula D VII, ff. 41b, 57b, 95.
93. Cott. MS Caligula D VII, f. 94.

13   Conclusion

1. *SC*, ii, nos. 132, 141.
2. Rapin, V. 71.
3. *LP*, i, pt. 2, no. 2391.
4. *MC*, no. 660.
5. *VC*, ii, no. 174.
6. *VC*, ii, no. 283.
7. *MC*, no. 651.
8. St. MS 146, ff. 96–8b; 104.
9. Ibid., f. 105.
10. Ibid., ff. 95, 110.
11. p. 28.
12. Hall, p. 425.

13. Goring, pp. 230–1.
14. Hennell, p. 196.
15. Goring, pp. 232–40.
16. Polydore, p. II.
17. *SC*, ii, no. 151.
18. HMC *Middleton*, pp. 131–2.
19. PRO, E 101/59/5. (For the dating of this document see Goring. Appendix IV.)
20. *APC*, iii, 225.
21. Ibid., p. xiv.
22. Stone, p. 207.
23. *SC*, x, 579.
24. Cott. MS. Cleopatra E IV, ff. 214–20, printed as Appendix II to L. Stone's *The Political Programme of Thomas Cromwell* (*BIHR*, xxiv, 1–18).
25. G.R. Elton, *Parliamentary Drafts, 1529–1540* (*BIHR*, xxv, 117–32).
26. BM Loan 15.
27. More, pp. 46–9.
28. La. MS 863, f. 54b.
29. Goring, p. 274.
30. Ibid., pp. 277–8.
31. Rymer, xii, 477–8.
32. Cott. MS Caligula B I, f. 49.
33. Goring, pp. 12–13.
34. Mid. MS Mi. O. 16.
35. 3 H. VIII, c. 5.
36. Above, pp. 82, 120.
37. *LP*, i, pt. 2, no. 2227.
38. Harl. MS 283, f. 4.
39. *LP*, xix, pt. 2, no. 297.
40. 3 H. VIII, c. 5.
41. 7 H. VII, c. I.
42. 2 & 3 Ed. VI, c. 2.
43. Noyes, p. 50.
44. Fortescue, i, 125.
45. p. 102.
46. *VC*, ii, no. 252.
47. Macquereau, p. 40.
48. Fleuranges, pp. 143–4.
49. *TRP*, i, 171.
50. pp. 17–18 (27 H. VIII c. 63).
51. *LP*, xix, pt. 2, no. 505.
52. *LP*, i, pt. 2, no. 2391.

INDEX

(Page numbers of illustrations are in italics)